The Mess & Mystery of Missions
KAWAJA BYE-BYE

Dr. J Alan Perry

"I am a stranger in the earth; do not hide your
commandments from me"

The Mess & Mystery of Missions
Kawaja Bye-Bye

A McKinney Publishing Production Printing History:
First Edition, November 2022

Book interior and cover designed by Grace Cremé

For copyright permission, please contact: McKinney Publishing www.McKinneyPublishing.com

ISBN: 978-1-943518-33-3

Printed in the United States of America

To Elizabeth,
who was (and still is) willing to walk through the mess together
with me, because of the mystery—Christ in her

— ACKNOWLEDGEMENTS

I am indebted to the sacrifices of others, so here I thank them for their part in writing our story, while living in the mess and the mystery…

Laura Freidenberger, who became "us" while we were living in East Africa, faithfully managing our finances in the US, and enabling us to remain on the field. We couldn't have been there without her service in this way.

Chris Katsekpor, my mentor while we were on the field, and our Regional Leader, who was always concerned for the well-being of our children. He is a picture of humility and meekness in this life.

Christine Perkins, our Area Leader for many years, a strong advocate for what would enable us and our teammates to remain on the field and thrive, not just survive.

Charles Fielding, author of Preach and Heal—not only was his book a great encouragement as we set out to understand how medicine and the Gospel went together, but he also gave me valuable feedback in the early writing process.

African theologians Pastor Hillary in Yei, under whom we were privileged to learn and grow; and Pastor Jimmy in Moyo, who welcomed us as "missionary refugees" and allowed us to simply participate as members of the local church.

Jim Garrett, dear friend, and elder at Tulsa Christian Fellowship, who always responded with decidedly encouraging words whenever he received our email updates, even in the middle of the night. His book, The Doulos Principle, was an integral part of growing our faith.

Dr. Kiden, who served us in our times of weakness, walked alongside us as we saw the Lord expand His work, suffered with us as she and we walked through loss, and continues to serve her people long after we returned to the US.

Dr. Graham and Linda Poole, our Aussie friends and co-workers, whom we learned to love amidst the stresses, personality differences, and surprising cultural nuances! We all grew as we did work and life together.

Kitty Moyer, our faithful friend, teammate, and nurse who cared for our children in our absence and their sicknesses.

Katherine Young, our Kiwi friend and nurse who taught our children piano, and brought all the details of the hospital together, salvaging organization out of the chaos.

Dr. Matthew and Maggie Loftus, our teammates, a gifted writer and missionary doctor who continues on teaching Family Medicine in Kenya and trying to coordinate medical missionaries within Pioneers.

Dr. Ben and Jenny Roberts, eye surgeon at Tenwek Hospital who operated on me three times, who both sacrificially give of themselves to this day in western Kenya.

Dr. Joe Kim, whose early planning of the hospital and advocacy for our African family dwelling (complete with two toilets, anticipating the diarrheal disease to come!), was instrumental in getting us off on the right foot in South Sudan.

Glenn and Karen Rumrill, our sending pastor and his wife, whose parting words in 2011, "you'll have stories to tell…" certainly came true, though none of us realized the cost of acquiring such stories.

Our children, who spent their formative years in another culture, learning what it is to be a foreigner on this earth…
Alex, a great big brother to his many younger siblings who left for East Africa.

Lillian, who embraced the challenge of moving across the world just before her 12th birthday, and often worked beside me in the hospital and refugee camps.

Sophia, quietly observant and always remembering, our treasure-keeper of memories, who stepped out of her comfort zone many times to care for others and interact with those who were very different from herself.

Evangelina, passionate about whatever she puts her hands to, willing to risk and try new things, deeply thoughtful about what she does, and desiring to follow the Lord where He leads Logan, hungry to learn about flying, music, and the Lord, and in the process, teaching us and influencing others.

Olivia, a great question-asker, modeling what it means to be focused on others, and seeking the Lord through His Word Hazel, who captures images in her art, worth many thousands of words; her insights into the things of God continue to astound us.

Given, our HIC (head-injury child), who is still funny (in a good way!), and serves so well with excellence and without complaining.

Winnie, our jena akir leben (youngest child) who grew up in East Africa, facing risks unbeknownst to her, and now going after life with gusto.

Thank you, all y'all, for your part in the Body of Christ, and in our lives in particular.

Dr. Jeff & Elizabeth Perry
November 2022
Colorado, USA

ENDORSEMENTS

It's not always easy to explain what life is like for medical missionaries, who are toiling in difficult conditions to care for patients and teach others how to do the same. Jeff Perry's stories (some of which I also lived through) may not always feel uplifting, but they give the reader an up-close-and-personal view of the mission field with all of its blood, sweat, dirt, and tears. Through it all, these stories help us to trust and seek after the Lord who watches over and cares for all of us.

Dr. Matthew Loftus
Medical Missionary in Litein, Kenya,
Writer at MereOrthodoxy.com,
2022 Zenger Prize Winner

As General Editor of AskaMissionary.com, I have received and published brief answers to over a hundred questions from aspiring missionaries. In this book Dr Perry and his wife Elizabeth powerfully share their modern-day journey into full-time missions. Their honesty, love, and willingness to persevere will be an in-depth inspiration to everyone who reads this book.

John McVay, MDiv
COO of In His Image International

The subtitle of "Kawaja Bye Bye" is "the messiness of missions," which seems a gross understatement as you read of the adventures, challenges, dangers and all-out messiness of the Perry's mission years in South Sudan, establishing a hospital in one of the most underdeveloped and least medically served regions of the world. This book is sure to ungird your prayer and love for missions, as well as make you stronger in your faith.

Charles Fielding, MD
Medical missions emeritus and author of "Preach and Heal"

"Little by little, one travels far". If this was true for Tolkien's Middle Earth, it is also an apt description of the missionary life. In the remote corners of this broken and hurting world, humble disciples are seeking to make Jesus known - following the dusty footsteps of the Way, the Truth and the Life. The journey is often slow, with suffering and setbacks and unexpected twists and turns - so disorienting, at times, that a sense of progress can be hard to discern. Yet, little by little, one travels far.

It has been a privilege for our family to have walked, 'little by little', with the Perry family, for many of their South Sudan years. In 'The Mess and the Mystery of Missions', we read their raw reflections of a ten year journey in cross-cultural life and mission. Amidst discouragement and disappointment, disease and disability, death and the demonic, we are invited to see, with them, 'the hope of glory', as the mystery of the eternal Christ, is revealed in the messy, yet always maturing, lives of his people.

"Little by little, staying close to Jesus, one travels far"

Dr Graham Poole BSc(Med) MBBS FRACGP GradDipDiv
General Practitioner - Launceston, Tasmania, Australia
Missionary Doctor - His House of Hope,
Yei, South Sudan (2012-2016)

TABLE OF CONTENTS

Perry family, Yei, South Sudan (2011)— clockwise from left: Eva, Hazel, Sophia, Elizabeth (Mom), Olivia, Jeff (Dad), Lillie, Logan, Winnie, & Given

Introduction

Elizabeth sat on the dust-coated floor of Mama Peace, the seamstress, and sifted through her rejects to find strips of material at least two inches wide. The local tailors made beautiful outfits from the multicolored African cloth, while the extra strips of fabric fell to the floor at their feet. Elizabeth had approached several of them to ask if she could buy their scraps. At first, those in the marketplace were suspicious. Why did she want their rubbish?

After paying the equivalent of $1-2, she went home with a bag full of linen. The tailors and other customers had trampled on the pieces. She washed them, flattened them with her charcoal iron, cut them to size, and began sewing. From this mess, she proceeded to piece together fabric blocks and assemble a large quilt. She made a small cushion for Mama Peace out of the scraps from her floor. She was amazed at what Elizabeth had fashioned out her leftovers.

Elizabeth enjoyed making quilts from new fabrics, but she was restored on a deeper level when she took what others considered a mess, and from it, created something extraordinary.

I like to read inspiring missionary stories that show how God worked through a bold man or woman of faith who committed their life to a people group, discovering the key of the gospel to birth the local church.

This is not one of those stories.

Between great martyrs of the faith, missionary statesmen of old, and those that leave the field in burnout or disgrace of moral failure, there are many who are none of these. Some leave the field, scratching their heads, saying, "What just happened?" They anticlimactically step back into life, much like the disciples returned to fishing after Jesus was crucified and raised, not sure of what to do next. Yet it is through messed up people such as these that God chooses to demonstrate the mystery He wants to communicate to the world.

This is a book about what many missionaries experience—messiness, difficulties, unfinished work, heartache in relationships, pride, lack of gratitude from those we serve, and loss. These hardships are true for anyone seeking to follow Jesus, for "indeed, all who desire to live godly in Christ Jesus will be persecuted" (2 Tim 3:12; not exactly a feel-good memory verse for Sunday School). Yet in cross-cultural mission work, the persecutions are often amplified.

There are many missionaries who have stories such as ours. Some are more dramatic, more hopeful, have more tangible results, or are more tragic. Most of these will never be written, due to busyness, insecurity, shame, difficulty with capturing the rigors of life in words, confusion about their experiences, or death. I am grateful that God created a space for me to record, together with my family, how and what He is teaching us.

Mission work is messy. It almost never looks the way the missionary expects it should. A counselor in East Africa reported that most missionaries struggling with emotional issues complained that they weren't engaged in the work they had planned. When asked further, they were doing good work, advancing the kingdom of God—it just wasn't the particular work they had anticipated. It had turned out messier than they anticipated.

Non-Western communication is not linear. It is circular, returning to the important points several times from different angles. The main idea is often found in the center, surrounded by examples and stories. As we reflect on our time on the East African mission field, the stories resurface with different memories and lessons. As such, this work is written in a slightly non-Western way. I will follow some parts of the story in a linear, Western way, to allow the reader to understand the flow of events. In other parts, as we delve deeper into the heart of these messy experiences, will revisit the same events with a different theme.

My hope is to capture the meanings more than our particular story.

It is a great mystery, but Jesus chooses to reveal Himself to the world through us, His followers. The Church. And the Church is messy. Paul rejoiced in the midst of suffering and explained the mystery: as we go through this mess we call "life," we reveal the great mystery—Christ in us, the hope of glory. This mystery is good news for a world that is in a mess. True discipleship happens as one follower watches how another handles the mess and manages to keep his or her eyes on the mystery.

I hope that our story is an encouragement to **those who are currently on the mission field**, struggling with the messiness of missions. For those who have served in cross-cultural missions, may it help you reflect and process what the Lord did in and through you, as it has for our family. For **those that send and support missionaries**, my hope is that you will get a glimpse into the difficulties facing those who serve in cross-cultural missions, increasing your understanding and honing your prayers.

I hope all will ponder this glorious mystery—that amidst suffering, and despite our messiness, God continues to use the Church to "open their eyes so that they may turn from darkness to light and from the power of Satan to God, that they may receive forgiveness of sins and a share among those who are sanctified by faith in me (the Church)" (Acts 26:18, CSB). The mystery is about belonging. That is, us belonging to God, God belonging to us, and us, the Church, belonging to each other.

As Elizabeth took scraps of fabric from the floor of an African tailor and fashioned a beautiful quilt, so God takes our messy attempts at obedience and draws others to know and worship Him.

*Now I rejoice in my sufferings for you, and I am completing in my flesh what is lacking in Christ's afflictions for His Body, that is, the Church. I have become its servant, according to God's commission that was given to me for you, to make the word of God fully known, the **mystery** hidden for ages and generations but now revealed to His saints. God wanted to make known among the Gentiles the glorious wealth of this **mystery**, which is Christ in you, the hope of glory. (Col 1:24-27, CSB, emphasis mine)*

Perry children, Moyo, Uganda (2018)—clockwise from left: Logan, Sophia, Eva, Hazel, Olivia, Given (with our dog Kawaja), Winnie, & Lillie

Chapter 1:
Llamas & Leavings

We made a big mistake. We prayed. Not a well-defined prayer for protection or healing from an illness, which I would recommend to keep it safe, but an open-ended prayer. One with potential follow-through required. We were hoping God would give the rubber-stamp of approval to our current course in life: a large house in rural southeastern Colorado, medical director of a community health center system, active in our local church, doing ministry in our life and work, and raising a family with seven children.

So we asked Him, "Is this what we'll be doing for the next many years, or do You have something else for us to do?" Truthfully, we were asking because we were thinking of putting in a swimming pool, so our home would be a welcoming, fun place for our kids to be with friends as they grew up. May this serve as fair warning to the reader: *prayer may require obedience.*

After four years of grueling, non-stop call delivering babies in small-town America, my community health center finally hired four other doctors. I would share call—finally, life would be manageable! We deserved a bit of a breather, and felt fairly confident God would grant us this. He surely wanted what was best for us, and our trajectory must fulfill His plans. Perhaps we should have asked this question before buying the $350,000 house... but we were young, and overwhelmed with work and young children. And we were still working out what it meant to be married and deal with our entrenched patterns of sin. We were naïve and sincere. Apparently, this is a "dangerous" combination—at least to one's flesh and the things of this world.

One week after beginning to pray in this way, my friend Craig called. "Would you help us plan a hospital in South Sudan?" he asked.

We were surprised by this blunt request, and the abrupt, unexpected response to our prayer. For some people, they get a vision. Perhaps because we were a bit dense, God had to literally call us with a telephone. Later, we learned the whole story. Another doctor with whom I'd trained did see a vision—while driving along the freeway. It was of an orphan and the words "Sudan." He called a friend, who searched "orphan" and "Sudan" on the Internet, and came up with the organization Harvesters Reaching the Nations. This doctor got involved with Harvesters, served on their board, and later asked Craig to join the ministry.

We were intrigued that God had answered so clearly. We had never considered Sudan. Some people have a love for a particular people group since childhood and know they are called to them. But we had been receiving emails from Harvesters for a few years, and we usually didn't read them. I had long been interested in mission work, ever since being at Urbana '90 with InterVarsity Christian Fellowship. After several trips to southern Mexico during college and medical school, studying and using Spanish over the years, and marrying Elizabeth (whose father is a Spanish teacher originally from Cuba), I assumed that if God called us to cross-cultural missions, it would be in a Latin American setting. Elizabeth and I had even met doing inner city ministry in a Latino neighborhood in Hollywood. It made sense and would be most efficient for Him to call us to work in a Spanish-speaking country—we already had the language down so we would be more useful, more quickly.

Apparently, God isn't concerned with efficiency. Rather, we found that He will have a 40 year-old learn Arabic in the afternoon heat of rural Africa because He is most concerned with our dependency on Him, not on our abilities. Being eternal, He's got plenty of time. He doesn't need to be efficient as we understand efficiency.

The first meeting with Harvesters happened nine months later, and by lunchtime Elizabeth and I looked at each other and knew we were going to Sudan. It was obvious that an onsite presence was needed, or the hospital would never get off the ground. More importantly, we were drawn to see if He would really have us do this.

One month later, Elizabeth "fell" pregnant (the East African way to say it) with our eighth child. Four months after the meeting, we were on a plane to southern Sudan with six children plus one in utero (our oldest son Alex stayed home as he was finishing high school). We thought it was efficient that we got one child in without a passport, visa, or plane ticket!

During our three weeks on the ground, we found out that we could do life there, though it was a challenge. Our kids embraced the happenings at the orphanage and compound where the hospital would be built. We sensed that Jesus did in fact want us to return. Still, I wondered if building a new hospital was the way to go. Shouldn't we simply support the few that existed in the area?

The day before we left, we had a brief meeting with the Bishop of the Sudanese Evangelical Presbyterian Church (EPC), over the ministry. I wanted to be sure that the local leadership wanted the project.

"Do something small, do it well, and be an example to the rest of southern Sudan," Bishop Taban said succinctly.

With that, we felt the release to proceed with letting our lives be turned upside down. Less than a year after buying our house (in a very dead housing market), we put it back on the market. Our realtor thought we were crazy. Our families thought the same. Later on, we even found out that many of our most faithful prayer supporters in our home church didn't think we'd ever get everything together to leave!

Given was born just a few months after returning from our survey trip to Sudan, increasing us to eight children at home. Winnie followed just 14 months later. They were precious joys, and at the same time we were confused as to the slow, winding path on which the Lord was taking us. We wilted as we saw no progress on raising support, few viewings of our house, and the massive student debt that we were still working to pay off. Maybe the Lord should have called someone with fewer children—we now had nine. We didn't see how we'd ever be ready to go.

Our house was large, on six acres of land (read "lots of grass to mow and weeds to control"), and in an economically depressed area. What's more, the nation-wide housing slump slammed our region. Prices plummeted, and few were buying—especially in our rural community. Elizabeth and I lamented our sorry state one night during a dinner at Christine's, our favorite local restaurant.

"It's like we actually have to trust God," I said to Elizabeth.

We were "practical atheists." Sure, we believed in Jesus, but in practice, we often functioned as if there was no God.

We realized it's easy to say we trust God, but in truth we had worked out how things would happen logically. We didn't really have to trust Him, even though we said and thought we did. But when we were put in a situation where we couldn't reason our way out, we discovered our lack of trust. In that moment, we knew we couldn't depend on ourselves anymore. We actually had to trust God. We had to believe that He could take care of the practicals of our life.

We were there.

Common sense vs. omniscience

Our land had a great corral for large animals, and Elizabeth and the kids were itching to put something in it. During a visit to Elizabeth's parents, we saw an ad in the local paper. "Llamas available, free to a good home." They were former show animals and quite old. In other words, it was "llama hospice." The owners would deliver them to us and give us all the equipment along with them. It was a good offer… but we were trying to move to Africa! The common sense in me said "no way."

On the other hand, it might be another many years, and we didn't want to put our lives on hold indefinitely. And just maybe they would help keep the weeds down in the pasture, and improving our "curb appeal." Our realtor had mentioned we needed to keep it mowed better.

We returned to our home on a Sunday evening, and spent a few days thinking about it. On Wednesday morning, I asked the Lord to give me some nudge of confirmation if we were in fact to take the llamas. The only reason I could see to justify them was to control the weeds. I went to work, and one of my first patients was one who suffered from schizophrenia.

"I think I drove past your house, doc," he said.

"Oh, yes?" I replied warily. Being a small-town doctor, anonymity was hard to maintain, but I preferred that my mentally ill patients didn't know where we lived.

"Yeah, isn't it the one on County Road 18.75? The one with the weed problem?"

I chuckled to myself at the confirmation, and we took the llamas a few days later.

So did they help? It didn't seem so. The summer passed, the weeds died, and the corral turned to dust alternating with mud. We still didn't have any real progress on raising funds. It was now two years since our survey trip. I completed my additional two-year work commitment to Valley-Wide Health Systems, the community health center with whom I'd worked for over seven years. We realized that we would never be able to devote ourselves to the preparation needed unless I left the medical practice and did something else. So, I resigned and began doing shift work in the Arkansas Valley Regional Medical Center emergency room. This allowed us the flexibility to begin traveling and speaking about what we believed the Lord was calling us to do.

We had added another baby, Winnie, and Alex had gone off to college, so now we were ten. As we contemplated travel, and the cost of hotels, we realized we needed to come up with another option. Though we vowed to never own one, we soon found ourselves the proud possessors of an R.V.—a 34-foot trailer! We planned our first trip, to the South, in January 2010. Even as we prepared to leave, things on the trailer weren't working right. Chuck Shipman,

a retired pastor from a local church, came over to help us fix it up, and told us the real meaning of R.V.: "repair vigorously."

As we left on the trip, the llamas watched us go from the muddy yard. We didn't bother cleaning up the house, as we hadn't had but 3 showings in 2 years, and who looks at buying a house in Colorado in January?! Besides, with two kids in diapers and multiple toddlers, cleaning up was not entirely possible, especially when trying to leave for a 3-week trip. Five hours after leaving, while looking for children's clothes at a thrift store in Amarillo, we received a phone call.

"I have two showings for tomorrow," said Tony, our no-nonsense realtor.

"Are you kidding?!" I asked, pausing from disbelief, excitement, and horror all at the same. "We didn't leave the house ready to be shown at all!"

"No, I'm serious—one is a new surgeon who's coming to town, and he and his wife want to look at your house!"

We promptly got on the phone with our pastor at the time, Glenn Rumrill, and his wife Karen, and explained our predicament to them.

"No problem. We'll take care of it!" he said, which was his standard response. They organized a cleaning crew from West Side Bible Church, and started sending us pictures to show what they had accomplished. In several of the pictures, we honestly couldn't tell which room it was, because we'd never seen it so clean and well organized!

The showings went well, and one couple even came back for a second look. They returned on a Sunday morning, having only looked inside the house. A fresh blanket of snow had fallen over night, masking the muddy earth beneath. They stood with their backs against the metal fence rail and several of the llamas walked up silently behind them.

"When they turned around and saw the llamas, I could see in their faces that your house had just sold," Tony later recounted. "Those llamas sold your house."

To this day, whenever I talk to Dr. Jackson, who bought the house, he gives me a detailed account of how the llamas are doing (one is still alive as of this writing). It turns out that his wife's passion is rescuing animals, and now the property is a veritable sanctuary for them.

Over the next 18 months, we sold the house, bought a smaller (and cheaper) house in town, worked to pay off the last of student loans, and traveled and spoke with many individuals and churches. Between selling and buying houses, we lived in our 34-foot trailer for four months, parking it behind our church—going from a 7,000 square foot house to a 240 square foot space. And then Alex even came home from college to visit for a few weeks!

We hoped to pay off our school loans a few months before we were to leave for Sudan, to have a little saved. Then we paid taxes. Because of all the extra work we were happy to receive in the last year, our taxes were more than I earned in my first year out of medical school.

We paid off our last loan by phone on the way to airport—on June 28, 2011—and had nothing saved.

We barely had our heads above the financial waters and had to once again *actually* trust God.

When you pray, are you ready to obey what God might reveal?

Have you ever been in a situation where you had to actually trust God?

Chapter 2:
A New Playing Field

We arrived in Yei, Sudan on July 2, 2011. It was still Sudan—for one week. Yei was a crossroads town of at least 150,000 people, a melting pot of many tribal groups from within and an assortment of foreigners—Indians, Pakistanis, Ugandans, and Kenyans. It was recaptured from the Arab government of Khartoum in 1997, and served as a secondary post of the embryonic nation about to be birthed.

Yei was nestled at nearly 3,000 feet elevation and crisscrossed with undulating ridges, sloping down to the Yei River, and eventually into the River Nile, 100 miles away. Fifty miles to the south, the borders of Sudan, Uganda, and the Democratic Republic of Congo came to a common point.

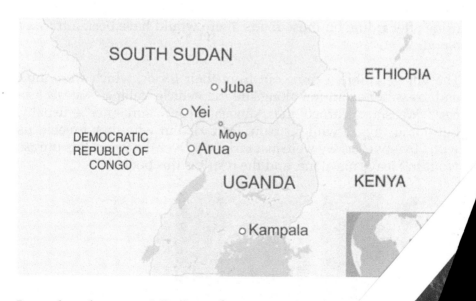

Jagged peaks rose oddly from the more gentle hills ´ north. Remnants of old coffee and banana planta´ seen on the fertile slopes, remnants of the Bri´

28

the early 1900's. The land was lush and green for nine months of the year, granting three abundant growing seasons to the people.

The dry season followed. Three months with little to no rain, turning the moist ground into cement-like hardness, and clouds of dust swirling with any wind or passing vehicle. The dust made its way into every crevice of house and car and sucked the moisture out of humans. Cracks opened in the earth as it became drier. The old people used to tell the young ones that the earth was coming to an end and that it would swallow them if they weren't careful.

Passing through Yei, it seemed like an Old West town—dirt streets, elevated sidewalks in front of the many small shops—though instead of cowboys with pistols, there were lanky African men in worn fatigues, with AK-47's slung over their shoulders. Three miles out of town was our new home, Harvesters. The white hardtop Toyota Landcruiser carried us over the rutted roads, occasionally slamming our backs against the thinly padded seats. It was like a poorly refereed boxing match in which my opponent was landing repeated kidney punches. I'm pretty sure that if we had tested our urine after riding on those roads, there would have been a trace of blood.

The village children came out from their *tukuls*, which were mud and grass huts, and ran alongside the vehicle, calling "*Kawaja bye-bye!*" We soon learned that kawaja meant "foreigner"—usually, but not always, a white person. I puzzled at why they greeted us with "bye-bye" as we were just arriving. Over the years, this phrase wouldn't leave me alone, and the result is this book.

The teak road in rainy & dry season—same location on the road to our home

We approached Harvesters through a green, living tunnel carved from the teak forest. If one looked closely, the large, hardwood trees were carefully planted in neat rows—again, leftovers from plantation days of the British. The leaves were unnaturally large, big enough to have just one leaf shade a person from the sun. During dry season, all of them fell, creating huge mounds, a favorite hiding place for snakes. Therefore, the locals set fire to the leaves, with flames reaching 20 feet in the air, yet the trees themselves never suffered more than a little carbon marking.

One week after arriving, on July 9, 2011, we celebrated the inaugural Independence Day in our new home, which was thereafter known as "South Sudan." We watched as the orphanage children marched out of the gate toward town, and then later joined the celebration at EPC (Evangelical Presbyterian Church) at the invitation of the Bishop. The children's choir from Harvesters danced in rhythm, dressed in new, matching outfits made of vibrant African fabric. "Higher, higher; lift Jesus higher; lower, lower; lower Satan lower," they sang as they brought the words to life with their actions. It was a hopeful time, filled with the possibilities that freedom and self-governance allowed.

Olivia with giant teak leaf

Three weeks later, we were directed to bring our Sudanese pounds to the bank and exchange them for the newly printed South Sudanese pounds (SSP). We had no idea how much these little notes would influence the course of the newest nation in the world, our lives, and the hospital we were asked to establish.

During the first nine months on the ground, the hospital was not yet birthed. We knew it wouldn't be done before we came, and planned to oversee the completion. We felt it wouldn't fully materialize until we actually showed up. Gloria, a missionary nurse who joined us, somehow missed the memo that the hospital wouldn't open immediately. This produced a lot of tension amongst our newly forming team, and she struggled with impatience and discontent. She took her frustration out by criticizing the leadership and ministry. After four months of difficult conversations and interventions, the founders of the ministry asked her to leave. We were off to a rough start. After five months, we lost the only teammate we had and still didn't have a hospital. God was in the process of breaking us down to build as He intended. And He wasn't done with Gloria and us, but would later show us the power of forgiveness and redemption in that relationship (more on that in chapter 18).

Neither was our home complete when we arrived. We moved into it two weeks after our arrival, despite lack of interior doors. Those came over time. We busied ourselves with setting up our lives, schooling, and learning the rhythms of life at the orphanage. Bond, one of the older boys, planted umbrella trees and a "living fence"—a succulent plant used as a barrier around local homes. The sap from this plant burned his eyes because it was toxic, which was part of its usefulness in keeping unwanted visitors out.

Language confusion

We sought out someone to teach us language. At first, we had some of the older orphans try to teach us Juba Arabic, the trade language of South Sudan. It was a simpler version of Arabic, mixed with tribal words, similar to the blending of Arabic and the Bantu languages of the coast of East Africa, which produced Swahili (Kiswahili).

This didn't go so well. The children at the orphanage were from various Sudanese tribes, being taught by Kenyan, Ugandan, American, and some South Sudanese teachers and missionaries—in English. Amongst themselves, they used Juba Arabic mixed with words they remembered from their various "mother tongues"— thereby creating a jumbled mess of vocabulary. We discovered that the older the individual, the more time spent in Juba or further north, the "cleaner" the Arabic would be (closer to classical Arabic). Over the centuries, Arabs had dominated the region, with the British following in the late nineteenth century. The British bumped into the French, who were colonizing from the west of Africa, somewhere in the low jungle area where we were then living. They apparently became tired of fighting disease, each other, and the native peoples, so they decided to sit down and send messages back to Europe as to how to divide up the lands. While they waited for a reply, the soldiers settled in for card games, drinking, and eating together. Eventually, word came back—they would divide Africa down the middle, with the French taking the west, and the British, the east. Hence, the Francophone and Anglophone (French-speaking and English-speaking) areas of Africa were established.[1]

Today, if you travel 20 miles to the west of Yei, you will reach the border of Democratic Republic of Congo (DRC), and suddenly need to speak French! I soon discovered that some of the local doctors were Congolese, and they wrote their medical notes in French. When our watches needed to be repaired, we took them to "Zozef" (Joseph), a little old man from DRC who had a roadside stand by the first roundabout as we entered town. Elizabeth spoke to him in French, and we paid 10-15 SSP ($2-3 US) for his work.

Loving the people = language learning

After six months of language confusion, veteran missionary Rhondda led us to a proper language tutor, Kezia (kuh-JZEE-uh). Rhondda helped us understand the importance of learning language; *not just as a means to an end, but integral to knowing and loving the people of the culture.* Being a student of the language kept us in a posture of humility, as we sounded like babies and toddlers while learning. People didn't just laugh with us—they laughed at us! But to not try to learn their language (which embodied the ideas and values of their culture) would have been rude, indifferent, and dishonoring—the opposite of love. By making even crude efforts to listen and speak in their tongue, we hopefully communicated our desire to respect and learn about them.

Kezia not only taught us Juba Arabic, she also unwrapped layers of insight about the people of South Sudan that were only revealed by delving into the language. She was a godly woman, who grew into serving as a lay chaplain in the hospital, praying with and counseling the many women who later came through the doors.

We learned that the "j" and "z" are interchangeable for an Arabic speaker of English, as are "p" and "f," as in Arabic there are several letters that are between these sounds, making translation a bit fluid. This made for some interesting twists.

"Doctor, there are some fufils that need to be seen," said nurse Esther, by which she meant there were students in the clinic.

Even funnier, and more humbling to us, were our names. I was often called (and sometimes actually written on official documents), "Dr. Ferry" (or "Dr. Fairy"?). This was a real test to my security as a man, but when Dr. Poole joined us, I didn't feel so bad about my name anymore. We were the missionary doctors—Dr. Fairy and Dr. Fool.

Years later, my name was changed again, this time by a Kampala generator dealer, where they frequently interchange "r" and "l"—such as "Kampala Load" meaning "Kampala Road" or a "LAV-4" being a Toyota RAV-4. Blending my first name (Jeff) with last name to become Dr. Jerry, and changing the "rr" to "ll," I became Dr. Jelly.

The "S" and "Sh" sounds were also debatable. Our guard Samuel was a gentle, faithful man. Early in our tenure there, we asked him to step into our sitting room to teach us how to say John 3:16 in Juba Arabic. He dutifully recited the verse, with his AK-47 assault rifle on his shoulder. Using the "sh" sound instead of "s," he once invited several of our children to "S-it down" on the bench outside our house, which he repeated emphatically several times, thinking they didn't understand him, judging by their stunned expressions and lack of movement. They were shocked, but later understood that he wasn't being inappropriate—only that pronunciation is flexible, and words of profanity don't usually transfer across cultures. They are deeply ingrained and particular to ones upbringing.

A man came to see me in the one room clinic at the orphanage, while we were waiting for the hospital to be built. He was over six foot three inches tall, with the telltale scarration of his forehead, indicating he had been through the coming of age ritual for his tribe, the Dinka.

"I have a problem with a rose," he said with intense, yet hushed tones.

"I'm sorry... I'm not understanding. You have a problem with what?" I pressed.

"You know, a problem with arose."

"I still don't quite understand."

"I have a problem with the fenis... it cannot rose!" he said in forced whisper, slightly annoyed at my slowness.

Oh...erectile dysfunction! I said to myself. And so we discussed the matter. It was not a floral crisis after all.

Language differences within

When our Australian and Kiwi (from New Zealand) teammates arrived, the humorous yet challenging issues continued! Who knew you could say the same words, all be speaking "English," but with entirely different meanings? Some differences were amusing and obvious. The "soccer field" became the "footy pitch." "Running shoes" were "joggers." "I'm wired up as a 2 IC" meant "I'm best suited as the 'second in command'—to support the leader." We laughed at each other's "accents"—then truly grappled with the fact that I saw my speech as normal, and all others as having accents (demonstrating my ego/ethnocentrism). It wasn't until we had been away from other Americans for multiple years, that we started hearing our American accent.

Other differences were insidious, leading to serious misunderstandings and assumptions about each other's motives. "Whateva" to us sounded like, "go ahead and do what you're going to do; I don't care, and I don't like you; I'm writing you off anyways." To our Australian teammates, however, this meant "I'm truly okay with any of these options, and you are more important to me than the particular outcome of this decision, so please go ahead and choose." The challenge was to begin to really hear each other's words as the speaker intended, not with the meaning that the listener brought to the conversation. But first, we had to uncover those words that bothered us, were different, and interfered with the life of our team. This took time and direct conversation, such as "when you say this, what do you mean?" It also required that we give one another the benefit of the doubt. It seemed inefficient, but as we were discovering, God is not concerned with efficiency, but with how well we learn to love one another. No matter how long it takes us to get it.

Birth Pains of a Hospital

Mama Veronica attended the church next to our house. She was pregnant, and called us when she suspected she was in labor. As we were on our way to the airstrip to pick up visitors, we dropped her at the government hospital. We all wished our hospital was ready for use, as she almost delivered in our van! She gave birth 36 minutes after we left her at the hospital.

Several years later Mama Veronica delivered twins at *His House of Hope*. She called Elizabeth to walk with her as her labor pains started. But first, she made tea for them at her tukul while Elizabeth became increasingly nervous. As they walked the half-mile to the hospital, she had to pause multiple times for contractions, raising Elizabeth's concern that she would end up delivering 36-week twins in the teak forest.

Our home was about 50 meters from the hospital, so during those early months, we could watch the slow progress on the hospital from our bedroom windows. With each death wail from the surrounding tropical forest, we wondered if we might have saved that life if the hospital was built and running. I felt like a carpenter with a few nails, some lumber, but no hammer. Bringing Western medicine will eliminate many of these deaths, I thought to myself. In the meantime, during school holidays, two South Sudanese students began meeting with me to talk about science and faith. James L. and Aaron had grown up in and around Harvesters and were both interested in medicine. They occasionally followed me as I visited other hospitals and saw patients in the one room clinic at the orphanage.

Tutoring and discipleship with James and Aaron

In early January 2012, we hired our first staffs— two laboratory technicians. Through visiting other hospitals and clinics, and talking to our new staff, I learned that blood transfusion, malaria treatment, and delivery management were most important to saving lives in this setting. A strong lab department helped us practice medicine in a more directed manner—rather than guessing at what was going on. Opening the lab was a key first step. I was grateful that God had seen fit to give me some familiarity with the lab. I had grown up watching my mom work as a laboratory technologist, and I had spent one year during medical school doing a fellowship in the Pathology department.

Moving Day

March 20, 2012 started like most Tuesdays in Yei—oatmeal, family devotions, still 85 degrees inside... but was interrupted by a call from the nurse. One of the older housemothers had vomited 700ml (~3 cups) of blood and was very sick. I arrived to clinic as the second bottle of normal saline was going in, and staff devotions were underway. Despite the fluids, her blood pressure was very low (69/57) and heart rate high (120), indicating she was in shock from acute blood loss. She probably had a bleeding stomach ulcer.

The insides of her eyelids were completely pale, suggesting severe anemia, so we quickly checked a hemoglobin level—a test we had just started doing. It was 2.9—a level of anemia that would have killed most people (in the West, we give blood if the level is less than 10, with normal being 12-16). Likely she had lived with anemia for a long time, due to malaria and poor nutrition, but now it was at a life-threatening level. We knew that if she didn't receive a transfusion quickly, she would die.

At the same time, we were discussing which day we should move to the new clinic. Nurse Bosco emphatically said, "Today we should move," and all of us agreed. This would be the day, and not only that; we would have our first critically ill inpatient that night.

Several of the staff swept, cleaned, and organized the rooms in Bet Eman ("House of Faith") - *His House of Hope*, while others saw the steady stream of patients arriving at the one-room clinic next to the orphanage. Meanwhile, Frazer, our lab tech, and I started discussing how to transfuse her. We could run the necessary screening tests and type and cross-match the blood, but our centrifuge had just broken the day before, and we did not have the bag or tubing to collect and give the units of blood. By the grace of God, our sister clinic in town (at EPC) had the blood giving sets and a working centrifuge.

Meanwhile, despite over two liters of fluids, the patient's blood pressure was decreasing (55/40). She had vomited blood again, and it was obvious she was actively bleeding. We stopped and prayed that the Lord would sustain her, allow us to coordinate the transfusion, and that His power would restore her body through these interventions. At the next check of vital signs, her blood pressure had increased slightly for the first time.

We tested the patient's blood type and started looking for donors. All of the family members available were NOT compatible, so we started asking staff. In East Africa, one's identity is largely based in the tribe. An African does not primarily think of himself by political boundaries (South Sudanese, Kenyan, or Ugandan), but by tribe. Our patient was a Kakwa, while the two staff donors we found were Dinka and Kikuyu (a Kenyan tribe). They freely gave anyway.

In the early afternoon, family and staff carried our first patient (now unconscious and critically ill) to the new clinic on a backboard. It was the end of dry season, so the teak trees were bare, the ground parched, and dust and smoke permeated the air. The place seemed as spent and close to death as was the patient. The lab tech drained blood from the donors and started the transfusion.

Miraculously, the patient continued to improve, woke up, and stabilized. This abuba (grandmother) survived after several units of blood and medication to help the ulcer, though she never returned to work at the orphanage. We had a picture of the truth that through Christ's blood, we are reconciled to God and with one another, and that He will call worshippers from every tribe and nation.

So, with this auspicious beginning, Bet Eman was finally operational—in HIS timing. I felt like a carpenter with a few more nails, some mismatched lumber, and a largely unproven hammer.

Examining the first inpatient at Bet Eman

As we opened the hospital doors to the community, people began coming—many more for antenatal care than for delivery. Finally, our first delivery was performed— in room 3 of the clinic, with a nurse, my wife Elizabeth, and the student James helping. When we realized she would deliver a premature baby, we scrambled to unpack and clean the incubator that was delivered by Samaritan's Purse. She pushed the baby out while lying on a flat exam table, and it was not a happy occasion. The baby was severely premature and had anencephaly (lacking the top of the skull)—a condition that does not allow a baby to live. The baby died within minutes of birth. Elizabeth and I had walked through a similar delivery with our friends just the year before. These were the same friends that invited us to join this work—and we wondered at this sad, difficult beginning to His House of "Hope."

Not just numbers anymore

In ten plus years of delivering babies in the US, I had never had a mother die during childbirth. In South Sudan, 1 in 9 mothers died in or around the time of childbirth. These were shockingly poor numbers on paper, but I never really thought of how, or even if, they would affect me.

June 22, 2012 began with a woman presenting 4 hours after giving birth at home. She was having severe bleeding and the placenta was still inside. I easily removed the placenta just as the bleeding stopped. The nurse was struggling to take her vitals—unable to get a blood pressure reading. As I looked up at the patient, I realized the reason the bleeding had stopped, and why he couldn't get a blood pressure on her. She had bled out and died.

We then performed a successful C-section on another patient, followed shortly thereafter by a vaginal delivery that was uneventful.

The next morning on rounds, I discovered that a patient who was 31 weeks pregnant no longer had a fetal heartbeat. She had been admitted several days earlier, shortly after hearing her mother had died. The history was scant, other than they had traveled on some bumpy roads to reach her mother's village. She had improved slightly with treatment, but the exact nature of her condition was unclear.

Her heartbeat was fast, liver enlarged, her uterus somewhat tender, and her lungs were filled with crackles (popping sounds). The possibilities ranged from partial placental abruption (separation), pulmonary embolism, acute fatty liver of pregnancy or other cause of hepatitis, phenobarbitone toxicity (a medicine for seizures, which she took for epilepsy), pneumonia, or amniotic fluid embolism. The differential diagnoses were many, and due to the lack of diagnostic equipment, I couldn't specify more. I say this, even though we had more than most hospitals in South Sudan. Our staff and the family also suspected poisoning in the differential—a common way for people in South Sudan to get rid of someone of whom they were jealous.

As we attempted to stabilize her and decide whether to induce her delivery or remove the baby by Caesarean section, she suddenly died.

The family and our staff guided us that we needed to remove the baby from the mother so they could be buried separately. Local tradition was to bury the baby in the foundation of the mud tukul in which the family lived, whereas the mother would be placed in a grave between the tukuls of their compound.

So, a C-section was done for the deceased mother and baby. It was a nearly bloodless procedure, silent and grim. As nurse Bosco and I worked late that night to close the incisions, it was an opportunity to teach him surgical assisting skills without the pressure of a live patient.

After the surgery was done, the lab tech, Frazer, started drawing up large amounts of formaldehyde, as we next had to become the morticians—to preserve the body until burial. In three days, I had lost two mothers. I began to realize that though we aimed to practice Western medicine in South Sudan, we were on a new playing field. The objective numbers of 1 death for every 9 mothers were now a stinging, subjective reality—real people for whom I was trying to care.

Death summaries

The playing field involved social, spiritual, political, and other issues. There were a myriad of factors that contributed to people not coming to the hospital for labor—or if they did, they didn't come until they were near death and beyond saving. At this point, regardless of the level of care we provided, we could do nothing.

The patients might lack a vehicle, and when in labor, they were in too much pain to walk. At times it was raining, dark, and the road was impassable by bicycle or motorcycle. The husband may have been reluctant to take her to the hospital because of the potential cost, and accepted the risk of her death (and everyone in the family has always delivered at home previously). Never mind that the cost of a burial was much greater than delivery at the hospital. If labor started at night, they might fear going out because of the risk of violence, animals, or evil spirits...

We quickly discovered that death was a way of life in South Sudan. We would try to figure out the cause to the best of our limited diagnostic ability. One morning, our longest-standing nurse was brought in with cardiac arrest. We struggled to resuscitate her, but couldn't. I wrote her death summary based on my Western medical training—she probably had a heart attack or blood clot in her lungs, as she had a history of high blood pressure and had been put on birth control pills a few weeks earlier. Maybe this was correct.

The hospital staff took rotations to attend her funeral. As medical director, I was called on to say some words on behalf of the hospital. It was close to 100 degrees Fahrenheit, and her rapidly swelling body lay on a bed surrounded by a white mosquito net. A large network of plastic tarps on teak poles shaded the nearly 300 people from the midday sun. The husband, a local pastor, had rented enough plastic chairs for everyone. I said my words, Elizabeth and I paid our respects to the family, left our gift of sugar, and walked the half-mile back to the hospital compound in the heat.

The next rotation of staff included Dr. Nadia, a young Australian doctor who had just joined us for a time. When she arrived, the family asked her to read the death summary and explain to the crowd how they could take care of their health so the same thing wouldn't happen to them. It was all so strange to us—a very different playing field.

Later, I heard that most people in the community were sure that she was in fact poisoned. From time to time, we heard the fear of poisoning, usually stemming from jealousy. If someone succeeded in life, he became a target because others envied him.

Our Ugandan staff were often fearful that the South Sudanese cooks would try to harm them through poisoning their food. Fear also was a way of life in South Sudan. It seemed like a bit of overdone paranoia to me.

Then one day as we did rounds in the pediatric ward, the nurse called me over.

"Look at this porridge," she urged me.
I looked closely, and saw many tiny shards of glass. "What happened?!"

"The patient's mother-in-law put glass in the porridge because she was angry with the patient. We've already chased her from the ward."

I might not have believed it if I hadn't seen it. I was definitely on a new playing field, and I doubted some of my previous death summaries. I underestimated the brokenness of the people. Perhaps many of these deaths could not be explained with medical reasoning.

Supplies and help

I also underestimated the mammoth task of keeping a hospital supplied. In the West, we just ask, and the medical tools we need are usually available. In Yei, we struggled to get needed supplies to the hospital—either purchased regionally or donated and shipped from abroad. Certain medications and supplies were just not available—not made, or not supplied except through a governmental or NGO program. When we found the supplies, the process of coordinating shipping and fulfilling the requirements to import them were overwhelming and sluggish at best.

Before we opened, I sat in our South Sudan home with Dr. Tony

Park, creating a massive ordering list. Samaritan's Purse sent a useful container of supplies to get us started. And by the end of 2012, the Lord had brought a missionary team to carry these burdens with us—nurse Katherine Young, Dr. Graham and Linda Poole and their three children, and nurse Kitty Moyer. When they arrived, we had been open four months, but it seemed like a year. We were already dragging. I developed an abscess on the back of my neck while also struggling with typhoid fever. I wasn't seeing the "rewards for obedience" I remembered from Scripture (Deuteronomy 8)!

It was a rude awakening, that bringing us didn't bring Western outcomes. There were harder cases, more compromised patients, less trained and fewer staff, and fewer resources. I realized the local doctors fought against these same barriers. Many of them knew what needed to be done, but were not able to bring their knowledge to bear on making many of the patients better.

They too were like carpenters lacking tools. My early judgment of local doctors went away. I realized that the provision of care (including when we became the patients) was affected by the setting in which we now were— their culture, their beliefs, and their government and infrastructure. And this was in a time of peace and relative prosperity for South Sudan. I didn't yet realize how much more economic instability and civil war would complicate matters. These would make it a field nearly impossible on which to play. And through these stressors, we would be thrust into complete dependence on God, which is the best playing field.

How do you view language learning? Is it optional, depending on the type of work you do, or integral to living amongst another culture?

What assumptions do you bring as you follow God's calling in your life?

In what ways are we are blessed when we obey—materially, health-wise, and / or spiritually?

Chapter 3:
Mzungu Matatu: *How NOT to travel in Africa*

"Are you still in Mombasa?" It was Christine, our Area Leader with Pioneers, calling from her home in Nairobi.

"Yes," I replied warily. We were in the midst of an attempted holiday after a harrowing first few months in our second term, including civil war, blindness, and near-death of a child.

And that was all in just five months.

"Why do you ask?"

"The British Embassy has just issued an order for all British expats to get out of the area."

"Good thing we're not British!" I thought nervously to myself. But rather, I said, "What's the concern?"

"They have good reason to believe there will be a terrorist attack in Mombasa—a bomb or the like," she explained. Mombasa is located on the south-central coast of Kenya—south of Somalia, home to an increasingly active terrorist group at that time. "Where exactly are you now?"

I groaned to myself, but felt a strange surrender. There was nothing to do. At the very moment she called, we were packed in a sea of cars waiting to get on a ferry to cross from the island on which the city was located, back to the mainland. It was a Friday, the Muslim holy day (jamaat), so the ferry was packed with hundreds of passengers returning from prayers at the mosque, in black, full-length Muslim garb. If the terrorists were targeting Western Christians like us, they would surely injure many of their own. I felt oddly safer amidst the crowd, and we were in gridlock, so there was little we could do.

We had gotten out of South Sudan for a "rest" from the civil war, which had started some six months earlier. And now we were in the midst of a terrorist alert in Kenya—out of the frying pan and into the fire. We proceeded onto the ferry, crossed over, and made our way back to the home in which we were staying. Nothing happened—in Mombasa. But the next day, there was a bombing in the market—in Nairobi. Good enough, as we would be traveling back there in a few days, then further upcountry to have a third, unexpected eye surgery on my right eye *(more on that soon)*.

Such went our attempts at "holidays" (times of rest or vacation) from the intensity of the work. It was recommended, even required, that we get out of country to rest every three to four months. At first, this seemed excessive, but once the work really got going, we realized the wisdom in this request. Not only was the medical work grueling, but the culture stress wore us down. Those who have lived in another culture long-term can affirm this. After about three months of constantly filtering new experiences through a different cultural lens, we found ourselves getting snippy and becoming compassion-fatigued.

Car-buying "vacation"

Our very first trip out of South Sudan was for the purpose of buying a car in Kampala, Uganda, 400 miles south of Yei. We thought we'd take some time to rest, but we had no idea how complicated it would be, and all the laws we'd be breaking as we drove the vehicle back to South Sudan. We made the two-day drive to Kampala. I then began the search for a suitable vehicle, going about the city on a boda boda (motorcycle taxi) with a mechanic that worked with Harvesters. The traffic police ticketed us because the two of us plus the driver were sharing the boda. This, despite the fact that most bodas had four to five people on them, plus a few dozen chickens and assorted items!

Once we found one to purchase, the complexities of buying a vehicle in one country, but registering it in another (where the church would help obtain some tax exemptions), began to emerge. We discovered that we had three days to make the two-day drive, 350 miles to the border, where the Ugandan Revenue Authority (URA) would make sure we actually took it out of the country. They had waived the usual 30% tax as we planned to register it in South Sudan. We didn't really understand this until later, though, and we couldn't leave immediately because the van needed seats (a luxury, apparently)! The van was a 1994 Toyota Hiace 4-wheel drive diesel van. This was the same body type as thousands of taxis throughout the region— "matatus" as they were known.

We took it to the garage straight away. They would install seats, luggage rack, and protective bars. The owner told us it would be ready in the next day or two. On the second day, the car dealer started calling, agitated that we had not left. It was then that we learned of the time crunch we were facing. He knew we hadn't left because he was required by law to pay for an escort from the URA to ride with us all the way to the border. We would also have a driver with us, as we had never driven the road north to Yei. I started visiting the garage more and more, and saw that the work was frustratingly slow in getting done. On the third day, I stayed at the garage until it was done—refusing to leave until I left with the vehicle! The welding and bolting continued until close to midnight, sparks flying in the dark from the crew of 4-5 Ugandan men and the owner from Seychelles. I finally drove the van back to the guesthouse for a short night of sleep.

Early in the morning, we loaded everything on the roof, covered with a giant tarp (known as a "carpet" by most there), and headed out of the city while still dark. The driver stopped on the outskirts of the city to pick up the URA escort, Abdul, a small Ugandan Muslim man with an alarmed look on his face.

"You can't have all these passengers!" he said. "You are only allowed the owner, driver, and URA escort."

"But we weren't even aware of that law," I explained. "At this point, we can't make alternate plans for all of us."

We proceeded nervously. There were 14 of us in the van—driver, escort, the ten of us, and two others from the ministry that were riding back with us. We were so new there, we weren't aware how safe or feasible it was to arrange another way to travel, and we were not about to split up and travel separately. Yet, we realized how many infracted, unwritten laws were beginning to mount against us. We were already two days beyond the date we were supposed to be out of the country. Our fears were realized before we even made it out of the city. Passing a police station, we were flagged down. Abdul and the driver got out and a heated discussion ensued with the traffic police. Would our journey end before it started?

After a few minutes, they returned with worn expressions and the verdict—we would continue after paying a fine of 60,000 shillings (~$25 USD at the time). We did, and resumed the drive—and the traffic police stops continued almost without fail. I realized that driving a vehicle without "number plates" (license plate) in Uganda was like flying a banner saying, "I might be stealing this car—please stop me and harass me, and while you're at it, ask me for money!" When the white-uniformed traffic police saw this "matatu" carried 10 "Mzungus" (foreigners) and several others, they found even more reasons to question us, fine us, and generally chew us out for not obeying the laws we had just learned of that day. I began to have a visceral response to seeing white uniforms along the road (which continues to this day), and we realized that if we kept our speed up as we drove past, and avoided eye contact, they weren't likely to shame themselves by running after us.

The children were largely undeterred, though. Abdul sat between the driver and me in the front bench seat, as we alternated driving, while the children sang "Rabuna huwo Rabuna kweys" in Arabic (our God is a wonderful God). Checkpoints continued, including one just after crossing the River Nile, which was a small URA office. We explained our delay, tried to not bring attention to the 14 of us in the van, paid more fees, and were eventually allowed to proceed. We finally pulled into Arua (a town in northwestern Uganda) in the evening, where we would sleep before proceeding the rest of the way the next day. Abdul was nearly panicked as we indicated we wanted to drive into town to get some food for the children.

"You are not allowed to drive around anywhere except directly to the border," he insisted. "There are more traffic police in town who will stop us!"

"Yes, but the children need food!" Elizabeth replied.

The next day, we finally reached the border, almost a week after we should have been there. After some mild reprimands and more fees, the URA agent let us pass after listening to our explanation and apologies.

We crossed into South Sudan, where we learned we would have to leave the vehicle! It needed to sit in the South Sudan customs lot for nearly a week before an agent could help us clear it. We had to wait for exemptions to clear, as it would be licensed under a South Sudanese church. We unloaded the van, hired several smaller cars, and all piled in.

The cars' suspensions were low, but that didn't stop them from speeding over the rutted "Kaya Road" that led from the border town of Kaya to Yei, 50 miles away. Upon reaching the town center, they abruptly stopped and demanded more money to take us all the way, despite our struggles earlier to explain to them that we lived 3 miles outside of town. With our limited Arabic, their limited English, and our feeling of being "taken," we called the Bishop and then our compound director in our desperation. (We later realized with embarrassment that this was a small thing to bother him about, and it was a common problem.) A lorry (truck) from the ministry came to pick our belongings and us from the side of the road in the center of town. We finally reached home, exhausted from the journey.

This was our first "vacation." It was definitely cheaper to drive than fly, but either way it was a chunk of change to travel with ten people. Before we left for the field, Dr. Duininck, one of my teachers in Family Medicine, made the insightful statement that "anything times eight (or ten as it had become)" is a lot of money! He, his wife and 6 children had moved to Ghana for two years, and said that with a hint of "get ready for the 'sticker shock,' but God will amaze you that He can handle it." Visas to get into Uganda were $50 per person (later increased to $100)—not bad for a single person, but for the ten of us, it was $500 (later $1,000) just to set foot in the country.

Elusive rest on vacation

After more than six months of living in South Sudan, we still had no hospital despite many hours of groundwork. We had only been out of the area once. So when we requested money for our next holiday, the well-meaning office staff with our mission sending agency told us that we really weren't meant to take extravagant vacations on the field (though they required us to leave every 3-4 months). We laughed, and felt a mixture of frustration and humor, remembering our first road trip to bring the van in. We told them that we had to leave South Sudan to have any sort of respite, and that we were "vacationing" in another developing country—hardly extravagant!

So it was that we embarked on our first "real" holiday, four months after purchasing the van. Things went fairly well at first. We stopped at the border to stamp out of South Sudan, buy temporary Ugandan registration, car insurance, and Ugandan visas. The first 100 miles were on murram roads. Murram is the red, fine dirt which when compacted and dried by the intense sun of the tropics, turns nearly as hard as pavement. Unfortunately, people usually drive on it, or rains create washboards and potholes before a nice, even hardening can occur. Often we would come across a lorry that had taken a rut wrongly and ended up on its side. This would then block the precious little part of the road that was drivable, and someone would create a "side road" to get around the blockage.

We were happy to finally be on the open road on our own, but it was slow going, and we didn't want to ruin the van we'd worked so hard to acquire. So we took our time. Other drivers whizzed past us, sending up clouds of swirling dust. In places, the roads were deeply rutted. We learned that taking these ruts at an angle allowed us to cross things we didn't think were navigable. The van had a long wheelbase and wasn't raised like other 4-wheel drives, so we scraped bottom if we weren't careful. Even when we had crossed into Uganda, the roads didn't get any better (until Arua, another 50 miles south of the border, where the tarmac started).

As yet another low-set, small car passed us at breakneck speed, I thought in amazement—how do their vehicles hold together? I listened to ours rattling down the road at a pedestrian pace and prayed Ephesians 1:17 often—"in Him all things hold together. May this be true of our van also!" As I pondered this, I noticed black spots on the pale red dirt road in front of me. The black spots congealed into a thin line of fresh oil glistening on the dry ground. The thin line grew thicker, then arched off the side of the road, where it ended at the same small car that had just passed us. They had stopped because of their cracked oil pan. Apparently, they were also subject to physics.

We breathed a sigh of relief upon reaching pavement, and stayed in Arua for one night, allowing the kids the opportunity to swim in the only pool in the region—though the water had a very questionable green color. The next day, as we crossed the "Albert Nile" bridge (so named as this portion of the river flows out of Lake Albert), we snapped a picture of the sign (not the bridge, as we had been told to not take pictures of critical infrastructure such as this). We did so for Grandma Grace, from our home church in Colorado, in memoriam of her husband, Albert, who had recently passed away.

Before reaching the other side of the bridge, we saw several uniformed men running after us—with AK-47's. Thinking it wise to slow down and stop for police with automatic weapons, we waited for them to catch up. The officers demanded the camera and began inspecting the photos, insisting that we delete the picture and threatening to take the camera. After listening to our reason for taking the picture, and seeing that only the sign was visible, they allowed us to keep the picture. Naturally, for a small fee.

We planned to spend a few days at a hotel in Murchison Falls National Park, where we would be able to see some of the traditional wild animals of Africa. The only animals we had so far seen in South Sudan were mostly dogs and cats—the giraffes, lions, and rhinos had been killed for meat or driven away during the many decades of war. As we got near the hotel, another car was blocking the road as they had stopped to look at something to the left. We pulled up behind and saw that it was a mother elephant with her baby! Suddenly, a baboon lunged in the right side window and started grabbing things from the kids. As I turned to the right, I noticed something else—the father elephant, moving rapidly toward us. The children slammed the window shut, causing the baboon to withdraw, as I "hooted" (honked) the horn to urge the car ahead of us to move. As they realized our danger, we both pulled out quickly, narrowly avoiding the wrath of Daddy Elephant. Many have been killed this way. African elephants in the wild are not the docile creatures of circuses and zoos.

The hotel was quite nice, perched on a bluff overlooking the Nile. Elizabeth had tried to secure rooms with cooking facilities, as we prefer her cooking and it saves money!

"Do you have anything besides full room and board?" she inquired several times. No, they didn't. The hotel only offered full board, and the meals cooked by an Indian chef were quite elaborate. Each meal was a buffet with various forms of meat, which we hadn't had much of in the previous seven months. There was also Indian food with curry, and desserts.

Upon awakening the next morning, Hazel was feeling sick, so Elizabeth stayed with her while the rest of us embarked on a morning drive to see the animals. We saw a few, and upon returning, several more of us starting feeling nauseated. By the end of the day, seven of ten in the family (sparing only Elizabeth, Logan, and Olivia) had "two-bucket" disease—both vomiting and diarrhea. So while a few in the family enjoyed the nice meals, the rest stayed in the rooms. The bathroom floors were quite nice—cool, smooth, clean tile. That was the main experience for most of us. Despite Elizabeth's pleadings, the hotel refused to reduce our payments, even though we barely ate anything.

Logan avoided the illness, but injured himself by running into the immaculately clean sliding glass door to the balcony. It was quite a time. By the third day, we were mostly well, but our time was up. We hadn't seen much (besides the bathrooms), so we decided to take a "shortcut" through the southern part of the park, in hopes of seeing something interesting on the way to Kampala. We drove down the hill from the hotel, with the Nile on our left. We stopped at an open area of dirt near a large tree, at the river. A sign indicated this was the ferry landing. The flat, metal ferry was stationed at the edge of the river, just large enough to hold four or five cars. This didn't give us a huge amount of confidence, seeing as hippos and crocodiles inhabited the waters. Years later, Hazel anxiously remembered this experience as we prepared to cross the Nile on a larger ferry downriver.

We safely crossed the Victoria Nile, and on the other side, the park changed almost instantly from dry savannah to dense woodland.

Our van, being old and not so fancy, had no air conditioning. We enjoyed the initial drive in the shade of the trees, with the windows open, looking for wildlife.

Soon, the most predominant wildlife found us—tsetse flies. The area used to harbor large amounts of East African sleeping sickness (trypanosomiasis) and they certainly still had plenty of flies around that used to transmit the disease. I later learned they are attracted to fast-moving vehicles and light colors (the van was white, and we were driving as fast as we could on the dirt road). The bite of the tsetse fly hurts like a hard pinch, we soon learned! We all started frantically swatting away at the large black flies, as they bit us even through our clothing. With windows shut, we drove on, and gradually eliminated the flies in our van.

However, the "shortcut" was not fast. The drive continued to drag on, and as the day wore on it got hotter. The windows were dripping with humidity, and we began to succumb to the temptation to open the windows to get some moving air again. We felt relief, and there seemed to be no flies any longer! After a minute or two, however, the flies discovered us. So we shut the windows quickly as we killed more flies and sustained more bites. This cycle repeated itself untold times until we finally emerged from the forest and reached tarmac (pavement) again, much to our relief. *That day, we started our list of how **not** to travel in Africa.* It would be many years before we consented to enter the park again. We also began to realize that vacations in East Africa didn't provide much respite compared to our home in South Sudan. We would have to say "bye-bye" to our expectations of relaxing vacations.

Mzungu Matatu

Other trips came with unexpected additions such as bringing the South Sudanese twins we had just started to adopt (with few official papers to show we weren't leaving the country illegally with them). Another ended with Given, then four years old, sustaining a serious brain injury and a road that had just sustained a serious rain injury. I will leave that trip for a later chapter.

There were lighter moments, and we did get used to being mistaken for a matatu. People would flag us down, and then notice that we had South Sudan number plates and that we were mzungus (Swahili equivalent of kawaja). We then made the sign (fist in hand) that we were "all full." We chuckled at the signs along the way with acronyms like "SLAP" (which ironically stood for the "Society for Less Advantaged Persons"). The traffic police continued to have a close relationship with us since we were an oddity, frequently stopping us. We learned to have our papers ready, smile, and "give appreciation" (say thanks) for them doing their job.

Google Maps & God's provision

The advent of Google Maps being available nearly everywhere in the world gave us a sense of security as we traveled East Africa. On our way to a Christian camp for our kids on the shores of Lake Victoria, we followed Google. It took us the shortest route. That's all I can say it was. Not the quickest, safest, or easiest route! We started getting concerned when we exited the uncommonly good, tarmac roads and started up a mountain on a dirt road. We climbed up one mountain, down the other side, and up another. It was picturesque as we passed through coffee and banana plantations, with views of the lake every so often. But the one-lane road was wet from the recent rain, and sloped dangerously off on each side to the drainage ditches. Between mountains, it was a miry mess of mud, requiring 4-wheel drive.

"How on earth do buses make it through this?!" we puzzled, realizing that Google had not taken us the

Winnie (front) & Given point out an important feature of our "Mzungu Matatu": 4-wheel drive!

best way. We eventually made it, but got verbal directions from a local for the return trip!

One more lesson for traveling in Africa: don't put all your faith in Google Maps. Unfortunately, we didn't learn that lesson the first time. A few months later, we again resorted to following Google while traveling through Kenya to visit a missionary and South Sudanese colleagues working at a remote mission hospital.

The route seemed reasonable at first. Then it had us turn off the main road. It was dry, with newly paved road, and in the right direction, so we proceeded. It was beautiful, wide-open savannah with Mt. Kenya off in the distance.

Then the tarmac ended. We only encountered safari vehicles, and there were no more road signs. It was rocky and slow going, and we cringed as our suspension rattled over the rough road. Finally, 20 miles and an hour later, we reached tarmac again. Relieved, we entered a small town.

I slowed down for the inevitable speed bumps, and it was then that I felt our brakes were different. The pedal was soft and our braking sluggish. The brake pedal went slowly to floor when I pressed it in.

"Something's not right with the brakes," I announced to Elizabeth.

"Should we stop?" she inquired, though perhaps the real question was *if* I could actually stop! We both looked around with trepidation at the mostly deserted buildings. There was no sign of any businesses, much less a garage. Fortunately, the road into the town was on a slight uphill, so I proceeded slowly as we surveyed the scene. "It looks like there is more of a town ahead," Elizabeth noted. "And Google says there is a Total service station to the right."

We decided to veer right when we reached the main road, though our fond feelings for Google were at an all-time low. We drifted ahead and saw the Total station on the right. I glided in, and had just enough brake power to stop the car in front of the service bay. A lone mechanic was working on a car next to where I had stopped. He looked up, and I asked if he could help us with our brakes.

His name was Boniface, and he immediately slid under the front end of the Landcruiser and found the problem: a broken brake line. He found a replacement part, installed it, refilled the brake fluid, and bled the brakes. During this time, Elizabeth prepared lunch for the family, and she asked the station attendant if Boniface was a good mechanic. "He's the best around," she said with certainty.

Within an hour, we were back on the road. We traveled on, the road following the northern side of Mt. Kenya National Park, with steep declines in places. After 2 hours of driving, Elizabeth noticed the brakes becoming soft again. We were again in a flat area, passing through a small trading center. She pulled off to wide, unpaved parking area on the left side of the road. "Perhaps we just need to top up the brake fluid," I said hopefully.

As we lifted the hood, two Kenyan men came over. "Do you need some help?" the older one asked.

"Maybe... we just had our brake line replaced, and the brakes are soft again," I explained.

"Perhaps you need to bleed them again," he suggested.

"Are you a mechanic?" I asked.

"Yes. But I'm just here having my car washed," he said, gesturing to a white sedan nearby. "We can take a look at the brakes."

We accepted, as I wasn't skilled at repairing brakes (or anything on a car, for that matter). He found a leak at a joint of the newly installed line, tightened it, and bled them more thoroughly than before. Within 20 minutes, we were back on the road, without any further brake issues.

As we were passing the same place on our way back a few days later, I noticed the building in front of which we had stopped. It read, "God Provides." Indeed.

Public transport

Bond was a young man who grew up at Harvesters and was a good friend to our kids. He was the one who planted trees and "living fence" around our house when we first arrived. When we had to go to Juba, Harvesters sent him with us, along with several boys who needed to get paperwork done there. They rode with us to Juba. We proceeded by plane, the boys stayed in Juba, but James returned by public transport—the same day.

"It was a horrible journey," he began. "I found a vehicle returning to Yei late in the day, and waited with it until the driver had enough passengers to make the trip worth his time and money. The more, the better—they stuffed so many in the back of the Landcruiser, sitting side-by-side, that I couldn't move my hips at all."

They departed at three in the afternoon. The journey was 100 miles, and usually took 6 hours if the road has been graded. But it had not been graded, and it was rainy season. He and the 13 other passengers moved along until halfway to Yei, and then it started raining heavily. The passengers were all men, except one Ugandan lady with a newborn baby. She had retrieved the baby from her sister in Juba, after the sister had died. The top of the Landcruiser was overloaded with everyone's luggage.

It was past six in the evening, and it grew dark. The road from Juba to Yei was hilly and mountainous. It had six or seven hills as it gradually rose 1,500 feet in elevation. The driver asked the male passengers to get out and help stabilize the car as they went up the hills, as the brakes were weak and he was worried about slipping backwards on the wet, muddy road. He proceeded slowly, as it grew dark. It was still raining heavily. They finally reached Lainya at eight in the evening, just over halfway to Yei.

The passengers wondered why the driver failed to turn on his headlights. The reason was that they didn't work. They proceeded very slowly, as the potholes and ditches along the road were treacherous and he could barely see them. A few of the passengers grew angry with the driver and his faulty vehicle, so they got out to sleep in Lainya and await another vehicle to take them all the way to Yei.

One of the passengers volunteered a flashlight, which they took turns holding outside to show the driver the road ahead. It was still raining heavily. But soon, the flashlight's battery gave out and they could only see an opaque haze in front. The driver then took to relying on other vehicles' headlights to guide them. When a vehicle passed, he sped up to follow them, but inevitably couldn't keep up for long, as he feared going too fast with his weak brakes. If they came to a bridge, the driver had the remaining 12 passengers get out and point out the bridge as he proceeded slowly across it. They walked across and re-entered the vehicle.

At some point, they realized the vehicle was on its side! It happened slowly, in the dark, and Bond now found himself on the downside, with his back to the side of the car that rested on the ground. He and the others on that side held the other passengers up with their legs, suspended in their seats above. Somehow they managed to climb out of the back of the vehicle. No one was hurt, as they were going so slowly. The passengers were furious, hurling insults at the driver. It was still raining, and it was sometime before midnight by this point.

"I was so tired I almost cried," Bond continued. "All I wanted to do was go to sleep. But now the driver made us male passengers push the vehicle upright onto the road again!"

They continued the journey slowly in the dark, unsure if they would ever make it to Yei that night. More bridges followed, and they got out at each one, lest they fall off the bridge with him. Finally, they passed the airstrip on the outskirts of town, but faced a new worry as they approached the checkpoint by the army barracks. The military usually harassed vehicles that passed into town so late at night.

When they reached the checkpoint, the soldiers saw the muddy, beat-up Landcruiser with no headlamps, and the bedraggled, muddy passengers within. All they could do was laugh and wave them on. They apparently didn't seem like a threat.

They pulled into Yei town, thankful to finally be at their destination. Bond memorized the license plate number so he would never ride in the same vehicle again. But he wasn't quite home. He had to search for a boda driver to take him three miles through the teak forest, but all of them refused because it was so late, and they feared he would rob or hurt them along the way. Thanks to the mercy of God, Bond found a driver he knew from school, and the boy agreed to take him back to Harvesters. It was well after midnight when he finally reached the compound, wet and dirty. He could sleep at last.

"That was the worst journey I ever had," Bond declared as he concluded the story of his road trip.

Taking public transport was inexpensive at best. It was always messy, uncomfortable, not for the faint-at-heart. At times, public transport was life-threatening. It was a way we tried not to travel in Africa.

Fish sauce

Times out of the country were also shopping trips. One of the great ways that Elizabeth loves us as a family is by cooking tasty food. The first year in South Sudan, we ate only oatmeal, rice and beans, with the occasional overcooked greens. But as Elizabeth explored the market, and we met Pakistani and Indian businessmen in town, we realized there were more possibilities for variety in our diet (they ate the foods they liked!). One of our favorites was Thai food, which required that we bring some key ingredients that weren't available locally—coconut milk and fish sauce.

Returning from a time in Kenya, we had a bottle of fish sauce packed inside a duffel bag. Fish sauce is a powerful weapon in the culinary arsenal—a little goes a long way. Just a hint of it makes certain soups what they are. More than a little, and it is overwhelming.

I was just finishing with immigration at the Juba airport, when I heard a commotion in the baggage area. Elizabeth was standing with the children, while several tall South Sudanese men in uniform were yelling angrily at her. It was hot, as it usually was in the capital city, and no air was moving inside the stifling building. The acrid smell of too many sweaty people in a small space already permeated the airport. As I made my way toward them, the usual ambiance grew more intense and took on a rotten, almost fishy odor. They were all gesturing toward a blue bag with an oily puddle forming around it.

During loading and unloading, which was not done in the most gentle of ways (read—they threw and dropped our bags), the glass bottle must have shifted to the bottom of the bag, and shattered during one of the times it was dropped on the concrete floor. They were very upset with us, complaining that we had made the airport smell badly. We were frustrated that our bags had been thrown around so roughly, and that they were blaming us entirely for the less than savory smell of their airport. What were we to do? They seemed most concerned about expressing their anger toward us. We quietly picked up the bag and moved it outside the terminal, where I bought a large plastic shopping bag to put around it—as they wouldn't allow us to board our next flight until we did something to contain the stench. The moral of the story? Traveling is messy, so you'd better pack carefully and pray for peace to deal with angry people along the way.

Flying south for the summer

Near the end of our first term, we decided to get out of East Africa, where we might feel a bit more relaxed. It was January, the middle of the hot, dusty dry season in South Sudan, and the middle of summer in non-tropical South Africa. Fortunately, their temperate summer was far cooler than our dry season!

We found cheap flights to South Africa, and a train that could take us from Johannesburg to Cape Town. Perhaps this would be a time to finally rest from the intensity of the first few years of opening a mission hospital!

Add to the list of how not to travel in Africa—"flying on airlines from countries that you are surprised to hear are operating an airline." We later heard stories of "Air Mali" (most haven't even heard of that country, let alone that it has an airline), where carry-on luggage has included a dead goat, with blood dripping from the overhead compartment. Our experience wasn't quite that graphic, but the airline from Rwanda did have its issues.

We flew from South Sudan to Uganda on a small prop plane (with the usual Ugandan airline with whom we traveled into South Sudan), where we waited in the airport for our flight to Rwanda. It was a 12-hour wait. We couldn't leave the airport or we would have to pay the $500 visa fee. We boarded around midnight, landing in Kigali, Rwanda around one in the morning. They had assured us there was a transit lounge where we could rest and get food, but upon arrival, there was no one from the airline, and no such place to wait. It would be another 8 hours before our flight to South Africa. We found a group of seats that were together and tried to rest. There was a bar open that had a few snacks and drinks (purchased with Rwandan currency—our fourth currency used within 24 hours: South Sudanese pounds, US dollars, Ugandan shillings... later that day we also used South African rand). We took turns dozing a few minutes here and there, and when the ticket counter opened, we discovered they had failed to provide a ticket for one of us when we departed from Uganda. After much hassle of proving we did actually purchase ten tickets, they hastily provided a hand-written voucher for the missing ticket, and by this time, the flight was about to leave. We rushed to the gate, thankful to have all made it on the last leg of our journey.

Unfortunately, our baggage was not so fortunate. Upon our arrival to Johannesburg, South Africa, we were relieved at the cool climate, modern airport, and overall organized manner of the place. We patiently waited by the baggage claim, but not one of our 7 checked bags appeared. None. We had only the clothes on our backs and a few items in our small carry-on bags (after this we always travel with several changes of clothes in a non-checked bag!).

We gave them information on where we'd be staying (Rosebank Union Church had graciously offered us their missionary house), and proceeded to the church. The couple managing the church properties, Duncan and Sandy, helped us settle in and listened to our situation.

"Fortunately, our church has a clothing closet," they said. So we headed down there, and everyone found a few outfits—most memorable were the Barbie pajamas our girls wore... not something we, or they, were "into."

After some days in Joburg, we were booked to travel by train to Cape Town—a journey of around 1,000 miles, enabling us to see the countryside of South Africa. We debated whether to book a sleeper car, or just do economy seats. To save money, and because they didn't have any sleepers available, we went with economy. It was interesting to us that they spent considerable time on the website discussing that train travel was safe. We thought, "this is South Africa—compared to South Sudan, how bad could it be?"

We made our way through the underground train depot in Joburg, and finally arrived to the train. It was virtually empty, which was good, because all of our luggage (our bags had eventually caught up with us 4 days later) had to be stowed where we were sitting, as there was no luggage compartment underneath the train, nor any overhead storage of note. We slowly pulled out of the station, through the industrial areas of the city laced with graffiti and factories billowing smoke. As we entered the peaceful countryside and the landscape opened up, it seemed like a fine choice to travel this way!

True, the seats were not very comfortable—they were hard plastic, not adjustable, and more like a subway or city bus seat. This was okay for the first hour or two, during the daylight, without many other passengers on the train. But as the 33-hour trip progressed, more and more passengers boarded, and soon seats were at a premium. We had to squeeze together, and move our luggage closer too. Some of the smaller children stretched out on the bags to try and rest. As evening wore on, and darkness set in, some of the other passengers started drinking. With our children and luggage to guard, Elizabeth and I had to remain awake. Several drunken men sat on the armrest of our seats and made themselves quite obnoxious. We were the only white people on the train, which we were accustomed to from several years of living in Africa, but this was different. There was an underlying hostility, similar to an American inner city. It dawned on us that South Africa's history of apartheid and racism produced a tension between us and our fellow passengers that we didn't face in most other African nations.

Olivia performs one of many puppet shows to occupy her sisters during the 33-hour train ride

At one small rural station, mechanical problems led to a three-hour time of sitting on the tracks. As the train's toilet was by now nearly intolerable for our little girls (especially as it was simply a seat over a hole that opened directly onto the tracks below), we took shifts going to a real toilet in the station. We finally resumed the journey, now in our second day on the train. The land became dry, almost like the "desert" grasslands of our home back in eastern Colorado—complete with bushes that resembled the dry sagebrush that becomes tumbleweeds. We then climbed into mountains, through a long tunnel, and then down towards the Atlantic Ocean through fertile, green valleys with vineyards.

We were in need of a shower, teeth-brushing, and sleep, as we were worn down by the constant need of vigilance. Once in Cape Town, we were incredibly relieved to be off the train. We went directly to the ticket office to get a refund for the return portion of our trip, which they did without any hesitation. We would not return the same way we came, but would find some other means. The city train that took us out to the YWAM base where we would stay was much nicer than the train from which we had just exited after our 33-hour ordeal.

Upon meeting us at the train station, the man picking us up looked at our oldest daughter, Lillian, with confusion and asked her how she had got to the station.

"This is our daughter," we replied, not understanding why he was acting this way. True, this was South Africa and Lillian was our only completely black child, but still it was strange.

"No, you are Ann, the daughter of the Westing family," he said assuredly, with a smile that let on a hint of uncertainty. "But how did you get down here to the station?" Perhaps he thought the girl had come along in his vehicle without him knowing.

"No, this is really our daughter, Lillian," we again responded, and he seemed to give in to this fact.

"You look exactly like the daughter of a family at the YWAM (Youth with a Mission) base," he explained. Sure enough, once we arrived there, out came a girl who was the spitting image of Lillie. Same facial features, same skin tone, same braids and hair length, and even similar glasses! It turns out, she had been adopted from Namibia, and she and Lillie hit it off. They say everyone has a twin, and Lillie found hers in Cape Town.

It was "summer" there, but it was quite a bit colder than South Sudan. Still, we braved playing in the surf at the ocean beach nearby because we could. We could, that is, until they changed flags—indicating there were sharks in the bay, too close to allow swimming. In spite of this, it was a restful time in the city.

We managed to book a flight back to Joburg, after arranging to transfer some additional funds to us from the US. Previously, we didn't have enough money to fly, but some gifts had come in which allowed this—at just the right time, as the Lord is known to do. The best part of our last few days in Joburg was spending time with families from the church at which we were staying. Duncan and Sandy drove us to see a few museums, Andre and Jenni had us over for a barbie (barbeque) and swim, and Len and Carol had us stay in their home since the missionary house wouldn't be available. Len even accompanied us ice-skating! He took a few falls, and we later learned he actually broke several ribs. I watched cricket with him, and gradually noticed that it was the same teams playing as the day before. As I looked closer, I noticed it was the same player batting as the day before. When I asked more about it, I discovered that he had been at bat since the previous day (it was a record or near-record at bat, but also highlighted the pedestrian pace of cricket... it makes baseball seem like a blur)!

True Rest

We stumbled upon one of God's great mysteries: belonging to the global body of Christ. The best part of our travels was meeting and being encouraged by the Church. To be somewhere far from home yet feel welcomed as if we were family, simply because we were children of the Father, was an incredibly rich experience. Belonging is the core experience of the gospel.

Escape, comfort, and "vacating" our normal, messy life were illusions we couldn't attain. We needed to say "bye-bye" to this hope. We stopped seeking and praying for smooth travels, and started praying that we would have peace whatever happened, that He would keep us, and that He would be glorified in how we handled whatever hiccups presented themselves.

He wanted us to rest only in Him.

As the hospital grew, we realized we shouldn't be living from vacation to vacation. We needed to build in a way to regularly rest. As God brought others to join us, we found that having at least three doctors and three nurses allowed time to take a day of rest to prepare our bodies and hearts for the full days that followed in the week. Yet even with a schedule that allowed for a day of rest, there were always things that came up.

One of those times came at the end of a long Saturday call. The doctor who was scheduled that weekend had an unexpected family tragedy, and the other doctor who was to cover Sunday fell ill and was unable to work. So, we broke the news to the kids that Daddy would have to work again the next day.

"It's like when Jesus healed the man on the Sabbath... sometimes we have to do what is needed on our planned day of rest. So, I'll need to 'heal' on this Sabbath," I explained to the children.

"But Dad, you treat, Jesus heals... like it says on the sign at Tenwek," said Logan, our then 11-year old son who had traveled with us to the mission hospital in Kenya by that name.

Touché! He certainly spoke the truth, one of which we need to be reminded. Our rest came as we grew in our understanding that He was doing the work, and our job was to rest in that truth.

The Sabbath "...is a father's gift to indulge his children." (Mark Buchanan, The Rest of God, 220)

How do you understand and indulge in His gift of the Sabbath?

When people ask how you are, how often do you respond, "busy"?

How do you take time to stop and rest in God? Or do you feel too busy to do so?

Chapter 4
Kasulu: *The Messiness of Discipleship*

At *His House of Hope,* we only hired Christian staff. Well, at least those who identified themselves as Christian. We were a mission of the church, with a vision and mission to share the truth and love of Jesus with our patients and community. We were looking for those who could do the medical work, while we trained and encouraged them both professionally and in their faith.

Rose and Boniface were both Clinical Officers. They were responsible for diagnosing and prescribing treatments in the clinic and hospital. Both were interns, but Rose struggled with her knowledge base. She was learning slowly, but she had several young children to support and was highly motivated to do better. Boniface was intellectually sharp, but struggled with rudeness. Well, he often didn't struggle with it—he just went ahead with it.

One busy, hot afternoon, Rose saw a 3-year-old girl in clinic with severe malaria, suffering with dehydration and labored breathing. She rightly assessed that the child should be admitted, and brought her to the inpatient Pediatric ward, where Boniface was on duty.

"What is the hemoglobin? Where are the labs?!" he immediately challenged.

"It is not done yet," Rose defended. "But the child needs to be admitted."

Boniface proceeded to get very angry, and Rose's temper flared to match his. A full-out argument ensued (yes, amongst the mission hospital staff). I later heard that Boniface actually threatened to beat her. The next day, I called them to the office to discuss the matter.

To avoid shaming either one, I brought them in separately at first. I expected the stories to vary, each one leaving out the details that would incriminate themselves. It didn't happen that way.

"And so then I told her, 'I will beat you,'" Boniface explained matter-of-factly. I was shocked. He was non-plussed. Apparently this wasn't unprofessional behavior in his mind.

When Rose was called in, she told the same story. Her response to his threat was telling.

"If you are a man, do it," she had come back to him.

"Okay," I started. "It is not acceptable for our staff to beat or threaten to beat each other. How do we proceed now with working together?"

"It is okay," Boniface began. "I was angry last night, but today it is over."

"Yes, it is okay now," agreed Rose. We talked through further details of the incident and they agreed to address disagreements differently next time. And we prayed together.

Discipleship was truly messy at *His House of Hope*. Once we embraced the messiness, we could get down to the business of making disciples and teaching others to obey what Jesus taught.

Is there a Starbucks nearby?!

We soon realized that the only way to know a person's character and faith was to see his or her behavior over time. In fact, I learned a mathematical formula for character. Character = CB/T; that is, character equals consistent behavior over time.[1] We learned that everyone needed to start with a probationary contract. After a month, once we saw their behavior, we could end it if it seemed we couldn't work with them—no questions asked.

Prior to coming to South Sudan, my vision of "discipleship" was sitting down to a cup of coffee to talk about the Bible, what God was doing in someone's life, and pray (preferably at a coffee house or the like). As the hospital grew, our discipleship moments became sitting down with a staff member in the office to (again) talk with them about not coming to work drunk, but trying to do it in a way that didn't bring too much shame on them. How did we do that "sandwiched" between positive feedback, using indirect communication that is integral to an honor-shame culture? I was not in Kansas anymore (and I can say that with integrity, as our part of eastern Colorado is often referred to as "western Kansas").

We realized there was a large gap between what people say in a job interview or Bible study and what they do in the rest of their lives. Come to think of it, this is true anywhere in the world.

"Kasulu, Diktor"

One day, a female staff member named Betti came to me complaining of vaginal bleeding.

"Tell me more," I prodded. As it turned out, she was pregnant, and didn't want to be. Over the weekend, she had taken a large dose of Quinine (a medicine used to treat malaria) in order to abort the baby, but was now having quite a bit of bleeding.

We did an ultrasound, and amazingly, the baby still had a heartbeat. "Rabuna (God) wants you to keep the baby,"

I pointed out—"she is still alive."

"Kasulu, Diktor," Betti pleaded. Just clean it out, Doctor. "I have problems at home—I can't have this baby right now."

I arranged for her to talk with our pastor that day, to talk through these issues. She was released early from work, and returned the next day saying everything was fine. She hadn't met up with the pastor, but simply resumed work and wouldn't talk about it any further. About four weeks later, she miscarried. We continued walking with her, hoping that God would draw her deeper and open up more conversation.

Betti wasn't the only woman we encountered who tried to kasulu (clean out) her baby from within herself. A child was once on the ward with the name Shadrach. During rounds, the father was there (which was uncommon), and I commented that I liked his name.

"Yes, and he is a twin. His brother is Abednego, because they came through the fire and lived," he explained. "The mother tried to abort them early in the pregnancy, but failed."

Another woman came in, 4 ½ months into her pregnancy, with bleeding and leakage of amniotic fluid. After examination and ultrasound, we diagnosed her with premature rupture of membranes (bag of water). There was no fluid, but baby was still alive. Over the following days, she stabilized. The bleeding stopped and with antibiotics on board, she didn't develop any fever. This made us hopeful that the baby might hold on until he was able to breathe on his own once delivered.

One day during rounds, as the clinical officer, nurse, and I talked with her, she began crying. She admitted that she had taken drugs to try to end the pregnancy many weeks before, but had now asked God to forgive her and wanted the baby to live. We prayed with her that the baby would continue to remain inside—that God would sustain him until he was ready to live on the outside. She remained comfortable for several more weeks, but early one morning, she began to bleed and have pain. The baby delivered, but was still too small to survive.

Abortion was not terribly common, as children are a valuable commodity. Women are expected to "produce" (have children) within a year of marriage, or the husband's family will think there is something wrong with her. The husband will then go out and marry an additional wife. "Producing" made and kept a woman valuable to her husband (and his family). Yet for some, especially those who conceived outside of marriage, abortion seemed the only option. Misoprostol is a useful medicine to control bleeding after birth, but sadly, many in the area have learned that it can also be used to cause a miscarriage. The many stressors of life for an African woman lead some to make decisions out of desperation, but then later regret, and suffer guilt and shame. If a married woman had an abortion, there was often considerable backlash from her husband's family, since she was expected to 'produce' more children.

Discipleship 101

Discipleship is a messy thing—especially when done in the course of daily life. Disciple simply means follower. We understood discipleship to be inviting others to follow Jesus as we ourselves followed Him too. That meant finding out where people were in their "following" of Jesus. My favorite time to have impromptu conversations about faith was in the operating theatre, a technique I learned from my long-time mentor from Colorado, Dr. Lee Schmucker. With a captive audience of the anesthetist, surgical assistant, scrub nurse, circulating nurse, patient (unless under general anesthesia), and any other observers who may be in the room, he would lead out in some deeper, non-medical questions. As it wasn't a Bible study or formal meeting, we often heard what was really in someone's head and heart.

"What's the most important thing in life?" I asked during one late night surgery in South Sudan. It was hot, accentuated by the operating lights, suction machine, and all of us dressed in cloth gowns and caps. Through the drips of sweat, the scrub nurse pondered my question.

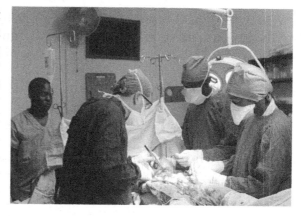

"To make money," she finally offered.

A visiting resident doctor from the US was our surgical assistant, and he waited anxiously to see how I would respond, eager to correct her. At that moment, though, I didn't feel led to give her the "correct" answer (such as "to glorify God and enjoy Him forever"), but to simply understand where she was in her "followership." For now, we knew what she really thought. Over the course of months and years, there would be time to try to influence her with truth—but only the Holy Spirit would change her.

The first aim in discipleship was to know what one truly believed.

I'm on the way coming

Besides abortion, we uncovered other behaviors amongst our staff that revealed their character. Arrival to work was influenced by weather, family emergencies, travel conditions, and political instability. It was not uncommon to have staff not show up after a holiday, as they were "delayed" on the way. Our first response tended to be anger at their unprofessionalism and lack of commitment to the patients and fellow staff. (Our anger coincidentally revealed our need for further growth and discipleship as well!)

"Where are you?!" I would begin if I reached them by cell phone, with obvious irritation and disapproval in my voice (*not* reacting in a Godly way).

"I'm on the way coming. I was delayed…" would be the response. Which meant, "I've thought about the fact that I need to get ready to leave, or at least I'm *thinking* about it now that you've called…"

This led nowhere good. Over time, some of our more helpful staff pulled us aside and gave us a cultural lesson in not shaming them, but expressing concern.

"Ask 'are you okay?' first," they guided us. The reality was that there were a lot of things that could delay someone on the way to work or back from holiday. They experienced illness more often, were more susceptible to the weather as most were "footing" (walking) to work over dirt roads, and family deaths were common—and considered priority, even over work responsibility. For those of us from the West, "professionalism" and "work ethic" usually superseded "personal emergencies." We would be sure to be released from work before not showing up. But in South Sudan, it was opposite: the assumption was that responsibility to family released them from work.

Still, we had a hospital to run. Patients got sick and staff that worked the night shift couldn't keep working through the day and again the following night. We pressed on to be sensitive, yet sought to have enough staff around to take care of the patients. Some staff got it, and they began to self-regulate a bit. We also moved forward in building on-site staff housing and had a van that picked up those that lived in town—eliminating many of the excuses for not showing or arriving late. It was an ongoing delicate balance of concern and correction.

After one of many such tricky conversations with staff, Elizabeth asked me how it went.

"It was a good conversation!" I said.

"How do you know?" she inquired.

"He smiled and nodded…" I trailed off, realizing that most likely, the staff member had simply said what I wanted to hear, to please me and not bring shame on himself or me by disagreeing. The only way we would ever know if our "intervention" had brought about real change was to witness a change in behavior.

Our cultural lesson in discipleship was to show concern for the person before we tried to correct his or her behavior.

Shotgun Medicine

In our teaching, we discouraged our staff from the all-too-common practice of "shotgun medicine," in which a clinician would order all lab tests, and then prescribe multiple medications, not being entirely sure of what the patient actually had. First, I had to explain what a shotgun was.

"Rather," I explained, "practice 'AK-47 medicine'—one bullet, directed from the rifle, at the target you want to hit!"

They smiled and "clicked" in agreement, and a few even laughed. They seemed to jive with this description, as many of them probably had an AK-47 hidden in their tukul. Perhaps I had discovered an analogy that worked well in a country accustomed to war. I then

went on to explain that most of the diagnosis came from the history and exam.

But did they really get it? One of the few, encouraging moments came when Loki, one of our Clinical Officers, was teaching the other staff.

"Ninety-percent of your diagnosis should come from the history and physical exam," he explained, echoing my words. These moments of confirmed understanding were rare, and we treasured them.

The Patient is Somehow Not Well

We were in a team meeting at our home when my phone rang. I was on call, and it was Bosco, the nurse on duty. The hospital had only been open for a few months, and we were still learning one another's cadence.

"Hello, Bosco, how are things at the hospital?" I began.

"Hello, well, things are okay," he said.

"And are you okay? What is your question?" I continued.

"We are well, it's only that the patient is somehow not well," he said deliberately.

"How do you mean? How is the patient not doing well?" I inquired, thinking she might be having a fever and in need of paracetamol (like Tylenol).

"She is not breathing," he said matter-of-factly.

"Oh!" I exclaimed. "I will come right away!"

Katherine, the missionary nurse, and I ran the 50 meters to the hospital and assessed the situation. The patient, sadly, had "coded"—she had stopped breathing, and as we didn't have continuous monitoring to alert us when the heart or breathing stopped, we didn't know exactly how long it had been. We attempted resuscitation for a few minutes, but it was apparent that she was not going to be saved.

After this incident, others on our missionary team developed a "red-yellow-green light call" system for the staff to use when calling us. They would first indicate it was a "red light call" meaning we should stop what we were doing and come immediately, "yellow light" meaning we should get there within a half hour or so, or "green light" meaning it was just a question and there was no real urgency. Then they would describe the situation. Developing a medical culture of being "on-call" and doing triage was one of the issues we faced in the "professional discipleship" of our staff. We found that the staff gradually embraced this system as they saw the clarity it brought to patient care.

"This is a red light call…" was what we heard thereafter.

Radioactive Rocks

There were many such times that our hopes of finding staff with good character were dashed to the rocks. But there were glimmers of hopes… and rocks that glimmered. Peter was one of our first staff members, integral to setting up the lab, and later grew into a staff manager. He was consistently reliable in handling money (largely because he asked to not be given too much responsibility over it) and was loyal to us over his tenure of almost six years. He did, however, lack judgment at times, such as when he cornered me one day in the hospital.

"Dr. Perry, can I ask you something?"

"Sure," I said, wondering what the request might be.

"Can you carry some uranium across the border into Uganda for a friend of mine?"

"Uh…no," I replied, stunned. "For a number of reasons. It's radioactive, it's illegal, it's used to make nuclear weapons, and it's never a good idea to carry things across an international boundary for someone I don't personally know!"

A few months earlier, a friend of ours had visited and taken a small clump of hardened dirt out of South Sudan as a memento. He was stopped in the airport in Uganda, where they confiscated the dirt, detained him, and almost arrested him. I could only imagine how they'd take to me trying to smuggle out uranium.

After Peter made his request of me, I mentioned the incident to one of our short-term volunteers, and he laughed in disbelief. Surely one of our staff wouldn't present such a ludicrous request! The following day, however, he approached me with an incredulous look on his face.

"I didn't believe he had really asked you that, but just now Peter asked ME the same thing!" he explained.

I honestly don't think Peter understood the implications of his request, and most of our experiences with him were positive. He was hard working, honest, and extremely loyal to us and to the mission of the hospital. Discipleship was more challenging, and a lot weirder, across cultures.

Teaching medicine and truth

Once a week, we had ongoing medical education sessions for all our medical staff, at their request. They were eager to learn and grow in their professional skills.

Each day at *His House of Hope* started with devotions, in the center of the hospital. Staff, patients, and their families would gather as one of our "translators" (recent high school graduates gaining experience in the hospital) picked a tune on the traditional "harp" or dugu (which literally means "beat"). Most songs were sung from the local songbook, Shukuru Yesu (Praise Jesus), some in Juba Arabic and others in English.

Over the years, the small staff devotions had outgrown our office, and there were often up to 80 people attending. Some were tribal and Muslim patients and families that had never entered a Christian worship place before. A South

Sudanese nurse, chaplain, or a Western missionary would give a brief message from Scripture. Once a week, Dr. Poole, Pastor Hillary, or I would lead an ongoing Biblical series, through a book of the Bible or topic—intending to equip our staff with the basics of the Word of God. We wanted to be sure that if they spent a year or more at *His House of Hope*, they would have had access to spiritual food, not just professional development.

The Safe is not Safe

As we poured into the lives of our staffs, we came to discover their character. Sometimes it was so messy that we had to do damage control to prevent others from harm.

Joseph was a lab student at the government hospital in town. He came to do a brief rotation at the hospital, and was very enthusiastic about his experience. Even before he graduated, he was calling me to express his desire to work with us. Upon finishing his courses in early December, he came by for a visit, dressed in a long, flowing African - Arab garment with traditional cap as well. This outfit was called an "abizalabiyah" (ah-bee-jaw-lah-bee-yuh) in Juba Arabic, sometimes pronounced "jolly-bee-uh," or as we affectionately referred to it, a "man-dress." Those that wore them said they were extremely comfortable and cool in the hot weather. Joseph was slightly short, smiley, and had a bit of a belly—which was rare in South Sudan. He was well spoken, pleasant, and excited about the possibility of starting with us after the New Year. I told him to bring his papers by so we could review them and consider an interview after the holidays. We were thinking of adding another lab tech, so the timing was good.

We ending up hiring Joseph, and he did well initially. Our head lab tech noticed some inaccuracies in his work, which he addressed, and they seemed to improve.

After about six months of working with us, Joseph requested an advance on his salary, plus some assistance from the hospital, in order to travel north to complete a part of his studies that he hadn't completed adequately. Our missionary team discussed it and decided to help him, in exchange for him returning to work as soon as the course was done. He called me on a Friday morning to confirm he was on his way to Juba by car, from where he would fly up to Rumbek where his school was. (I later learned he had started at this school, but transferred to the one in our town. In the process, he explained, there had been a problem with one of his courses, and he had to retake the exam—but they insisted on him sitting in on many of the classes again, prior to retaking the test.)

The next morning, Joseph even sent me pictures on social media of him on the plane. I chuckled at his careful documentation of the trip. I figured he wanted us to know that he was truly making the journey for which we had advanced and gifted him money.

Shortly after this, even though I was off-duty for the weekend, Dr. Poole called me with obvious tension in his voice.

"Sarah (the missionary nurse on duty) arrived this morning to find the door to the office unlocked, and the safe is gone. She thinks she may have left the padlock unlocked last night—and feels awful about that."

I wasn't sure what to say. "Well, it is part of the night guard's duty to ensure all the doors are locked," I began. I stopped and fully grasped what he had just said. "The whole safe is gone? Do we know what was in it?" The safe was medium-sized, and would have required a few men to move it quickly.

"Yes, the entire safe. Linda thinks it had the equivalent of about $1,600 USD, plus some documents. Fortunately, we didn't have the month's payroll in it yet."

The rest of the morning was like a bizarre, South Sudanese version of "CSI" (an American television show about crime scene investigation). The Yei Police and the CID (Criminal Investigation Department) gathered testimony from several staff members, starting with the night guard, who is always the first suspect, and held responsible for any major theft that happens during his shift, even if he simply failed to prevent it. We walked around the compound, and noted footprints in the mud by the back fence. On the opposite side of the fence was a deep, triangular, safe-shaped indentation in the ground. We could all visualize a few men hoisting it above their heads and lofting it over the top of the fence. From there, it was only about 30 meters to the road under the cover of teak trees, where it could be quietly loaded onto a motorcycle in the dark of night.

Witnesses had curiously seen Juma, a nurse who had been on duty the night before, return in the morning to clean his motorcycle. Even more suspiciously, he forced the night guard to wash it for him. We had been having problems with Juma for some time—he seemed to be an instigator of dissatisfaction amongst the rest of the staff. He had organized several secret staff meetings to plan a strike, though Dr. Poole had calmed things down when he learned of it. Juma was under discipline for this and other issues, and he was fairly upset with us, "the administration."

The police decided to bring in Juma, the night guard, and several other staff for further questioning. One staff member they sought was Joseph. They were very interested in him, though he had been gone for over 12 hours before the crime had occurred. And I had a date / time-stamped picture on my phone of him on the plane early in the morning following the crime. And the plane had departed from Juba, a five-hour drive from Yei. He was now in a town hundreds of miles to the north, to complete his coursework, after we had paid for his flight there. I felt the police were barking up the wrong tree, and I really didn't want to fly him back to Yei, and then back to Rumbek again. Fortunately, the Bishop intervened, and the police backed off. Joseph had a strong enough alibi.

The guard was kept in jail while he awaited trial. They let Juma and the other staffs go. No leads were found on the whereabouts of the safe. The guard refused to say with whom he had worked, but we knew there was someone, and most of us still suspected Juma. He knew a lot of people in the area and in the legal system, so it would be hard to pin anything on him. We ended up putting him on suspension until conclusion of the police case—which dragged on for almost a year.

The police informed us that we would need to buy chains to lock up the guard in jail—or else they wouldn't guarantee they could keep him from escaping. So, we bought the chains. Several months later, as little seemed to be happening with the case, I was called down to the police station.

The police station was a run-down cement building in the center of town. Yei had no paved streets, and the parking lot in front of the station was no exception. Dust swirled in the hot air as I walked into the small office as I was directed. Scores of papers were held in large three-ring binders on the warped wooden shelves that encircled the office.

"How is the progress on the case?" I asked.

"There is nothing new. It may take some time. And we need you to file the complaint." I thought we had done that long ago! "Since it is taking so long, and the jail is full, we wanted to see if you can bail him out," the officer explained.

"Pay to release the man responsible for stealing from us?!" I clarified in disbelief. "No, we won't be doing that."

Several months passed with no further news. One day, an officer arrived at the hospital. He requested that we give some money to support the guard, as he was without food. I wasn't aware that we were also expected to feed him while he was in jail for his crime against us!

Some time later, we came to the conclusion that nothing would happen with the case. The guard had served almost 9 months in jail, and was likely not the mastermind of the heist. He was originally from DR Congo, so he had few friends and no family in the area. He had done his time. We knew proceeding to a court case would gain us nothing, but rather lead to more loss—of time and money. We dropped the case, and the guard was released.

Joseph had returned after four months in school, and resumed work. There were concerns. Several times, when he was on night duty, units of blood went missing. One morning, a family member of a patient reported that Joseph had requested 600 SSP as a fee for collecting the donor's blood to give to the family member. We met with him, the money was returned, and he was given a formal "explanation letter" (the Labor Department discouraged the use of "warning" or "disciplinary" letter). In that meeting, and several times in the previous months, his temper flared in concerning ways.

It was then 2016, and the economy was crashing. Our employees went on strike, with Joseph and a few others leading the uprising. This was despite our efforts to compensate for the spiraling devaluation of the South Sudanese pound by adjusting their pay. While in a meeting with the County Commissioner, Mayor, Labor Department, and all of our employees, an officer who was present from National Security noticed Joseph in the crowd. Afterwards, he caught me.

"What is he doing here? He is a very bad man!"

"He's been working with us for a year and a half. Why do you say that?" I responded.

"He led a protest at the Yei Health Sciences Institute, and created many other problems there and at other places. He should not be here!"

Over the next few days, we developed a plan to reinstate contracts with our employees. Given his recent "explanation letter," we chose not to continue Joseph's contract. I gathered the administrative staff, the head laboratory technician, missionaries, the guards, and Elizabeth to witness how he received the news (at Elizabeth's suggestion).

He became violently angry, and likely would have hit someone, had there not been so many present. Right there in the office, he threatened the life of his supervisor, our Ugandan head lab tech. He left, and the guards were given strict orders to not allow him back on the compound.

Over the following days, several staff members came to me to share more about Joseph. One nurse gave me the details.

"He was at the hospital the night the office was robbed," she confided.

"But he had traveled to Juba and flown out the next morning," I countered.

"No, he was here. He brought in a woman for treatment of syphilis. She was impregnated by him."

"His wife?" I asked.

"No, this wasn't his wife. He impregnated quite a few girls—that's why he was sent away from the Lab school in Yei. He was here, and he was definitely involved in the robbery."

"Why didn't you say something last year when it had happened? Would you testify about this?"

"Oh no. I couldn't," she said. "He goes around with a lot of bad people—I can't say anything more about it."

"I understand… it's not worth putting your life at risk."

The witness protection plan was certainly not developed in this new nation. Witchdoctors and poisonings were easy to come by, and I knew that revenge killings were common and almost untraceable. The legal system had a long way to go before reaching maturity.

However, since the man from National Security had recognized him, and bits of information leaked out to the police and National Security, Joseph was now a wanted man. He went on the run, and wasn't apprehended. Over the following months, the civil war escalated, and staff and missionaries started evacuating in waves. With many horrific killings, fear, and chaos in the government and country, Joseph was forgotten.

That is, until we bumped into him in northern Uganda over a year later. Elizabeth and I were strolling through the open-air market in Moyo, Uganda, where we were then living.

"Hello, doctor!" Joseph began, somewhat sheepishly.

"Hello, Joseph," I replied cautiously. "Where are you staying now?"

"In Juba, working with an NGO." He was obviously sizing up how we were going to act toward him. Would we be angry? Would we try to bring in the police?

The conversation continued awkwardly, then we parted ways. There were far greater criminals in South Sudan, who had murdered scores of civilians. At that time, the government of South Sudan was in chaos and civil war raged. There was no use reporting him to anyone.

Discipleship was messy, and it didn't always end with a redemptive twist.

Forgiveness

There were a few who demonstrated a desire to follow after Jesus— by their consistent behavior over time. Charles was an excellent nurse-midwife. He came to us in the middle of 2015, and picked up skills very quickly. When I was on call, and came to evaluate a pediatric patient, he was awake and actively checking and rechecking the patients (as opposed to sitting idly or sleeping... both of which happened with some staff on night shift). He began taking more of an interest in caring for the neonates and premature babies.

After he had been with us for more than six months, he was adept at resuscitating a premature infant, maintaining one on CPAP (continuous positive airway pressure, a type of breathing support), and carefully attending to feedings and problems that arose. Several times, I came in for rounds in the morning, only to discover that a preemie had had several episodes of apnea (cessation of breathing) during the night, but Charles had stimulated him, breathed for him with a bag-mask, and adjusted his feedings and CPAP appropriately.

When the staff went on strike in March 2016 (more on this in chapter 7), I was sad to see Charles serving as the employee spokesman. He was articulate, I knew, and was likely pushed forward by the others because of his well-spoken manner. During it all, he had a pained expression on his face, yet carefully chose his words to be as respectful as they could be, given the situation. The subject was difficult, and in the end, the strike was resolved. Employees were reinstated once they signed a commitment to address future disputes without going on strike—since a strike endangered patient care.

When Charles came to the office to discuss the reinstatement, he declined to sign the commitment. Heavily, he asked for a letter of reference as he sought out another job. I provided him this, and he left.

Two weeks later, Charles came into the office. He looked at me, averted his eyes downward, and shakily began to speak. "I want to see if you will forgive me. I want to return to work here, if you will have me. My current job pays more, but I want to be involved with the work we were doing here, and continue to learn more about caring for the neonates."

This was unheard of—I had never had a South Sudanese, especially a man, ask for forgiveness. Occasionally one might apologize, or act in such a way that communicated they were sorry, but I had never heard one say it outright. "Of course I forgive you, Charles, though I noticed that you were always careful to be respectful even in all the hard things that were said."

"I left because I didn't think you would allow me to continue working here after my part in the strike," he continued. "But I really wanted to come back, so here I am."

Charles rejoined us, and continued as a strong link in our staff until he and the others had to evacuate due to civil war.

Discipleship: "Living in the grey"

We struggled with feelings of deep hurt when those we came to serve betrayed us. And we were encouraged, but didn't declare that they had "arrived," when people showed good character. We struggled with disillusionment and depression when others spoke badly about us despite our efforts to do right. But then, if they treated Jesus in the same way, and He was perfect, why should we expect to be treated better than He? We never understood all that led to our staff and patients' decisions, but we saw the consequences of sin, the availability of forgiveness, Jesus' offer to cover shame, and the sovereignty of God over life.

God can kasulu (clean) our sinful choices and clean our hearts before Him—so we can stand without shame before Him again. "*Then I will sprinkle clean water on you, and you will be clean; I will cleanse you from all your filthiness and from all your idols… I will put My Spirit within you and cause you to walk in My statutes*" (Ezekiel 36:25, 27a). Only the Holy Spirit can convince someone of sin and enable him or her to follow Him over time.

We are now more cautious in our estimation of a person's character. Only time will reveal what is in the depth of those we walk alongside, following Jesus. "Suspend judgment," one author suggests.[2] "Live in the grey," as people's character is neither black nor white. God will judge; we are simply to teach them to obey everything He has commanded us, as we love one another (simple to say, but profoundly difficult to actually do!).

"*The sins of some men are quite evident, going before them to judgment; for others, their sins follow after. Likewise also, deeds that are good are quite evident, and those which are otherwise cannot be concealed*" (1 Tim 5:24-25).

Belief before behavior

Behavior is not the ultimate issue though. Faith is. Yet, the reality of ones faith is shown by what one does. We are saved by faith, but our faith is judged by our deeds (Matt 25:31-46, Rev 20:12).

If the missionary focuses first on behavior, there won't be a change in the core of a person's belief and worldview, and the potential disciple may end up blending their old ways with Christian ideas. The end result is often worse. Behavior should change as belief happens.

A young Catholic man from the Madi tribe in Moyo, northern Uganda, explained the coming of Christian missionaries to their area and the effects on behavior.

"Our people used to fear our own 'gods' (demons), so we didn't steal or lie. The child sacrifices weren't good (*yes, he actually said this*), but other than that, they used to act better than people these days. Now that Christianity is here, people steal and do other bad things."

I'm not sure his assessment was completely accurate, but it raised some questions. Did the missionary not fear God himself, and teach the Madi the same by his actions? Did the Madi understand God's grace to mean that they could go on sinning without fear of consequence? Did the missionary focus only on their behavior, or was the missionary's behavior worse than those he came to reach with the gospel? Would the forces of globalization spread by the merchants and traders (who came before the missionaries) have led to even worse behavior without the presence of the missionaries? Sadly, all of these circumstances are seen. Even within the last few years, stories of moral failure of missionaries continue. And teaching behavior rather than belief is easier, so this sadly continues as well. And globalization has and is happening, whether we like it or not. There is no stopping it.

But there is hope. As we follow Jesus and seek to love and share truth with those in darkness, beliefs change and faith grows. A young missionary family was living amongst an entirely Muslim tribe in the Blue Nile state of South Sudan. The people saw the quality of their lives and called them *kafir kweysin*—"good infidels" (non-Muslims). Six of the tribal youths went to the leaders, asking permission to convert to Christianity. The elders still remembered that Islam was forced on their people, so they felt they should allow their people to choose their faith.

"Yes, that is ok, but do it right. Go to the kafir kweysin and learn from them about God," the leaders said.[3]

The tribe had seen the good behavior of the missionaries, and some were drawn to learn of the belief behind that behavior.

"I by my deeds will show you my faith" (James 2:18)

The hardest part of discipleship

Discipleship is to "admonish the unruly, encourage the faint-hearted, help the weak, be patient with everyone" (1 Thess 5:14). Patience is a great challenge for most of us. Paul wrote these words, yet it seems he was impatient with John Mark for turning back on their first journey, leading to his split with Barnabas (Acts 15:38). Barnabas was willing to give John Mark a second chance. David Livingstone was reportedly quite intolerant of other missionaries and explorers who couldn't keep up with his breakneck pace in the interior of Africa, yet he had a great love for the African people and a burning desire to pave the way for the gospel there. But God used these great men of the faith to accomplish discipleship despite their shortcomings. And He can do the same with us, because thankfully, it doesn't depend on us. God is the one who starts and finishes the work in each of His followers. *"Faithful is He who calls you, and He also will bring it to pass" (1 Thess 5:24).*

Discipleship is messy, but it happens as we patiently follow Jesus alongside others. In the process, His mystery is revealed as Christ grows in us and in those we invite to follow Him.

What is your understanding of "discipleship"?

Do you believe that every "disciple" of Jesus is "saved"? Is it possible that someone might start following Jesus, only to receive salvation somewhere down the road? (see John 6:66—"As a result of this many of His disciples withdrew and were not walking with Him anymore.")

What are some of the challenges of discipleship across cultures?

Chapter 5
But God had Mercy

"Indeed he was ill, near to death. But God had mercy on him, and not only on him but on me also, lest I should have sorrow upon sorrow."
(Phil 2:27)

Death was so common in South Sudan that it tempted us to lose hope. This despite the hospital being called *His House of Hope*. But God had mercy on us many times, sparing us sorrow upon sorrow amidst the mess. He allowed us glimpses of His mystery. Of His glory.

Gates & Glory

It was rainy season, and we were preparing to fence around the hospital compound. First, we had to construct two segments of wall on either side of the drive leading to the hospital. Hinges were set in concrete pillars and the gate had to remain closed for at least 3 days while the concrete cured. It was a strange sight—a heavy metal gate with fifteen feet of wall on either side, but no fence beyond that.

It just so happened that we were closing the clinic for a few days during the third Independence Day of South Sudan, while keeping the hospital open for emergencies only. In the dark of one early Saturday morning, Jackline, one of the nurses, called me to a vehicle stuck in the mud. They had tried to make their way around the wall, while the gate remained closed because the concrete was still setting.

Jackline told me the mother had delivered a baby in a breech position while on the way, and it had died. They carried the baby back to the delivery room while others helped the mother into the hospital. I confirmed that the baby was dead, but then glanced at the mother—she looked as if she was still pregnant and in labor!

"She may have twins," said Jackline, who also noticed what I had seen. A quick look on ultrasound confirmed that there was still a baby inside! He was alive, but was positioned sideways in the uterus and not able to be delivered safely. We prepped for Caesarean section and quickly delivered the baby, alive and well. The mother required a vertical incision of her uterus, losing a fair amount of blood. But God had mercy, and she was given a unit of blood after the surgery, which helped her recover well. She went home five days later with one healthy baby.

We later discovered more of the story. She had an ultrasound several weeks earlier and knew that her twins needed to be delivered by C-section, but she delayed coming to the hospital because she feared the surgery. Once labor started, it was the middle of the night and raining heavily, and it had taken the family quite some time to organize a vehicle to bring her to the hospital.

Gates are interesting things. During the night, they are usually closed for security. They speak of the brokenness of man, in that we must guard ourselves from one another. During the day, they are open and allow people to enter and access whatever is within their confines. Speaking of heaven at the very end of the Bible, John recorded that "in the daytime (for there will be no night there) its gates will never be closed; and they will bring the glory and the honor of the nations into it…" (Rev 21:25-26). At that time, the gate at *His House of Hope* provided much-needed security in a broken, messy world, yet it was also a portal to the hope and healing that are only found in Jesus Christ.

A Tale of Two Mothers

Celina was a 26-year-old mother with a young child at home and 26 weeks pregnant with her second when she came to our hospital with severe anemia. Her husband had abandoned her recently. We measured anemia by the level of hemoglobin, with anything under ten considered abnormal. Her hemoglobin was 2.7. After transfusing her several units of blood, she had increased to only 4.0, and then her level began dropping again. Not only that, but her platelets (responsible for clotting the blood) were dangerously low as well, and she had bilirubin in her urine, indicating her red blood cells were hemolyzing (bursting).

We consulted specialists around the world and treated her with steroids and antibiotics, in case the anemia was being caused by her own immune system or infection. She didn't get better, even after many days. We all feared it might be an unusual case of HELLP syndrome, something seen in pregnancy—for which the only treatment is delivery. After praying and discussing with the family, we decided to deliver the baby (knowing it would not be mature enough to live yet) in order to hopefully save the life of the mother. We knew even delivery was risky, because she had little blood to lose, and poor ability to slow any bleeding she might have.

Upon starting to induce her labor, she was found to be already dilating some, which affirmed our decision and gave us some peace that we were on the best course of action. Just four hours after starting the induction, she delivered a stillborn baby. The fluid around the baby was suggestive of infection. Celina seemed to be improving the day after the delivery, though her hemoglobin was only 2.4 The next day, however, she worsened, and we tried to give her a different medicine to block the bursting of the red cells. She had no response, but only got worse each day. We began to transfuse her again, but she immediately developed fever, as her body was now reacting violently to any blood we tried to give her. She began to accumulate fluid in her abdomen, became short of breath, and slipped into unconsciousness. She died later that day.

Agnes was a 38-year-old mother pregnant with her ninth child. She was a cherished woman by many, including us. She was the wife of Pastor Hillary, the leader of our local church. We hoped it would be a simple delivery, as she had had many normal births—often at home. It was midday, and she was in labor. Dr. Poole came into the room where I was seeing patients.

"This one is going to need a Caesarean," he said in a grave manner, gesturing to the paper strip in his hand. The fetal heart tones were having recurrent, deep, late decelerations, showing that baby was extremely distressed. She was not yet close to delivery. The operating team was quickly assembled, and Dr. Poole and I delivered the baby girl by C-section. The left side of the uterine incision tore down and to the left, and it bled quickly, refusing to stop. We struggled to place several deeper sutures to cinch off the bleeding vessels. Finally, we were able to control it, and close her incision. But she had lost a lot of blood.

She showed signs of excessive blood loss immediately after surgery, with a heart rate speeding along at 130 beats per minute and a blood pressure of 70/30—critically low. By evening, she hadn't yet fully awoken from surgery. She was in shock. We tilted the head of her bed down, and took a blood count. Her platelets were diminished (30,000) and hemoglobin had already dropped to a dangerous level of 6.5. She needed blood, and quickly.

We were able to locate three donors with compatible blood, and started collecting from them—her husband (the pastor), a visiting missionary, and my wife Elizabeth. Most importantly, we prayed earnestly that night. I prayed that the Lord would not let her die, as we loved our pastor and knew he was integral to the community and church. To lose his wife at this point would not only affect him, but their children, and the entire community. We pleaded with the Lord for her life over that first night.

The next morning, she opened her eyes and responded a bit. Her vital signs began normalizing, and the baby was doing great. Elizabeth picked some flowers and brought them to Agnes in the hospital. She opened Agnes' gown and put the baby to breast, hoping to stimulate uterine contractions and give the baby much-needed colostrum. Later, we learned they named the baby Elizabeth, because she was the first to greet and visit her in the hospital.

Months later, Agnes was well enough to attend a women's workshop at the church, and she brought baby Elizabeth to visit Mama Elizabeth! We thanked God for showing them and us mercy, and sparing us all sorrow upon sorrow.

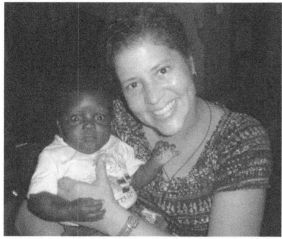

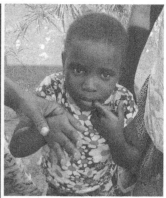

Mama Agnes and "Baby" Elizabeth at age 4 (July 2017)

Baby Elizabeth with Mama Elizabeth (December 2012)

Hope for an Entrance

Rose came to us when she was only 15 weeks pregnant. She was in pain and could not sleep because her abdomen was very swollen with fluid—from liver disease caused by Hepatitis B. The baby was alive and looked healthy, but the fluid was compressing the uterus. We had little hope that the baby would survive until an age at which she could breathe on her own. Because Rose was in so much discomfort, we decided to start taking fluid out of her abdominal space as often as we could safely do so. Therefore, every two weeks we removed 4 liters (about 1 gallon), using ultrasound to make sure we didn't damage bowel or uterus—and to check if baby was still alive.

Every two weeks, Rose showed up. She appreciated the relief of getting the fluid off so that she could breathe and sleep more easily. We were surprised when she reached 29 weeks—the age when babies are able to breathe on their own in our context. We gave her a series of steroid injections at that point to help the baby breathe if she delivered early. But Rose just kept on maintaining the pregnancy, and the baby continued to be happy!

Then, at 31 weeks, Rose's water broke. She had mild preterm labor, but the most concerning thing was that baby was back down (transverse), which would require a Caesarean section operation to deliver. This was a problem because Rose had low platelets due to her liver disease, so that she would likely have bleeding problems if we had to do surgery. Even more concerning was the 15-20 liters of fluid that would gush forth once we opened her up—a dangerous shift of fluid for her body, and one which she would possibly not survive.

We prayed and waited. Nothing more happened. We eventually let her go home on antibiotics and careful precautions.

Rose returned for her next fluid drainage, now near 37 weeks. The ultrasound showed that baby was now head down and still doing well!

Several days later, Rose returned after suddenly delivering the baby girl at home. Unfortunately, Rose lost much blood and was very weak. We stabilized her and transfused a unit of blood. She slowly recovered, fighting typhoid, anemia, and the fluid that kept accumulating. She was the first to receive a birth control injection at our hospital, as she and the family didn't want to risk another pregnancy for her. The baby did well, though she was also treated for an infection in her bloodstream.

We had little hope of this baby girl making an entrance into this world, but the Lord allowed her to do just that. He had plans for her and for many of these precious young lives who entered life at *His House of Hope*. We were learning to hope, and we continue to wait for what He will do in South Sudan through their lives. The ends of their stories are not yet written.

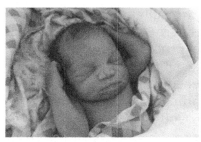

Grace Upon Grace:
The Struggle to Have a Healthy
Baby in South Sudan

Grace J. was followed carefully in antenatal clinic for several months. This, her eighth pregnancy, was hoped to be different than all the others. Her first baby had been born alive, but died after a few days of life. For the next six pregnancies, she faithfully attended antenatal care at the main hospital in Juba, South Sudan.

Her husband emphatically stated, "We did not stay and deliver in the village-- we were at the big hospital!"

However, each time she would arrive at a checkup around 35 weeks of gestation, only to find that the baby had died inside without any warning signs. He implored us to help them have a live baby this time. We carefully monitored her after 28 weeks, giving her steroids to mature the baby's lungs in case of an early delivery, and checking the baby each time on a fetal monitor (a "non-stress test"). Around 34 weeks, the husband began asking us to deliver the baby, but we were hesitant to bring baby out too early. At one visit, he asked to sign a consent form for a C-section operation ahead of time, in case we needed to emergently deliver the baby and he wasn't available. Their village was about 50 miles from the hospital, so he worried that we wouldn't be able to reach him if surgery was needed.

We kept her in the hospital, at our new Waiting Mothers Shelter, and monitored her daily until she was near term. At that point, we made the decision to induce labor. Grace was stable, but as soon as contractions started, the baby showed signs of distress, so we prepared urgently for C-section. Her blood pressure suddenly went extremely high, so we modified the anesthesia we were planning to use, gave her medicine to lower her blood pressure, and quickly delivered the baby by C-section. We were seeing the process which had likely killed the other babies replay itself before our eyes.

Thanks to the grace of God, it was a healthy baby boy. Grace struggled with a post-operative headache due to the spinal anesthesia, requiring me to learn a new procedure ("blood patch"), which worked (thanks to an email consult my nurse anesthetist friend, Charlie). It was a happy day when Grace and her husband took their healthy son home, reminding us all that our lives themselves are only due to the grace of God

Mary & the Triplets

Mary came to us when she was 27 weeks gestation. She was not quite 5 feet tall, and her pregnant belly was already impressively full. We sent her for ultrasound scan with Morris, the ultrasound tech whom we had trained, expecting to discover twins. Our area in central East Africa had some of the highest rates of natural multiple births in the world, so we were used to diagnosing twins. At one time, we had eight sets of twins in the hospital at the same time!

We had even seen naturally occurring triplets, though none carried them past 26 weeks, which in our setting (without a Neonatal Intensive Care Unit with a ventilator) was not compatible with life. One set delivered at 26 weeks, with all three breathing at the time of birth. They lived for almost an hour, breathing slowly with family and staff holding them, until they ran out of strength and succumbed.

With Mary, the ultrasound tech was a bit confused—he definitely saw at least two babies, but called me in to confirm. There they were, 3 babies lined up, all head down! Mary was already quite uncomfortable, and given our experience with triplets, we advised her to stay in the Waiting Mothers Shelter until she went into labor. We anticipated that would happen quite soon.

We gave her steroids to mature the babies' lungs, medicines to relax her uterus, and urged her to rest and drink plenty of water. Twice a week she would shuffle over to the Labor Ward where she would be monitored for an hour or so to see if all the babies were healthy and to assess if she was having preterm contractions. Surprisingly, she kept going like this week after week.

As we got closer, the babies all remained head down. I consulted with an obstetrician as to how to deliver them.

"Can we actually try to deliver them normally if they are all head down?" I asked.

"No, you need to do a C-section—too much can go wrong, with babies turning, cords entangling or falling out, and the risk of bleeding afterwards," she responded. So, it would be a C-section. The next question was when. We didn't want to wait until one of the babies was in distress, or Mary developed a complication, especially as she was such a petite mother. But we also didn't want to force delivery too early, for they would struggle due to prematurity.

One Sunday afternoon, April 10, 2016, I was resting quietly at home with my family, celebrating Winnie's seventh birthday. The on-call team had delivered a set of twins and two single babies during the morning hours. It was special to our kids to have babies born at *His House of Hope* on their birthdays—sharing that special day with a new life in South Sudan. Already, Winnie had four that shared that day with her! Then, as I prepared to rest for a little while, my phone rang. It was Dr. Loftus, the new addition to our missionary team.

"I think it's time we deliver Mary," he said. "Her right leg is swollen and painful—I'm not sure if it's the babies resting on her veins, or if she has a blood clot." I felt a jolt of adrenaline course through my body. There would be no Sunday afternoon nap for any of us. The triplets would enter the world today. We had received the direction we needed—the risks of continuing the pregnancy were now greater than the risk of delivering the babies. Mary was 34 weeks and 1 day of gestation (just less than six weeks from her due date).

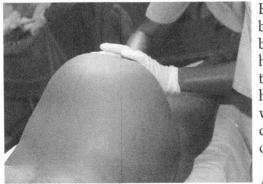

Everyone came out for the birth. With three premature babies coming, whom we had all been working hard to keep alive, we needed all hands on deck. The C-section went well, and all three were crying and kicking once delivered!

As we were closing her abdomen, her uterus struggled to regain its previous size, since it had held so great a volume. It was firm, but still hollow. After we closed her skin, she still was having too much bleeding, despite all the usual and extra medications. We had to pack her uterus with gauze and begin a transfusion of blood. She was on the verge of shock, with very low blood pressure. Before we took her out of the operating room, we prayed that God would have mercy. These three little babies needed their mother. It was difficult to find someone to breastfeed one baby who had lost his mother, much less three. Bottle-feeding almost never worked either, given the cost of formula, and more critically, the difficulty in properly mixing with clean water. We had seen a 2-week-old orphan die of amoebic dysentery, a severe diarrheal infection from unclean water source. So, we prayed that she would live.

The next morning, Mary began to wake up. However, because of the stress of surgery and her blood loss, she wasn't producing milk. We gave the babies fluids in the meantime, and as she got stronger, she started to feed them more. After two weeks, she was able to support their nutritional needs!

They were the first triplets to survive until discharge from the hospital. Winnie was excited to have seven babies share her seventh birthday! A week after the birth, we left as scheduled for home assignment, greeting the Poole family at the airstrip as they returned from their home assignment. None of us realized that the fighting would escalate and return to Yei. Mary and the triplets were seen once more at a feeding program in town during July. They were well, but her husband was missing, captured or recruited by rebels. A few months later, our team again had to evacuate—this time, for good.

In December, in the midst of a refugee camp with hundreds of thousands of people, one of our missionary nurses discovered Mary with the triplets (plus her 2 other children), still without her husband. God had mercy and spared her and her children. But the

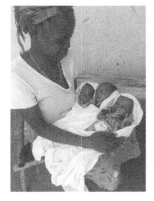 suffering was still so great, without husband or home, in a refugee settlement, in a country not her own.

It is a mystery why God has mercy on some, and not on others—but then again, He is God—and He is good. I trust He will let us know more in due time. We are grateful for the hope that these mercies give to the families and to us. We are thankful for the reprive from the mess of this world and a glimpse of His power.

When you pray for God to save the life of someone, are you open to Him choosing not to spare his or her life?

How would you explain the observation that God saves some but not others?

Chapter 6
Accidental Foster Parents

Olivia, our fifth child, was born in January of 2005, on a cold winter day in Colorado. Dr. Schmucker, my mentor and our family doctor, was cautiously overseeing Elizabeth's labor. Throughout the day and night, whenever her contractions got stronger, baby Olivia's heart rate would dip precipitously. We gave Elizabeth fluids and she changed positions, but to no avail. After a long painful labor, Olivia had to be delivered by Caesarean section. Elizabeth wept that she was unable to have a normal birth, as she had with our third and fourth children (our first two had been physically painless as they came through adoption). She wept even more when the spinal anesthesia didn't work, and she had to be put to sleep for the operation. It turned out that the umbilical cord was short and thin, so continued labor likely would have killed Olivia.

Elizabeth awoke to a healthy, strawberry blonde girl. Her first question was "Whose baby is that?!" which was a valid question since our first two were black and half-black, while our next two were white, but as our biological children are one-quarter black, they had some pigment and dark-brown hair.

"She's ours!" I assured her, confident of this as I had watched the whole process. I had seen the reddish hint to her hair as she gave her first screams and the nurse dried her wet head.

Olivia was different from the start. She was very energetic, but clingy. She wanted to be with us at all times. We tried to leave her in our home church nursery a few times, but she would scream non-stop, so we gave up and walked or held her during church and Sunday school class.

"You need to just leave her in nursery and let her scream it out," our new, young pastor wisely exhorted us, having no children of his own.

"We don't feel right about doing that—she will be ready in her own time, and then we will leave her," we countered.

"But you are missing out on the teaching," he asserted.

"This is just a season, and we will receive in other ways now, as we love our children. She is our responsibility and we are accountable to God for how we parent her," we replied.

"Well, I think you are being disobedient to me and to the Lord," he said, finishing the conversation.

Nonetheless, we did not feel at peace leaving her in the nursery. So we didn't. On our survey trip to Sudan in 2007, Olivia was almost three, and she blossomed. With blonde curly hair, she freely interacted with the children at the orphanage, and was usually surrounded by at least 30 of them. Our children were the first *kawaja* (foreign) children they had ever seen. It didn't faze Olivia at all. At the end of each day, her pale skin would be reddish brown from hours of playing in the dirt with her new friends. Olivia had emerged from the safety of her parents' care to be secure with people who were very different from her.

Upon our return to Colorado, she was confident and able to navigate the church nursery. The previous pastor had resigned. But then, her little temper developed, and she bit several other children. So in the end, she was kicked out of nursery! Lillie called her the "nursery drop-out" and Olivia's friend Elise still recalls the story of getting bitten by her.

As we approached our move to Sudan in 2011, then six-year-old Olivia started praying an unusual and persistent prayer. Every night, and every time she was asked to pray out loud, she would be sure to pray the same thing.

"I pray for twins, and that the twins would be boys, and the boys would be twins, and the twins would be boys, and the boys would be twins..." She definitely had the "persistent widow" aspect of prayer down. Perhaps she felt sorry for Logan, as the only boy at home now that Alex had gone off to college. At first, her prayer was that Elizabeth would give birth to twin boys, and then her prayers shifted to being for adoption if not birth. Every night, she asked God for twin boys in this way.

Several friends asked us if we hoped to adopt, since we had before and now lived at an orphanage. In our first year on the field, we were overwhelmed with all the new cultural differences, so the thought of adopting was beyond our comprehension.

"The only way we would adopt is if someone brought a child to our front porch," Elizabeth was heard to respond to such enquiries. We had friends and family lay down their lives to do foster care, with tales of heartache as the children went back and forth to toxic home situations. It seemed too difficult for us—if we were to ever take a child in again, it would be with the intent to be a permanent part of our family. Anything less would be too emotionally trying on us— and our other children. Or so we thought.

One cloudy, somewhat cool (for there) morning in April 2012, our assistant lab tech came to me as I surveyed the remaining parts of the hospital under construction. We had just "opened" a few weeks before, but were only using the clinic rooms, even for overnight patients.

"My brother's wife gave birth a few days ago, but she died, and the babies are not doing well," Kamba began. "They are at the Yei Civil Hospital, but they are sick and the family has no one that can take care of them. Would you be willing to take them?"

"Does the father want us to raise them as part of our family? That is the only way we would take them," I said.

"Yes, he can't do it. There is no one else—he wants you to take them. They are twin boys. He will bring them to you today, because they are sick."

I walked the 50 meters home quickly, and pulled Elizabeth aside. "Kamba has a relative that wants us to adopt his twin boys—the mother died after childbirth." We were shocked, amazed, and convicted—twin boys, brought to our front porch, with family wanting us to adopt them.

"What else can we do but receive them?" we agreed.

By that afternoon, we were meeting with the family—the boys' father, an uncle, Kamba, and our compound director from Harvesters (as a witness). There was much conversation, translated carefully multiple times to be sure we all understood each other well. We would adopt the boys forever. We would be their parents fully. We would likely still have the family visit or go to them to have the boys visit, but they would be with us and we would take care of them fully. Papers were drawn up and signed by the witnesses. Astoundingly, we ended the day as parents of a family with twin boys.

Logan with Taylor

The moment of reception of the boys on our porch, with Kamba watching on

Eva and Sophia on cloth diaper duty -- a full time occupation!

We returned inside the house to deliver the news to the children. They were overjoyed, ecstatic, elated. They jumped into care of these precious little ones.

We had always loved the name Hudson, and had been impressed by the life of Hudson Taylor, how he obeyed the Lord and become like the Chinese people in appearance, so as not to distract them from the message of hope he brought. So, their names became Hudson Jeffrey and Taylor Moses (the father's name was Moses).

Hudson was a bit bigger, stronger, and healthier, but he was still only 4 pounds. Taylor was 3 ½ pounds and quite sickly. He developed a fever and rash on his skin with many blisters. We decided it must be bullous impetigo, an infection caused by a type of "strep" (bacteria). He was started on cloxacillin as we gingerly tried not to break open the blisters while caring for him.

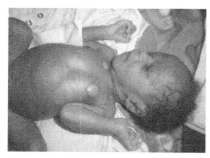

Taylor, with prominent bullous impetigo

Elizabeth was still nursing Winnie, our youngest, and she began nursing the twins as well. While her milk supply adjusted to the increased demand, we supplemented with formula. The staff at Harvesters provided us formula that had been donated for situations such as this— babies who had lost their mothers. Suddenly, we were back in the baby business! At the same time, the hospital was getting busier and we opened the inpatient ward. Taylor improved, and Hudson remained strong and healthy. The family came for a few visits, and affirmed their happiness about the arrangements.

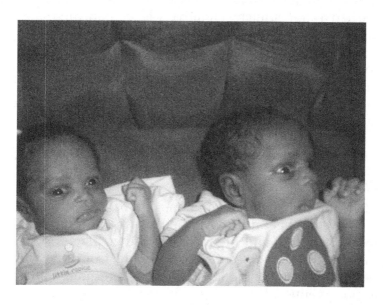

Even a week after joining our family, Hudson and Taylor were alert and responsive to their surroundings

The following month, we had planned a trip to Kenya to visit other mission hospitals and learn from their ways, followed by a conference in Uganda with our sending agency. We knew this would be tricky, so we went to the local authorities to learn what sort of paperwork would be needed to travel with them. Since they were under one year, they could travel on our passports. The county commissioner wrote a very official letter explaining that we were the legal guardians of the boys, with his office's stamp. We gathered all the papers originally signed by the family and witnesses. Then, we set off on our journey.

We had to first travel by ground to Juba, where we would fly to Nairobi. From there, we would go by ground to several mission hospitals in Kenya, and finally enter Uganda from the east. The twelve of us, the driver, his assistant, and our luggage crammed into the matatu which had no luggage rack. The driver was like many matatu drivers—he apparently had frustrated dreams of being a racecar driver. It was May, so rainy season had begun in earnest, and the road was riddled with large potholes. But our driver was determined to make it in record time, so he sped as fast as possible when he had a short stretch of relatively level road, then slammed on the brakes or swerved violently to avoid a large pothole. We were ill.

"Bira, bira," Elizabeth repeatedly pleaded with the driver. Slow, slow. He would slow down... for about two minutes, and then resume his previous race pace. We were relieved to finally reach Juba and make our way to the airport for our afternoon flight.

Juba was 10-15 degrees hotter than Yei, with few trees. Several rocky hills jutted up from its expanse as it straddled the Nile. In the previous ten years, it had exploded in growth, now reaching an estimated population of one million—almost a tenth of the entire nation. They had begun to pave their streets, and in a few places, the city looked new and organized. In other places, metal sheets were hastily put up to secure a compound from thieving. Many NGO's (non-governmental agencies) and government offices lined the various avenues. It was thriving, bursting with life, yet with a slightly unsafe, out-of-control feel to it all.

The Juba airport was large, with tarmac runways—the only of its kind in the young nation. A new terminal was under construction (and continues to be up to the time of this writing). It looked fairly impressive from the outside, but on the inside, not so much.

For such a large airport, the check-in area was surprisingly small. The floors were tiled with terrazzo (small stones mixed in cement), and a large scale stood in the center of the room, with counters for various small airlines forming a ring at the outside. We stood in the line (which was difficult to discern from the mass of people) and inched our bags forward, ushering the kids along as we took turns holding the two boys. It was now about one in the afternoon. Did I mention it was hot?

We were directed to place our bags, and then ourselves, on the large scale. It had a huge needle that spun slowly around, registering the weight for all to see, 100 kilograms for each round of the dial. So much for privacy. The airline was hesitant about us bringing the boys, but we showed them the letters we had.

"Do you have visas for them?" they also asked.

"No, we will get our visas upon arrival in Kenya, and they are traveling on our passports," we explained.

"But you first need to get stamped out of South Sudan," they directed us, motioning toward another line forming behind a wooden booth with a plexiglass window. We shuffled over to the line and waited.

Meanwhile, the children were thirsty, hungry, and had to go to the bathroom (it had been about six hours since we left home by now). So I remained in line while Elizabeth went in search of water, snacks, and a potty. She found the first two, and was directed to an area off to the side where the bathrooms were located. Despite being *inside* the terminal, the bathroom was a pit latrine.

When it was my turn at immigration, I presented our ten passports, twelve departure cards, and papers from the county government about the boys. The immigration official studied them for a while, and then scowled at the letters.

"These papers are only good for travel within South Sudan! You need letters and travel permits from the Ministry of the Interior!" he announced. Our flight was to depart one hour later.

"Where is that located?" I asked, hoping it was next to the airport. It wasn't. And it would surely take much time to get such documents! "If we do that, we will miss our flights and have to stay overnight here, reschedule our flights, and that will be very hard on the children," I explained. "We would be happy to get such documents, but we didn't know—we went to the highest government office in Yei and they told us this would be sufficient for us to travel. Can't you please stamp us out based on these letters?" I pleaded.

"No. You need to get the permit from the Ministry," he came back, undeterred.

I silently prayed. Please, Lord, this trip is hard enough on the children without adding more time here. Help. Not a fancy prayer. Just "help."

Suddenly, another man in the booth turned around and noticed me. It was an immigration official from the Yei office, who apparently had just been transferred to Juba. He recognized me and we greeted.

"Salaam, Diktor! You are leaving us?!"

"Just for a few weeks, for a conference," I explained.

"Ah, very good!" he replied, and then said a few words in Juba Arabic to the other officer. The first officer looked back at me, grunted a little, and started stamping our passports.

"You go," he commanded… which I happily did.

I returned to the family. "We almost didn't leave, but we're on our way now, thanks to God," I reported. Hastily, we showed our stamps and passed through security, where we were told to sit down and wait. The waiting area was without any moving air. The toilets in this part of the airport were flush toilets, but they weren't flushing—

they were overflowing. The doors to the outside were secured with a large chain and padlock. Confirming Einstein's theory of relativity again, time went very slowly as we waited for the call to board.

We were overwhelmingly grateful to be on the plane and in the air. Arriving to the Nairobi airport was like entering a different world—a modern airport that rivaled one in the West. The immigration checkpoint was thoroughly up to date, with computerized scanning of our fingerprints. I presented our ten passports and arrival cards, which indicated that Elizabeth and I each had an infant traveling on our passports. Elizabeth and the children stood by holding Hudson and Taylor. The official eyed us curiously as he stamped us in, perhaps trying to rectify the number of passports with the number of humans he was seeing, but he made no special mention of the boys as he did so. We were officially in Kenya now—but were the boys "officially" in the country?

From Kenya to Uganda with the twins

We had a great time with the twins as we visited Kijabe and Tenwek mission hospitals, to glean what we could from them. Leaving Tenwek, in western Kenya, we crammed the twelve of us into a *matatu* (minivan taxi for commercial hire) and began the long journey to Uganda for our Pioneers East Africa conference. As we neared Kisumu, Kenya (home of then President Obama's father and grandparents) around midday, the van broke down. It was a flat stretch of two-lane tarmac road, amidst a boggy area not far from Lake Victoria. Our driver hopped out, crawled under the vehicle and looked it over for a few minutes. He got on the cell phone and started talking rapidly with someone in Kiswahili.

"I'll be back shortly," he abruptly said, and flagged down a passing boda boda (motorcycle taxi).

"Okay..." we responded weakly. What else was there to do? We broke out the snacks and water, and opened the doors and windows to invite in whatever fresh air was available. We still had to pass through Kisumu, drive further to the border town, and then slog through an international border crossing and immigration with all

12 of us. And I didn't have much confidence in the paperwork we held for the twins. Would they stop us? Take the boys from us?

Travelling through Kenya with ten children

The driver miraculously returned in about half an hour, with a mechanic and some parts. Equally miraculous, in less than twenty minutes, the matatu was fixed and running. We were on our way!

We reached the border crossing in the late afternoon, and a sea of lorries and disheveled vehicles amassed in a confusing array. The driver encouraged me to get out of the vehicle and take all the passports to the immigration office to be stamped out. I went, along with some of the children, and filled out the departure cards, again noting the two infants traveling with us. The officer slammed the exit stamp in each of our ten passports.

"Where are the rest of the children and your madam?" he queried.

"They are all in the vehicle," I replied.

"Hmm," he grunted. "You go."

I again found our driver amidst the chaos, and hopped in. Sophia and Olivia were holding Hudson and Taylor, to give them a break from the car seats. They were in the far back of the van.

We pulled up to the checkpoint, and Elizabeth handed the passports to him. The official furrowed his brow and half bent over to look inside the matatu. He seemed a bit confused and overwhelmed by the sight of so many differently colored people in one vehicle. He thumbed open a few passports to locate the exit stamps, but seemed to tire of the process, so went very quickly. He handed them back to Elizabeth and waved us forward. We crossed into Uganda!

It was a rich time of fellowship, learning, and worship with the other Pioneers missionaries from East Africa. They welcomed the twins warmly as we immersed ourselves in their care. I came out of our banda (round house) one morning to find Josiah, a Maasai missionary, teaching Logan to throw a spear. A real spear. He was a joyful mzee (older African man), missing two of his front teeth, which is the custom in his tribe. Otherwise, he would "look like a donkey" (which is how they view the rest of us). We later took a boat ride with him and his wife, and they posed in the prow of the boat in a Titanic-like moment.

Adoption meets roadblock

We returned to Yei with the boys, and resumed life. Several weeks later, we were scheduled to meet with the family to complete adoption paperwork with the local government. One moderately warm morning in late June 2012, we arrived at the Yei River County offices. The buildings formed a horseshoe shape, with elevated walkways under the overhang of the roof. Various doorways led to the different departments. We were glad to have Pastor Hillary and Kamba with us.

The biological father, grandmother, and several other relatives were present. We sat in plastic chairs and an old sofa on the veranda, visiting pleasantly. We tried our limited Arabic, along with depending on our companions for translation. The social worker appeared from one of the doorways and beckoned the family members inside. They stayed for what seemed a very long time—perhaps 20 or 30 minutes. We became a little nervous. What were they talking about for so long?

"You come now," said the social worker as she stuck her head out of the doorway. We followed and sat in the dim office, lit only by the natural light of a few windows. "The family has decided that they are happy with you having the boys until they are five years old, and then they will come back to the family to be raised," she reported matter-of-factly.

We were stunned. That was impossible! Our children were already bonded with Hudson and Taylor. What had changed?

"But, we had many conversations with them before, that we would take them knowing they would remain with us until they were grown," I said shakily, trying to hold back my anger and beginnings of grief. "We have their signatures and witnesses to that."

"Well, that doesn't matter. They are afraid they won't see them, that you will take them out of the country forever. But they are happy to have you raise them for five years."

Did they, and she, not realize the amount of emotional trauma for the boys to be raised by one family for five years, only to be taken away to another family? Not to mention the pain it would cause our children and us!

"I'm sorry," we began. "We can't do that. Either we raise them entirely, or they raise them starting now."

There was muttering in Kakwa (the tribal language) between the family and the social worker. "They will think about it and meet here after two days. Be ready to give them back at that time."

We walked out of the office to our van, stunned. It felt like someone had punched us in the gut. We drove home slowly, while Pastor Hillary and Kamba shook their heads in disbelief and dismay with us.

"I can't believe they are doing this. The social worker convinced them not to give them away—they were going to do it, no problem," Pastor Hillary stated.

Delivering the news to the children was devastating. It was like an impending death. For the next two days, we all ached as we numbly continued to feed, bathe, and change diapers. The twins were clinging to life when we received them. Now, both of them were happy, chubby, and strong. Who wouldn't want them?

I remembered Olivia's years of prayer for boys that were twins and twins that were boys; a prayer that had been answered, but was now being ripped from us, it seemed. We were heartbroken—especially for our children, who had longed for the twins along with Olivia.

We drug ourselves back to the county office two days later, with the boys and all their belongings, accompanied by several of our kids. As expected, the family had decided to take over their care. The father's cousin had agreed to assume responsibility for them. She was young, and didn't smile as we placed Hudson in her arms. The grandma, a wiry little woman, took Taylor in her arms and warmed a bit to him.

We forced a smile and a greeting, then turned on our heels and got back into the car as soon as possible.

"Go, go," said Elizabeth, tears starting to flow. "Let's just get out of here." We pulled out without looking back.

After the failed adoption

I saw them a few times in the clinic over the following months—they had been given tribal names, and now went by Chandiga and Lotigo. The father and the young cousin raising the boys brought them to get formula and immunizations.

Many months passed. Nearly a year after we returned them to the family, we gathered up the courage to ask Kamba about visiting them in the village—at Olivia's initiation. We were fearful of finding them sick with malaria, malnourished, or worse.

Their village was several miles past the airstrip. We turned off by a school and followed a winding sandy road down a steep hill, navigating a few large boulders on the way. Given was suffering from malaria (even though we were all on anti-malarial medication).

Olivia got carsick, vomiting out of the van window while children from the village laughed at the sight of a little blonde kawaja girl getting sick. Not a glorious day for the Perrys.

We pulled our van into their compound, then walked the rest of the way. Their home consisted of a group of mud huts with grass roofs. The dirt was swept clean and they brought out a straw mat for the children to sit upon. Plastic chairs appeared for the adults, and after some time, semi-cold waters and sodas were brought for all to enjoy. Obviously someone had traveled a great distance and spent much of their meager South Sudanese pounds to get them. We gave them the gifts we had brought—baby books, clothes, and rations of sugar and flour— a common practice.

They brought out the boys. We hardly recognized them. Hudson, who was the bigger one before, was now the smaller twin. Taylor had a mild case of malaria, and both had reddish hair, a sign of malnutrition. They tried to have us hold the twins, but they would have nothing to do with us. They clearly had no memory of us. It was humbling. They seemed content enough with their family and culture. Before we left, a chase ensued, for a chicken. They finally caught one, and offered it to us as a gift. Hazel proudly held on to it, all the way home, and named it Astrid.

That was the last time we saw them. We continued to get updates from Kamba for a few years, that they were doing okay. As the civil war began, however, he lost contact with them. Born in April 2012, they would be six years old as I write this chapter. We have no idea where they are or if they are yet alive.

Accidental foster parents

We never planned to be foster parents, because of the pain we anticipated, and then experienced. What happened with Olivia's prayer? We realized that God *did* answer her prayer, though He never promised they would be with us always. Perhaps He concealed what would happen so that we would fully enter into the brief time we enjoyed with them. In the process, their lives were preserved, and the family was challenged to value them, organize how they might be able to take care of the twins, and get over their grief of losing the mother.

I stopped to consider the father's situation right after the birth. His wife had just died, leaving sickly twins for whom he wasn't ready to care. His wife's cousin worked for a hospital and orphanage run by foreigners. Moses, the father, was willing to do anything in his desperation, as he didn't feel capable of handling these children.

As we walked through this dark night of our family's soul, we pondered the wisdom of adopting children out of a collectivist society like tribal South Sudan. Many of those we respected in the community didn't feel foreigners should adopt South Sudanese children. Their identity comes from the community, and if the children lack knowledge of their birth family, they become lower class citizens. They are without identity, and even marriage becomes difficult. Certainly, they would have had more "opportunity," material goods, and a physically "easier" life with us. They would have had a family that loved them, but was very different than those from whom they came. Who's to say what is more important? Our lasting concern is for their physical safety, and more so, if they will get to know the Lord. Only then will their identity be found in Christ.

We don't fully understand why God had us walk through this. But we trust Him, and have seen Him heal and draw us into a place of deeper trust. He is good, and He is working these painful experiences together for good. One day we will understand His reasons—when we see Him face to face.

Olivia, the prayer for twin boys, face-to-face with Hudson

What have you told the Lord (out loud or in your heart) that you will *never* do?

What are the pros and cons of cross-cultural adoption?

How do you respond to God when circumstances don't turn out the way you'd prayed or hoped for?

Chapter 7
Bricks without Straw: *The Teaching of Disillusionment*

The Deputy Ministry of Health, second in command of the Ministry of Health in South Sudan, was coming for a visit.

"I want him to come see *His House of Hope*," the Bishop said with intensity and pride. He saw the hospital as the flagship of the Evangelical Presbyterian Church (EPC), a gem in the crown of the church. He wanted the government to know how well the church was caring for the people of South Sudan. The church was a beacon of God's power and honor in a broken country. "Show him around, do rounds with him."

Dr. Atok was an impressive specimen of a man. His muscular frame was contained within a finely tailored blue suit, his head topped with a cowboy hat, and he carried an air of confidence about him. He was a surgeon, trained in Germany for five years. We gave him a quick tour and introduced him to several staff members.

"This is Anna," Dr. Poole mentioned to Dr. Atok. "She is an orphan who has grown up at Harvesters, and we are training her to help in the hospital!"

Dr. Atok nodded, but didn't say much. We proceeded with rounds, where he gave some helpful surgical consults. He was obviously well-trained.

"We don't want any 'cowboy' missionary doctors of old," Dr. Atok said. "Only practice what you are trained and qualified to do in your own country. Refer to Juba if you have anything you can't handle. Of course, if there is an emergency and the patient's life depends on it, do what you need to do."

I agreed with him, and appreciated the limitations he put forth. I didn't want to do surgeries for which I was untrained, either! The visit ended pleasantly, shaking hands as cameras recorded the moment.

The next day, Elizabeth and I were called down to the EPC office for a meeting. The founders of Harvesters also came. The Bishop began.

"The Deputy Minister of Health didn't want to say anything in front of you, but you shouldn't have students working in the hospital. *His House of Hope* is not a health training institution, so everyone there must be a trained health professional in his or her field. They must have papers."

We were stabbed with disappointment. Mentoring these students from the orphanage and giving them experience in the medical field was our greatest passion. Furthermore, they were learning skills and had quickly become valuable members of the team. Our staff was limited, and some of them didn't like to work very hard. Late at night, if a woman needed a C-section, it was nearly impossible to pull a surgical team together and still have someone to look after the other patients in the hospital.

The community was happy to have us there, attending to pregnant mothers and sick babies. Hospitals and clinics (including the large government hospital) from all around were sending us their more difficult cases. We were struggling to keep up with the demand, though we'd only been open for a year.

"With all respect," I began, "they do everything under our direct supervision. In the US, we work with 'medical assistants' and phlebotomists who are largely trained on the job. They are under the authority of my medical license. I'm very used to supervising and training staff like these. I'm a faculty member with a medical school in the US."

"The Ministry of Health doesn't want anyone working in the hospital that hasn't completed training in the medical field," the Bishop restated. "They could close *His House of Hope* and EPC could be jeopardized."

"We were thinking they shouldn't have students in the hospital," said the founder.

We felt thrown under the bus. They wanted us to do the work, and more of it, yet were taking away five of our most helpful staff. They wanted us to make bricks but wouldn't provide the straw. "Moses" had come to "help" and now we, the "Israelites," had to do our work without the resources. The disillusionment had begun.

We struggled on with fewer staff. Later, we were allowed to employ the students as "translators," as long as they didn't touch patients. This at least allowed them to see and experience the healthcare setting. We also learned that once they had simply started in a school of nursing, midwifery, lab, or clinical medicine, they could resume helping with direct patient care. As some of the students did this, we were thankful to welcome them back during their breaks from school.

Inspections

"The Public Health Inspector is here!" announced Juliet, as I was finishing our second C-section of the day.

"Can you get started with her, and I will join you as soon as I can?" I glumly asked. A surprise inspection was the last thing we needed on a day like this. There was another woman in labor that was threatening to require a C-section. And we hadn't started rounding on all the maternity patients and premature infants on the wards.

Forty minutes later, I joined Juliet in the office. A middle-aged South Sudanese woman, not overly thin, sternly looked at a box on the floor.

"These are all past their expiry date!" the inspector declared. "I also discovered that the bathing shelter is not draining properly and the grass needs to be slashed."

"Oh, I am sorry," I began. "We review our meds monthly to make sure they are still within the dates. May I see them?" It was the second day of March, a Monday. The expiry dates of several of the medications were 28 February. Our staff had not yet cleared them from the medication cabinet, as the first had been a Sunday. Some of the medications were dated 31 January—our pharmacist later told me they had been cleared from the shelves in the pharmacy, but not yet disposed.

"Here is your fine," the inspector said as she thrust a paper toward me. I read the hastily scratched description of the infractions and "7,500 SSP"—then around $500 USD.

"This seems like a large amount for the problems you found," I said, mustering all the respect I could, despite my "justice-o-meter" needle passing into the red zone. We knew the condition of most area clinics. They were holding us to a higher standard, so they could bleed us for fines.

In other clinics, a nurse or clinical officer would briefly consult on a patient and order a battery of tests. Then they would prescribe several medications for each positive test result. By the time it was all done, the patient could only afford one or two doses of the many medicines. If it was only malaria, they usually had success, as the treatments were short and inexpensive.

Such clinics ran for profit. They would turn patients away if they had no money. The notes from the clinic, if any, revealed no or few vital signs, physical exam, or medical rationale for what they did. No doctor would be on call. Patient abandonment was common— "the doctor is not here this week." Medications would suddenly "get finished" (run out) and no replacements would be offered. Patients came to us with such stories and records of their experiences.

We had consulted on several patients who had surgery to remove their ovary or uterus because of pain, only to do an ultrasound showing a perfectly normal and complete uterus and ovaries. "Sham surgeries" were not uncommon at that time. Many locals were illiterate, and "doctors" would open up shop, diagnose a serious condition, and take them to the operating theatre. Once there, the doctor would sedate them, make an incision in the skin, explore a bit, then suture the skin closed again. More than once, we had pulled gauze and large fragments of placenta from inside the uterus of woman who had delivered elsewhere.

As I absorbed the fine before me, tension rose. Why weren't they dealing with the major problems of other clinics? Juliet and I tried to reason with the woman. I called the Bishop to seek his advice.

"Let me talk to her," he said brusquely. I gave her my phone, and they switched to Kakwa, discussing the matter in seemingly angry tones. Abruptly, she handed me the phone.

Bishop changed back to English with me, saying "You will pay her 1,000 SSP. Just take care to clear any expired meds off your shelves each month."

"Okay, we will do so," I affirmed.

A few good men and women

Good staffs were hard to find—ones that were competent and had good character. There was a third "C" that was a critical factor—cash. For decades, South Sudan had lived in wars (or rumors of war). This meant fewer trained health professionals. Those that were around were usually snatched up by a large non-governmental organization (NGO) that paid a hefty salary in US dollars. Once a part of an NGO, staff had little on-site supervision or ongoing education. The NGO cycle usually ran from January to December, with people negotiating each December for the next year. The NGOs depended on large outside grants, which might last one to five years, then abruptly end. Then, we would receive a candidate looking for us to match their previous salary, which we usually couldn't do as a small ministry under a national church.

Bet Eman – His House of Hope staff (2015)

We gradually accumulated better staff, as we weeded through the chaff. We were hopeful when we hired Emmanuel, an older "Medical Assistant" (like a Physician Assistant) trained in Khartoum many years back. He had a wealth of work experience, most recently with MSF (Medicin Sans Frontiers / Doctors without Borders). He asked for a large salary, and we compromised, paying him more than we would have liked, considering his experience. As always, we started with a one-month probationary contract.

Emmanuel was kind, but as we reviewed his notes, his medical reasoning was all over the place. He would order multiple lab tests after taking little history, and prescribe a seemingly random assortment of treatments. We began the process of remedial training, but he was resistant to much input. Then he got sick. Really sick—we had to put him on oxygen. It turned out that he had smoked much of his life, and now had COPD (chronic obstructive pulmonary disease, or emphysema). At the end of the probationary period, we decided not to continue his contract.

We did find some great staff, like Innocent. He was tall, soft-spoken, and gentle with the patients. And he was smart. He knew how to assess and treat critically ill children. He was able and willing to learn new skills. After about nine months with us, he sheepishly told me that he was going back for more schooling. I was sad, but encouraged him in his pursuits.

Several months later, we received a referral from an outlying clinic run by an NGO—and the referring nurse was Innocent.

"Is this Innocent that used to work for us?" I asked the nurse on duty, gesturing to the referral form. "I thought he was going back to school."

"Yes, Doctor, that's him. He didn't go to school. He got an offer for a higher salary from them, and that's why he left. We all knew," she gently informed. I felt like the child everyone was trying to protect from an embarrassing family secret. In this honor-shame culture, it was more shameful for Innocent to tell me directly that he was leaving for a better salary than to tell us a lie. He probably was thinking of going back to school eventually—after earning more at his new job. So maybe it wasn't a complete lie...

Innocent at least told us he was leaving. Loki, a talented young clinical officer, went on holiday. He was due back on a Tuesday, but didn't show. On Thursday, he called from Juba saying he needed a few more weeks to sort out some family issues.

"I'll return after the first of September," he gruffly said.

"We will allow it this time, but we'll need to sort out your time off. You don't have that many leave days left," I responded. We knew that unexpected crises came up often for our staff, and we tried to be understanding. Yet, we were trying to instill a sense of professional responsibility in our young staff.

September rolled around, and Loki did not resurface. I called but his number was not available. I asked other staff, and no one knew his whereabouts (or they weren't telling me—I knew their allegiance to one another, tribemates, was greater than to their kawaja employer).

We accepted the fact that he had "disappeared" to an NGO job.

Nine months later, I was in the pyat (meeting place) having dinner with our missionary team, when I received a call. It was Loki.

"Hello… Uh, do you think we could meet?" he began tentatively.

"Sure," I responded. "What's going on for you?"

"I am back in Yei, and I wanted to see if I could return to *His House of Hope*."

"Come on by and let's talk," I said.

Loki shared that he had been on holiday in Juba when he learned that Dr. Tom, a well-known Catholic missionary doctor in the Nuba Mountains, needed a clinical officer. The government from Khartoum was bombing the Nuba region of Sudan (just north of the border with South Sudan), and the place was in desperate need. Young and adventurous, Loki jumped at the opportunity and hopped the next flight to take the job.

In the hospital office, he was a different man than before. He was more humble. He wanted to rejoin us.

"Why did you leave Nuba?" I asked.
"It was too much. I couldn't take working amidst the bombing. It was just too stressful."

"You didn't tell us you were leaving. Technically, I shouldn't rehire you. It wouldn't be fair to the others to let you pick up where you left off," I continued.

"I know. I shouldn't have left that way."

We rehired Loki, but he started as a new employee. He had to forfeit his benefits, money that was saved on his behalf, because he had not left on good terms. Over the following few years, he grew as a clinician, and began learning to do C-sections. His surgical skills were good, though a bit cavalier in his cutting. He respectfully let me know that he wanted to apply for a new program that was training clinical officers to perform C-sections. I reluctantly supported his application; reluctantly, because I knew he would better gain the experience he wanted by staying with us. The program never materialized, though. Circumstances were brewing that were beyond any of us.

Disillusioned staff

As Loki applied for advanced training, the economy in South Sudan took a turn for the worse. Civil war had started in December 2013, and had smoldered on for two years. The cash reserves of South Sudan had dried up, in step with the flow from the oilfields. South Sudanese pounds started losing their value in lunging steps downward. Fifteen pounds to a dollar became 30 to one. Then 40 to one, 50 to one, and worse. Inflation followed, first with imported goods that had been bought with more stable currencies, then with local goods. Those that were paid in US dollars were protected from the changes, but the government wanted everyone to be paid in SS pounds. Only the larger NGOs paid in US dollars. Our staff, paid in SS pounds, found themselves with half the buying power they once had. We witnessed a desperate fear rising in our staff. Would they be able to provide for their families?

We began adjusting salaries, giving bonuses to help them through. The Bishop had seen this happen before, and he felt the currency value would stabilize after a few months. The exchange rate would improve from time to time, every time a hopeful bit of news or another peace treaty was signed. The two sides had signed many peace treaties since the civil war began. Even so, our staff became increasingly disgruntled. They saw only one solution—they should be paid in US dollars.

One morning, Charles and Loki came into the office to discuss salary issues on behalf of the other staff.

"Can we talk with you about our salaries?" they began.

I was tired. Dr. Poole and family were on their second home

assignment, and by this time, he had assumed much of the Human Resource management. When he was away, I had my usual duties, plus his administrative tasks, topped with the actual medical work of rounding on patients, doing surgeries, and teaching the staff. Dr. Loftus had joined us, and was quickly learning C-sections, but I was still "on" as backup all the time.

I responded briefly. Too briefly, in retrospect. "If it's about being paid in USD, not really. We appreciate the difficulties you are facing, and that is why we are adjusting your salary each month, in SSP, to match the rising costs of goods." We sampled the prices in the market each month and calculated a "consumer price index" which we multiplied by their salary. With this, we were hoping to keep pace with inflation. "That is what we can do for now. We cannot pay you in USD."

They were not happy. They saw this as the only solution, though the church and the government didn't want us paying our staff in USD. But I should have at least listened again. They didn't feel heard. They felt voiceless.

The next week, we held a staff meeting, and revisited the issues. Jay, the Executive Director, joined me. I carefully explained our system for adjusting their salaries.

"We multiply your usual salary by this index, so that right now, your salary will be 1.8 times as much as the salary you signed for on last December's contract."

Confused and angry faces looked back at me. One by one, different staff stood to "have their say." These sequential monologues, some as long as 15 minutes, were the way such meetings functioned. The tension rose as the speakers became more emotional. The discussion was going nowhere—nowhere good, anyway. After two hours of this, Kitty interrupted with an emergency from the labour suite. The meeting was adjourned—or so I thought. As two staff and I attended to the woman in labour, the rest of the staff continued discussing what they would do.

Two days later, the Bishop called, obviously excited. "The Minister of Health is coming in next tomorrow, along with the State Minister of Health, County Commissioner, the Mayor of Yei, and others. They want to sign the Memorandum of Understanding making *His House of Hope* a National Teaching Hospital of South Sudan!"

We had been working on this agreement for 16 months, and had all but forgotten about it. Suddenly, it was about to happen—complete with television, radio, and newspaper coverage. We burst into action, cleaning up the facility. We prepared a table and chairs in the pyat of the new male staff housing where the official signing would take place.

On the scheduled day, I hurried to the hospital to start the day early. I would try to get rounds mostly done before they came. Curiously, many staff had assembled for a meeting at the rear of the pharmacy. I proceeded to the ward, and found Dr. Kiden.

"What are they meeting about?" I inquired.

"They are striking," she said disapprovingly. "It is ridiculous. They shouldn't do this."

I made my way to the meeting, and Kamba, our Logistic Officer, came out to meet me. "They are refusing to work. They want to be paid in USD, or they won't return," he said, confirming my fears.

I stood and pleaded before the staff. "There are patients' lives at stake. Medical professionals cannot strike—it is abandoning patients. We must continue working as we sort out these issues." But they were resolute—save a few who had chosen to work despite the group's decision. They were being true collectivists—thinking and acting as a group to effect change from those in power—us.

I received a call from Bishop just before the official entourage sped to the front of the hospital for the signing ceremony. A police truck emptied its contents of uniformed men brandishing their polished AK-47s. The dignitaries stepped out of immaculate vehicles displaying South Sudanese flags.

I put on my "game face," though inside I was reeling. The Minister of Health extended his hand in greeting. He was a dignified, gray-haired South Sudanese man in a sharp black suit. I led him and the group around the facility on a brief tour. They noticed the many employees sitting in one area—only one or two working.

"What's going on?" the Bishop asked me discreetly.

"Our staff is on strike," I said.

"Okay, we'll deal with this after the signing is done and the Minister goes."

What should have been a victorious, joyful day in the life of *His House of Hope* was instead a surreal, bittersweet event. After signing the document and making speeches for the South Sudan television cameras, we walked back to the hospital and the waiting vehicles. The Bishop sidled up alongside me, put his large hand on my shoulder, and spoke encouraging words to me.

"You are doing good work here. Don't be discouraged. I will come tomorrow to talk with your staff."

That he did. But where he was usually undeterred, able to handle every situation, the Bishop was exasperated after his meeting with our staff.

"They are unreasonable!" Bishop exclaimed. "They will not listen." I knew if the Bishop couldn't get through to them, little would at this point. "I have informed the mayor, since the hospital is now within town limits. He should be given first chance to deal with this."

Meanwhile, we reduced services to a bare minimum. I informed the medical director at the government hospital of our predicament. It was a humbling moment of connection and understanding—they had been through the same ordeal before, and we were now at a moment of crisis, in need of their help. They prepared to absorb more deliveries, although the truth was that more women would simply choose to deliver at home.

The mayor ordered all staff to report to his office the following day. We provided the hospital van as transport, but only three staff agreed to go. Agripina was one of those who continued to work, and she told the mayor of other staff threatening her life—without mentioning specific names. We knew the names, because they had also warned several missionary nurses not to return, or they would be hurt or killed. The mayor was incensed that they were striking at a hospital, giving out death threats, and disobeying his order to come to his office. I later learned the staff feared they would be put in jail.

The mayor came to the compound the next day to meet with our staff and management. Politicians, National Security, and the media assembled for the show. I was seated up front with the other "big men" as the meeting began. The cultural norm was for uninterrupted time for each person to speak. So for three hours, while patients languished in the hospital, we sat silently, being lambasted by the very staff we had come to serve. They criticized and complained. These were some of the most painful hours of our time in South Sudan, and left a bitter taste in our hearts. We felt betrayed. We were disillusioned.

I said very little. The mayor and others spoke directly to our staff, pointing out that the war and the country's overdependence on oil as its only export were the real sources of the economic crisis. He exhorted them to not blame us, and that they should not be abandoning patients that needed care.

"There is a Labour Department with which to lodge your complaints. I will have that department meet with the management of *His House of Hope* to address your concerns, but you are all ordered back to work as scheduled—tonight!" he concluded.

"What will happen if they don't?" I later asked.

"They will be arrested," was the explanation. And no one wanted to end up in the Yei town jail.

The final two weeks before we left for home assignment was filled with reinstating staff that agreed to handle future grievances through the Human Resource Department of EPC, who would involve the Labour Department as needed. The staff that signed the agreement then went to EPC, where the Human Resource manager and elders prayed and sang with them. Those that didn't sign the agreement, left. Loki remained, but Charles left, only to return later, as recounted in an earlier chapter. There was no feeling of victory or vindication in the resolution of the strike. The healing began, but it was a slow, painful road with our staff.

The Teaching of Disillusionment

My disillusionment betrayed the fact that I suffered from illusions. Illusions that life would not be as messy as it actually is.

I hadn't fully realized the depth of our staff's brokenness. I hadn't expected the very ones we came to teach and work alongside would "bite the hand that fed them." Deep inside, I still believed others wouldn't slander me if I were obeying God. What was He trying to teach me through this?

The great missionary mentor Oswald Chambers warned that "... our experience of disillusionment may actually leave us cynical and overly critical in our judgment of others. But the disillusionment that comes from God brings us to the point where we see people as they really are, yet without any cynicism or any stinging and bitter criticism."

If we refuse to be disillusioned, and remain in our illusions, we end up expecting consistently good behavior out of bad humans who can't deliver. Only the Lord can. "Our Lord trusted no one, and never placed His faith in people, yet He was never suspicious or bitter. Our Lord's confidence in God, and in what God's grace could do for anyone, was so perfect that He never despaired, never giving up hope for any person. If our trust is placed in human beings, we will end up despairing of everyone." (Chambers, My Utmost for His Highest, 30 July)

If I allow God to administer the teaching of disillusionment to me, I must fathom new depths of grace and forgiveness for others, and better understand the mystery of His great mercy toward me. The object is to know what is in man (the mess that we are) yet not be bitter or despair. All this, while clinging to hope in what God can do for any person.

"Jesus did not commit Himself to them... for He knew what was in man." (John 2:24-25)

How have you experienced disillusionment?

How would you respond if someone treated you badly or slandered you, even though you were "just trying to help" him or her?

Chapter 8
The God of Accidents: *Bunks, Trucks, Bodas & Trees*

South Sudan is not a safe place. Then again, neither is Colorado. But we were accustomed to the dangers of Colorado—mountain climbing tragedies, traffic accidents, and mass shootings. In many developing countries, there is no safety net of an ambulance that comes to the call of "911," an emergency room with a CT scanner, or a trauma surgeon on call at all times. Messiness results from this lack of a safety net, because trauma happens.

Christmas in Yei often included increased robbery and fighting, as the men wanted to provide nice material things for their families. Somehow the birth of Jesus was lost on these individuals. Men and women usually used pangas (machetes) to cut teak poles for the roof of their tukul, but pangas also made good weapons.

Lillian, our oldest daughter, completed a nurse assistant course and sometimes helped me in the hospital. Late one night in December, a patient was referred to us after a panga fight. The referral note mentioned "minor cuts on head and fingers." Lillie helped me unwrap the thickly bandaged hand, to discover he was missing half of three fingers! We worked late into the night in the operating theatre, cleaning and completing the amputation of the fingers, leaving better stumps for those fingers.

Bunks

We first encountered the lack of a safety net with our second youngest, Given, then four years old. We were ready to return to South Sudan after collecting medical supplies and taking some time of rest in Kampala. I put Given and Winnie in their bunk beds for an afternoon nap, and turned to walk out of the room. Out of the corner of my eye, I saw her start to climb back down the ladder, when she got tangled in the mosquito net and plummeted to the tile floor over six feet below.

It sounded like a bowling ball dropped on concrete. She hit hip first, whipping her head even faster toward the unforgiving surface. An instant wave of sickness hit my gut as it did. Elizabeth screamed from the other room as I scooped her up and kept talking to her to keep her eyes open and fixed on me.

"What should we do?" Elizabeth asked. We thought quickly. There was a reasonably good hospital just half a mile down the hill. We could get her there quicker than trying to figure out how to call an ambulance, as there was no "911" service.

"Into the van!" we agreed. Our missionary friends Peter and Kate had just stopped by to visit, and they were immediately pressed into service to stay with the other seven children.

We arrived at the hospital, a multi-story modern facility, quite clean. However, no one seemed to move as fast as we would have liked. Given lapsed in and out of awareness. The left side of her skull was swelling rapidly. That is near her middle meningeal artery, I thought. Bad brain bleeds happen there… My last job before leaving the US had been as an emergency room doctor.

"Do you have a CT scanner that is working?" I said urgently.

"The doctor will come and evaluate her shortly," returned the nurse passively.

A few minutes passed, and there was no sign of urgency anywhere, from anyone. When the nurse returned, we again asked about the CT unit. Reluctantly, she admitted they had one, but it was not functional at the moment.

"We are leaving then," we asserted, as we lifted her from the bed and hurried out the doors.

We traveled about a mile before reaching a common point of "jam" (traffic jam) for which Kampala is famous. Then we sat. I was in the driver's seat, while Elizabeth held Given, now nearly flaccid and unable to keep her eyes open. It was still several miles to the hospital where we hoped we'd find the care she needed—but given the standstill, it could take hours. Lord, help! we cried.

Up ahead, we saw a few boda bodas alongside the road. While unsafe, they could weave through traffic and get you where you needed quickly.

"I'm taking her on boda," declared Elizabeth. I agreed immediately—I could see Given was lapsing in and out of consciousness. Elizabeth hopped out of the van, crossing lanes of traffic carrying our limp 4-year-old girl. I watched, helplessly stuck in traffic, as she rode off on the boda with Given cradled in her arms.

An hour later, I arrived at the hospital. They had been sent on to the only functioning scanner in the city of nearly 3 million people, a stand-alone MRI run by a Chinese entrepreneur. I made my way to them, almost 2 hours after we had parted on the road.

Given had a fractured skull, a large hematoma under her skin, and a subdural hematoma—a brain bleed—as we had feared. She was mostly conscious. Many hours later, back at the hospital, a Ugandan neurosurgeon checked on her and reviewed the images.

"We don't need to operate right now," he began. "Let's watch her overnight, and if she worsens, we'll need to drain the blood."

She did well, slowly recovering. Our return had to be delayed for a week, so we could recheck if the bleed was stable. A CT scan a week later showed that it was. We were able to make the 400-mile journey back north to Yei.

The drive back was horrendous. The last 100 miles were on dirt road, and it poured rain the night before. We slipped and slid. Going up the steep Kaya Hill just inside South Sudan, several lorries (large trucks) were stuck in the mud, blocking the road. I wondered if we'd make it home that day.

Locals had created a path around the blockage, but I was doubtful our van would make it. Our roof rack was loaded with medical supplies and belongings, our dear friends from Los Angeles, Chim and Fay, were with us (making us 12 in the van), and the diversion was steep and sloped to one side. We had been in 4-wheel drive all day, and now I shifted to low gear and summoned all the diesel I could, plunging my right foot to the floor on the accelator. We crept slowly forward as I prayed silently. I couldn't hear the engine anymore, but somehow we never stopped our forward progress. Gradually, the engine became audible again and we cleared the obstacle.

Given, Winnie, & Uncle Chim on the journey; Given endured the trip though she felt awful

Next up were the PUD's (puddles of unknown depth) that spanned the entire width of the road, filled with light brown muddy water resembling coffee with creamer. Others had apparently made it through, and we certainly didn't want to camp out in the rain-soaked bushland of South Sudan for the night. So we surged forward, praying the depth was not more than our little van could handle. Water seeped in through the floorboards and door gaskets. Still, it kept moving, even in water halfway up the doors.

Chim, our Indian friend from Los Angeles, laughed. "I love diesel engines!"

"What do you mean?" I asked, not feeling very light-hearted at the time.

"They are compression-fired—no spark plugs. A gas engine would have never made it through all this water without dying!" Chim was a diesel mechanic and owned a garage back in Los Angeles. I was thankful we owned a diesel van, even more so after the lesson I had just received!

We had never been so grateful to reach home. The next day, I cut the posts of the little girls' bunk beds, making them twin beds. Bunk beds and mosquito nets are like oil and water. They just don't mix.

Trucks

I was getting some needed projects done on my afternoon off call. Balanced on a chair, I hung a new grass mat at the end of our front porch to block the intense, late-day sun. Suddenly a sound of metal crashing into metal reverberated around the compound. Before I could hop down, screams pierced the sudden silence that followed, and my phone started buzzing.

"Come up here right now!" cried Elizabeth, who was meeting with another missionary inside her home, just next to where the accident occurred. "Two of the workers were just run over by the lorry!"

I sprinted the 50 meters to where she was, and witnessed the gruesome scene. Henry, a local laborer, writhed in pain on the ground, holding his lower abdomen and not moving his legs at all. James, the Kenyan driver and mechanic, lay just a few feet from him, with deformed legs bleeding through his overalls. We sent Dave, a missionary EMT (emergency medical technician) from northern Canada, to alert the team at the hospital and bring backboards.

The missionary team and all available staff joined in the trauma care. We took both men to the operating theatre to assess and stabilize them. The ultrasound showed that Henry had fluid in his abdomen. We would need to operate. James had obvious fractures of both femurs (thighbones), one of them open and oozing blood. Neither Dr. Poole or I were general surgeons—we mainly did C-sections. We called the doctors at the government hospital, but one doctor was away in Juba and the call to the other didn't go through. It was up to us to help them. We were scared, and prayed silently. It was a comfort to work together as a team, though.

Dr. Poole opened Henry's abdomen while I began to clean James' wound, control the bleeding, and splint his legs. Once I had done what I could for James, I scrubbed in with Dr. Poole. He "ran the bowel" to carefully inspect the intestines for holes—there were none. There was very little blood, but there was urine. We found the bladder had ruptured, so we sutured it. Still, he was not stable.

We were giving both men blood transfusions, as femur fractures can cause much blood loss, and Henry's blood pressure was dangerously low. Morris, the X-Ray tech, presented Henry's images to us. His pelvis was shifted, and we saw several subtle fractures. An unstable pelvic fracture is a grave diagnosis, especially in our location. We looked deeper in Henry's pelvis, and saw a deep purple discoloration forming behind the semi-transparent lining of his abdomen. We dare not open it, as his only hope was that the bleeding would compress the vessels as blood filled the limited space. We quickly ordered more blood for him, and closed his abdomen. Both men were alive as we left the operating theatre and brought them to the 4-bed male ward.

Henry's family members were trickling in, a stream of brooding anger barely contained by the banks of Henry's frail condition. Henry lay in the bed nearest the door, with James in the next bed. James had no attendants except a few Kenyan staff. Exhausted, I made my way home and left Dr. Poole covering the hospital on his call night.

About two hours later, I received a red-light call. Henry was failing. I rushed to join Dr. Poole at the hospital, where he and the team were "coding" Henry—giving him breaths with a bag-mask ventilator and compressing his chest to keep his blood flowing. I joined in the rotation of the desperate attempt to preserve his life, while Dr. Poole and I quietly discussed the next steps.

"How long have you been coding him?" I asked quietly as I squeezed the bag and watched his chest rise.

"Since about 10 minutes before you arrived," he responded while doing chest compressions. "He's just lost too much blood into his pelvis, and he's on his third unit of blood even now."

We both looked around us discreetly, sizing up the ever-growing crowd from the surrounding villages. It was dark out, and at that time there was no fence around the hospital. Clan members had heard about the accident at the kawaja compound and had silently been sifting in to surround the hospital.

In the very next bed lay James, the Kenyan driver and mechanic, with his two broken femurs. There was already bad blood between the locals and the Kenyans who worked for the foreigners. James was the supervisor who would be held responsible for any deaths resulting from the accident. He had given the order to start the lorry, while another worker had turned the key—without putting in the clutch first, apparently.

"Pandemonium is going to break out when we declare his death," we both agreed. I was grateful that James and Aaron, the aspiring Clinical Officers, were there that night. They stretched out their six-foot frames as they quietly stood guard over James in the adjacent bed.

We took a deep breath and ceased our efforts. I lowered my head and placed my stethoscope lightly on his chest, hoping to hear some miracle of a revived heart. It was still silent.

I stood up and soberly announced that it was finished. "Nina amulu kulu, lakini huwo mutu. Kafara." We did everything, but he has died. Our condolences. Our other local staff helped with further explanation, but it was pointless—they were too angry to listen.

Screaming and wailing began, and one older man in particular moved close, yelling "White man arabiya! White man arabiya!" It was obvious whom they blamed—the kawaja—white man—and the arabiya (vehicle) that he brought. And seeing as I was the nearest white man, in his grief and anger, he started swinging at me. All his anti-colonialist feelings welled up against me at the moment of his son's death. A younger relative rushed to restrain him from behind.

I was backed up against the wall of the small ward, with the old man blocking the only doorway in and out. James was to my left, guarded by several of the older orphans including Michael, James, and Aaron.

Before they could further organize, I was able to make my way out of the ward and into the office, the room next to the male ward. Our guards were notably passive—I realized they were of this clan also, and they seemed to be weighing their allegiance. Would they protect the kawajas, and risk later mob justice from their own kin, or would they stand by their own and risk losing their job later? For most, it was the latter.

We learned later that men from the community were organizing, coming from their homes with guns.

We then heard the sound of breaking glass as the crowd starting smashing lights and dishes. I hoped they wouldn't find the boards with nails in them that littered the nearby construction site of the new X-Ray building. I called the Bishop to notify him of the burgeoning riot situation.

"I will send National Security right away. Be ready—they will fire warning shots as they approach to scatter the people," he explained. The police were also on site shortly, to investigate the death.

Just as he said, when National Security arrived, the crowd dissolved away into the darkness of the tall grass all around the hospital site. It was after 10 pm. I sat in the office with the police, as they waited for me to complete the death summary. I tried to be careful with my description, knowing it would be a huge legal tangle, yet quick, so as to release the body to the family and defuse the scene. I finished, and handed the patient book and death summary to him.

"Where is the stamp!?" he ordered. "We need your seal—on each page!"

Of course. I was just learning the importance of the rubber stamp— and this surreal night would be sealed in my memory, pulled up whenever I read of a seal or stamp in Scripture. I opened the drawer and dutifully pressed the wood-handled rubber stamp on each page, followed by my signature on the blue ink lines I had just created.

The next challenge was that the family expected us to move the body to their home. He was an employee, injured in an accident on the job, treated at the hospital also run by his employer—now dead. It was all our responsibility. Mind you, we (the hospital missionaries and staff) had nothing to do with the cause, but the cleanup was left to us—and in doing so, we found ourselves the recipients of the blame.

Samuel, the guard at our home since the first day we had arrived, did choose to stand with us. He had a driving permit, though not much experience.

"I can take the body back to their home in the hospital van," Samuel offered. This was also our family van.

"That would be really helpful," I accepted, knowing that he was risking himself for our protection, and I was risking never seeing the vehicle again. It was a risk worth taking given the circumstance.

I followed the procession out after the body. Men carried Henry on a backboard, with women and children following. A lone African dog trailed dutifully behind, out into the dark night and awaiting van.

At home, Elizabeth and the children had heard everything, as our home was less than 50 meters from the hospital. In the chaos, someone had broken a security light on the water tower inside our yard. She had sat at the window and prayed throughout the evening. We were all relieved to be together again, shaken but safe for now.

I didn't hear back from Samuel until after midnight. "They won't let me leave. They have taken the keys and they want me to go pick some other people. I will try to come back as soon as they let me," he explained with a tremor of fear in his voice. When I awoke at 5 AM, he was still not back. Near daybreak at 7 AM, he finally arrived home, exhausted and shaken.

Several National Security officers remained as armed guards outside the male ward overnight. James was still alive, but needed orthopedic surgery and had a long recovery before him. And he needed to get out of the country—quickly. Unfortunately, he was embedded in what would be a complex legal matter. The ministry coordinated a medical evacuation flight for him back to Kenya that day. First, we had to get him to the airstrip, which involved crossing the center of Yei town—and get clearance for him to leave.

I drove, with a National Security officer seated beside me in the front of the van, literally "riding shotgun"—or "riding AK-47," as was the case. We were told to first stop by the police and immigration to get clearance before proceeding to the airstrip. It was there that we met obstacles. The police chief refused to grant exit permission for James. I haggled and pleaded, and assured him that Harvesters and EPC would deal with the legal issues, but he wouldn't budge. We were stuck, James lying in agony in the back of the van. His open fracture would become infected, and he might continue to lose blood from the wound. The plane we had chartered was waiting on the ground, 5 miles to the northeast of town.

At that moment, the Bishop arrived at the police station. He looked the police chief eye to eye, and they had a rapid-fire exchange in Juba Arabic. Suddenly he paused, turned to me, and said "You can go."

I didn't wait for an explanation—I just went and drove quickly to the airstrip (well, as quickly as was possible on the roads). We loaded him on the plane without incident, other than the pilot and crew borrowing my tools so they could remove a few airplane seats in order to fit James in on the backboard.

That night, we debriefed with the team.
"They would never really hurt us. I think they have respect for us as medical professionals that have come to help," said one missionary.

"That man looked like he meant to hurt me! Did you not see him trying to hit me?" I countered. "If National Security hadn't come, who knows what the riot would have become." Idealism and realism were bumping heads. It wouldn't be the last time we wrestled with these different viewpoints amongst our team.

We did agree that we needed a fence and better security. Dave, our Canadian EMT (emergency medical technician), summed it up. "It finally settled down when the man with the gun showed up."

James lived, and eventually walked after nearly a year of rehabilitation and surgeries. He never returned to South Sudan. The village chief, the family of the deceased, and the ministry reached a settlement. Thomas, the worker who started the truck, was initially put in jail for his own protection from mob justice. He was eventually released and re-integrated into the community.

Bodas

Boda bodas are the ubiquitous motorcycle taxis of East Africa. When you combine dirt roads, overloaded motorcycles, and young, risk-seeking riders, you end up with plenty of accidents. At *His House of Hope*, we saw the results of boda rides gone bad.

On one occasion, Lillie comforted a five-year-old boy who fell from a boda boda as I painstakingly plucked small stones from the gaping wound in his right cheek. It extended from below his cheekbone into his right eye, communicating with his right nostril through a shattered nasal bone. After cleaning and closing with 43 sutures, we addressed the open fracture of his tibia (shin bone). We loaded him with antibiotics and pain medicines and tried to get the family to take him to Juba, where an orthopedic surgeon could take care of the leg.

The most common cause of missionary death is traffic accidents, and a few hours of traveling in a developing country will dispel any doubt in this figure. When you combine road travel in East Africa with a motorcycle, it becomes the most dangerous moment in a missionary's career. **The following story illustrates the importance of taking rest in a timely fashion, the risks of travel, the challenges of getting medical care in a developing nation, and how God uses accidents to guide our steps.**

Adam was a young, energetic missionary, who loved working with the South Sudanese laborers on the compound around the hospital. After four months, he still hadn't taken a holiday, and we saw tell-tale signs of culture stress and fatigue. As his Team Leaders, we felt the responsibility to advise him, so he might thrive on the mission field, not just survive.

"Adam, you really need to take a holiday. Get out of South Sudan. Rest, breath, spend time with the Lord," Elizabeth and I gently prodded him.

"I will, but I need to oversee the fence project to completion," he replied decisively. Following the riot of the previous year, we had ordered one mile of chain link fence to go around the compound, and he was directing the crew that was making that need a reality.

"It will continue, and if it doesn't, it's okay. You can pick it up again when you're back and refreshed."

He resisted, but after another tough week, he began planning a trip—on his own personal boda. We were alarmed. It seemed unsafe for a new, lone missionary to travel the uneven dirt roads of South Sudan and Uganda. And he didn't own a helmet.

Our Kenyan compound director discouraged it, and when Adam mentioned his plans to a shop owner in town, the man said flatly, "You will die."

Nonetheless, he went ahead with his plans, and we had him promise to get a helmet at the first opportunity. He traveled safely to Arua, purchased a helmet, and continued on his way.

Late the following day, I received a phone call from Adam, though he sounded different.

"I'm somewhere in Uganda...don't know where I am..." he groggily started, followed by rustling sounds of the phone changing hands.

"Hello, this Dr. Juma in Nyadonga Health Centre. Adam has been in a serious motorcycle accident. We have his neck stabilized, but we need your direction of where to send him in Kampala."

Our hearts dropped within us. Christopher, another missionary who was friends with Adam's father, volunteered to go be with him. He and I made the unpleasant call to his dad, urging him to pull his car over to receive the news any father would hate to hear.

Days later, the story unfolded. He had met a few Australian guys also on a motorcycle tour while camped in Murchison Falls Park. They joined up and rode together the next day. Just before sunset, Adam was passing a truck when he hit a pothole and went airborne. He came down directly on the top of his head and his bike landed on him. The Australians were able to stop a passing van to transport him to the Health Centre. He was unconscious for 45 minutes.

The X-rays showed some rib fractures but the neck seemed okay. He certainly had a concussion. Once in Kampala, they were able to get him up, and in so doing, discovered that he had intense back pain. More X-rays revealed a "burst" fracture of his 12th vertebra (backbone). We were incredibly grateful that he had not severed his spinal cord on the normally backbreaking ride to Kampala, which would have left him unable to walk. As I rounded on our patients in South Sudan, the orthopedic surgeon called and described the planned surgery to stabilize his back.

Adam's boda after the accident

Adam's father arrived as they performed the operation. Adam and his dad then made the painful medical evacuation flight back to the US, with Adam in the first-class section so he could lay flat. He was kept numb with morphine, and a nurse attended to him during the entire journey. He went directly to the hospital in Little Rock,

Arkansas, where more surgeries followed to definitively stabilize the fracture. He survived and was able to walk, but his body has never been the same again.

Adam matured through this tremendous trial, and the Lord changed the direction of his steps. He remained in the US, married his sweetheart, Andrea, and together they sought God's guidance. Before recommitting his life to Christ, Adam had worked successfully in Hollywood as a cinematographer and grip. However, in his initial term in South Sudan, he was reluctant to use his artistic gifts, as his time in Hollywood had been a tumultuous time in his spiritual walk. He wanted to distance himself from his "secular" past.

Two years after his accident, Adam and Andrea came to Yei on a "re-survey" trip, given Adam's new physical limitations and marital status. During those weeks, they discerned they were not a good fit with the ministry in Yei, but they worked as a team to make a poignant short film recounting the struggles our family faced (see chapter 11). They explored other ministry platforms through which to return to South Sudan, but each idea was closed to them. At the same time, doors opened in the film industry again. The Lord continues to develop them as a family and guide their steps in serving Him, perhaps through helping missionaries tell their stories in film.

Trees

"The tree in the garden of Eden was definitely a mango tree," announced Pastor Dennis, one of the founders of Harvesters. "People here will die for a mango!"

We first heard this shortly after our arrival, and we chuckled at the bold statement. Surely this must be an exaggeration. Once the hospital opened, though, we began to see how the mango tree had a grip on local disease patterns. As the mangoes started to ripen, kids became impatient and started eating the green mangoes. A common history at this time was diarrhea, without any of the usual signs of dysentery, worms, or gastroenteritis (stomach flu).

"How many mangoes did you eat today?" would be the next question we asked. The answer was usually some number close to ten. The treatment was "Don't eat so many green mangoes."

Once they began to ripen, the harvesting began. Mature mango trees could hold thousands of luscious fruit. It was a cornucopia of delicious, sweet, nutritious, and free food. The only challenge was that the lowest branches were often 10-15 feet off the ground, with the top reaching 60 feet or more. And the best fruit might be in those uppermost branches!

A well-dressed, wise older South Sudanese man once showed me the proper way to get the sought-after fruit. He raised a long teak pole, surrounded the mango stem with the split end of the pole, then twisted until it came cleanly off. No need for dangerous methods!

Unfortunately, this art was lost. The younger generation had not learned it. The children at the orphanage preferred to test their aim with whatever object they could find. A rock, stick, piece of metal—it didn't matter. One particular favorite was a discarded piece of lumber (with rusty nails protruding from one end). The child would launch the projectile as high as he or she could, hoping to knock a ripe mango loose from the upper branches. The thought of where the missile they just launched might land didn't seem to slow them down.

As one can imagine, there were cuts and bruises galore. Sometimes, however, the thrower suffered too. One young girl came in with a board stuck to her palm. A nail entered at the base of her middle finger, but I couldn't tell which direction it angled. I studied it, cleaned it, numbed her finger, and then carefully sliced the skin around the nail so I knew which way to pull.

The most common history, though, was "fall from a mango tree." It was the South Sudanese equivalent of the inner-city America trauma history, "I was just walking along, minding my own business..."

(when these guys stabbed, shot, or beat me up). Over the years in Yei, we treated broken legs, head injuries, an 8 year-old boy with bilateral humerus fractures (breaks of both upper arms!), and even a pregnant woman falling and injuring her unborn child.

Timothy was a 13-year-old boy at the orphanage, and was a friend of our children. One Saturday afternoon, a week before leaving (for what we didn't know then would be for good), Timothy and several other boys climbed to pick mangoes from a large tree in the center of the compound. Lillie, Sophia, and Olivia were sitting in front of the old pyat near the tree, when they heard a loud snap followed by a dull thud, which they thought was a tree branch. Then the "branch" started moving—it was Timothy, lying on a pile of rubbish under the tree. According to the other boys in the tree, he had been over 30 feet high, and fell straight down.

I was called to the scene, followed closely by Dr. Loftus. He was awake, with no obvious cuts or deformed bones. He was moving his neck without pain, but was moaning and clutching his stomach.

"How did he land?" I asked some of the children who saw him fall.

"Flat, on his stomach," said Sara Lilly.

Dr. Loftus brought a backboard, and he and several others carried him to the hospital. Timothy was in so much pain that he dug his fingers into Dr. Loftus' arm, drawing blood. I ran ahead to alert the hospital team and get the ultrasound. In God's sovereignty, we had an Irish surgeon visiting for several months, so we alerted her, even though she wasn't on call that day.

We scanned him with the ultrasound and saw blood in his abdomen already—less than 10 minutes after the fall. His spleen looked like it hadn't ruptured— a common injury in such cases.

"We need to operate," said Dr. Lo Alcorn decisively. "And find blood to transfuse!" She rushed to prepare the operating theatre with the team, and the surgery began less than 30 minutes after the accident happened—quicker than in most locales, anywhere in the world.

Pastor Hillary and Elizabeth were of the same blood type as Timothy, so the lab tech started collecting their blood. Dr. Loftus scrubbed in with Dr. Lo, while I "floated" to coordinate blood transfusion, talk with the orphanage staff and missionaries, and support the surgery as needed.

He was bleeding quickly. As on the ultrasound, the spleen was undamaged. Dr. Lo located the bleeding—a large area of laceration in the liver. Repairing the liver is like sewing a sponge. As she struggled to locate the worst areas of bleeding and control them, we lost Timothy's blood pressure due to extensive blood loss. Then, his heart stopped beating. I reached under the drape and began doing chest compressions—Elizabeth's blood was running in as fast as possible, and Dr. Lo was trying to stop it from flowing out of his open liver. For 45 minutes we continued in this way—to no avail. Despite prompt trauma care, we lost one of our own—and our kids lost a friend.

I exited the theatre to bring the grim news to Pastor Hillary and the orphanage leaders. They were grateful for the extensive efforts, and understood he shouldn't have been climbing so high in the tree. His body was brought out to Room 1 in the clinic, where a crowd of over 500 people was assembling to mourn over Timothy. The 160 orphans, the staff, and many from the community gathered to wail loudly and take turns entering Room 1 to look at him one last time.

Timothy's mother arrived. She was a paraplegic who moved along the red dirt ground using only her hands. She cried out when she saw his body and understood that her recently strong, healthy son was dead.

It was a beautiful Saturday evening. I stood amongst the throng on the concrete slab of the new laboratory under construction. Our children stood in groups with their friends from the orphanage, weeping with them, and Lillie, Logan, Given, and Winnie went in to view Timothy's body with the others. After several hours, an orphanage vehicle transported the *beyit* (dead body) to the home of his extended family. This was a common local way of referring to the person recently deceased, which could be taken as disrespectful, but was simply a matter-of-fact term indicative of the frequency of death in that place.

Church was somber the next day. Many faces had clean streaks where tears had washed the dust off their black skin. The funeral happened later that day, and on Monday, life slowly resumed a normal feel.

Lillie met Timothy's older brother and Boy, a close friend of Timothy. "The day Timothy died," Boy said flatly, "I started hating mangoes."

She looked down at Boy's hands. "But you're eating one right now!"

"Oh, I know. But the day after, I started liking them again."

At our staff meeting that week, the more newly arrived missionaries were reeling with grief and concern for the children at the orphanage. "I think we need to debrief with each one and give them a chance to express their feelings. Perhaps they can draw pictures to express how they feel about Timothy's death," said one.

I looked around at Pastor Hillary and Mr. Mourice, the two African staff in the meeting. I noted they didn't join in the enthusiasm of the plans. They didn't contradict, either—but I could tell they were not on the same page as the well-meaning missionaries.

Afterwards, I asked Pastor Hillary more about how the South Sudanese grieved.

"When someone dies, everyone comes out to wail and grieve and show support to the family. But once the body is in the ground, they move on. *There is still sadness and remembering, but life must go on*," he explained.

Death was so common in this collectivist culture, people tended to be fatalistic—to give up, saying it was just God's will that they die. But to their credit, they were realistic—for all must die. They grieved openly, didn't deny their pain, and they did so *together*.

Those of us from the individualistic West often cling to an illusion of immortality, trying to preserve life as long as possible. When we lose a loved one, we struggle with accepting the death and mourning fully. And we tend to mourn alone or in small groups—for a long time.

The newer missionaries struggled with his death more than those who had grown up with him. They wanted to provide counseling to the kids that they themselves, not the children, probably needed. The friends and family of Timothy were sad, but could talk about him—a healthy place to be.

And they went right on eating mangoes. Hopefully, using a pole to harvest.

The God of "Accidents" (?)

Accidents are a way of life in East Africa. We serve a God who is Sovereign, who is in control, even of the seeming "accidents." There are messy effects—some painful, life changing, or life ending. But God works these in us, sometimes in ways that are visibly for our good, and other times, His reasons remain a mystery. It may be for someone else's good, or we may never see any visible good from the accidents. In all cases, He wants our circumstances to cause us to reach out to Him and grow to depend on Him more, because He is what we really need.

"To You, O Lord, I lift up my soul; O my God, in You I trust" (Psalm 25:1).

Given is our H.I.C.—head injury child. She is a little funny—and I mean truly funny, not funny in the head. She is smart, usually has a smile, is always willing to help, and is quick to ask for forgiveness when she isn't! And for those of you realists who struggle watching musicals, saying "No one ever just breaks into song like that in real life," you should really meet Given. For her, life is a musical! She really does break into song during the course of daily life! She brings great joy to our family, and we are grateful God has given her to us and allowed her to remain with us.

Our children walked through the death of Timothy, with their friends, and learned of the reality of death and the need to grieve. They saw that life goes on, even after the death of a child, a friend, one that still had much life ahead of him. They saw that grieving in community made the pain of loss easier to bear.

God uses the messiness and hardships in our lives to show the mystery of His glory.

"...as servants of God we commend ourselves in every way: in great endurance; in troubles, hardships, and distresses; in beatings, imprisonments and riots..." (2 Cor 6:4-5)

What is your current "safety net"? How might it change if God called you to a different situation?

How have or might you deal with terrible accidents or "near misses"?

How is God present amidst an "accident"?

Chapter 9
The Neglected Middle

I grew up in a middle-class, predominantly white suburb of Seattle. Science was king, and I was a willing follower. I learned later that the Pacific Northwest is one of the most unchurched areas in the United States. Yet even in this place, the spiritual world would peek out once in awhile.

"What's this?!" my classmate Janelle asked excitedly. We were three ninth graders, helping to organize the back storage room of the math and science building at our junior high school. She pulled down a box that looked like any other board game. It was made by a well-known game company and was labeled "Ouija Board."

"Let's try it," said Tim. We opened the box and unfolded the board carefully onto the small table.

"What should we ask?" said Janelle.

"Let's ask how old Mr. Larson is," suggested Tim, referring to one of our science teachers. The three of us gathered around the board that had letters of the alphabet and numbers ornately written upon it. We placed our fingers lightly on the triangular plastic pointer, with its three smooth bumpers resting on the board and a clear hole in the middle through which we would read the "answer."

The instructions said to ask our questions and let the pointer move around to the letter or number, so we did just that. None of us expected anything to happen. But then the pointer deliberately moved to "3" and then "9." We asked another question and the pointer moved to spell out the answer—this time in letters, with an answer that none of us would have known.

None of us had pushed the pointer—it moved of its own accord. We all felt the fear of something unknown, bigger than us, ready to pounce on us. We sensed we better not ask anything else. Scared, we quickly put the board away.

That day, I walked away knowing there are realities that can't be seen, and it's better not to mess with forces I don't understand. I hadn't learned about these in my Lutheran upbringing...

Encountering the "middle realm" in South Sudan

Twenty-five years later, I stood in the newly opened pediatric ward at Bet Eman in Yei, South Sudan. James, the student following me, was interpreting as I did rounds. I noticed an angry, somewhat scary-looking abuba (grandmother) in the first bed with a young child. We moved on to start with the sicker patient in bed five, next to the outside window.

"How did you all sleep?" I routinely asked the mother of three-year old Lillian, who was recovering from severe malaria with anemia. I expected to hear "kweys" (good).

Instead, she started a long, animated description in Kakwa, the local tribal language, while casting a glance at the abuba in bed one. Other mothers in the ward seemed to track with her and give the cultural "click" of agreement from the back of their throats. I noticed James' wide-eyed expression as she talked, and when she finished, he paused pensively for a moment before he started recounting her monologue to me. It was as if he was debating if and how to break the news to me.

"She is saying that she couldn't sleep at all because a wizard was outside the window all night harassing her and the others. He came as an owl and changed into his form of a wizard, and placed these cuts on her daughter. They all say that the abuba brought him here." She showed us several superficial wounds on the girl's stomach.

I wasn't expecting this type of response! A few years before, I would have seriously doubted this story. Before moving to Africa, our Area Leaders asked me to take a course about spiritual warfare. In the book "Spirit of the Rainforest," a shaman (witchdoctor) in the jungles of South America writes about his life in the dark spiritual realm. He describes moving about in the form of an animal, traveling great distances to discover something about an enemy or harass or curse someone.[1]

Just before this interaction, Elizabeth and I had been given a short book written by James Wio, a former witchdoctor from Yei.[2] He had become a Christian during an evangelistic event in Freedom Square, at the center of Yei. Wio had come to disrupt the meeting, but ended up being lifted in the air by unseen hands and dropped to the ground. As pastors came around him, they began picking up the charms and fetishes that fell from his pocket, including "a 'mobile phone'—the back of a tortoise and a snail shell connected to a marijuana plant which he used for communication with the devil" (Wio, 4). He surrendered his life to the Lordship of Jesus that day.

Wio describes his former life as a witchdoctor. People would come and pay him to curse someone they hated. He would enter a spiritual trance and "travel" spiritually, often appearing as an animal. He would then place a curse on the target person, who would fall ill and usually die.

However, he described that when he tried to curse ("tie") a Christian who prayed regularly and worshipped God, *not just one who attended church*, he looked and saw "something like a white smoke around his body. I tried to tie the person to pull him out of the smoke, but the smoke was close around him and the medicines could not touch his body. I tried everything but I could not harm him" (Wio, 22).

These two accounts from jungle witchdoctors on opposite sides of the world are strikingly similar. As I felt after the incident with the Ouija Board, there were unseen realities out there. Those forces meant harm, and the only way to guard oneself was prayer—to Jesus.

I think I prayed with the patient at that time. I hope I did. One of the nurses politely asked the abuba to leave, as the child's mother was there anyway, and only one caretaker was allowed. The next day, there were no reports of overnight disturbances, and Lillian and her mother went home after Lillian received a unit of blood—donated by James, the translator.

A local believer who served as one of our chaplains was caring for her 18-year old nephew. His father had asked that the boy live with her, and she provided food and shelter for him. The young man got increasingly involved with witchcraft, and resented the consistent faith in Jesus he saw in his aunt. One day, he "went into the river" to call on evil spirits to harm her. Local witchdoctors will go under water and stay for long periods of time where they describe contacting local spirits. They will promise to do something for the spirit if the spirit causes harm to someone they despise.

However, he was unable to cause any harm to his aunt. He sought out other ways to harm her, such as poisoning, but she discovered his intentions. She took him to the police station, and he confessed to going into the river and trying to harm her. The boy's father was then called and he took him back to the village.

Stories such as this were not uncommon in South Sudan. For those of us from the West, they seem like fiction. But, we heard these stories repeatedly from credible people, with key common elements. When I consider the reality of the spiritual world of which the Bible speaks, and present-day reports like these, it causes me to pause and re-examine my Western worldview, with its neglect of the everyday interaction of the physical and spiritual world. This is the neglected or excluded middle—that "middle realm" between the world we see and the God to whom we pray.[3,4] In this middle space, according to Scripture and the experience of many, there are angels and demons interacting with our lives. Angels and demons are created things, listed in Scripture along with things present, things to come, death, and life—things that we don't deny or neglect (Rom 8:38-39).

James and I with family of baby Lillian

The neglected middle surfaces in the West

Yet even in the West, we encountered stories of spiritual attack. On home assignment in Colorado, the new marijuana laws allowed easy purchase of the drug. While covering in the hospital, I noticed many admissions related to its effects. One man reported being chased by demons during the night.

Our neighbor Joe also sold and used marijuana—for pain control, according to him. He had cancer, and each day we'd listen for his telltale cough as he walked his Chihuahua, Penny, along the sidewalk in front of our house. He told us he had been given just a few months to live, so each morning when we heard his cough we knew he was still with us. We increasingly felt burdened for him. The kids prayed for him, Elizabeth brought him food, and we were finally able to arrange dinner together in our backyard one evening. Knowing he might not be with us much longer, I asked him about his spirituality.

"Oh, I'm very spiritual. In fact, I used to go to the church next door," Joe said.

"What do you think of Jesus?" I asked.

"Oh, he's powerful alright," Joe responded.

"Why do you say that?" I pressed.

"I woke up one night, and I was on my bed and demons were holding me down. I couldn't move and they were getting ready to hurt me and take my life," he explained.

"So, what did you do?" I asked, knowing he must have gotten out of the situation or we wouldn't be sitting at my picnic table.

"I called on Jesus, and they left me alone," he explained. "I know he's the only way."

We talked on, and his mind wandered. He seemed to have a grasp on the truth, but years of drug use and other choices had taken a toll on his clarity of thought. We continue to pray for Joe, and each time we return to the US, we have been surprised and glad to see him. His health continues to improve, and he started attending church again.

Pastoral consult in South Sudan

Back in South Sudan, a 23 year-old woman came in midway through her pregnancy. Her family carried her because she was unable to walk. She had been running all around town because "demons" were in her head. I checked baby, and baby was fine. Her labs showed she had a mild urinary tract infection. Seeing few signs of anything physically wrong, and not gathering a previous history of any mental illness, I called our local South Sudanese pastor. Pastor Hillary came and prayed with her. She cried out, and then relaxed. The next day, she went home, no longer tormented by the voices. She called the pastor a week later, and said she was still free from the attacks. These physical and spiritual realities often met at *His House of Hope*, providing the local church a needed inroad to bring spiritual healing to the community.

Arab & Greek Spirits

The neglected middle is not neglected by other major world religions. Several years later, I was sitting with Jamal, our Iranian Muslim mechanic, early in the morning as we waited for the auto parts dealers to open their shops. Our conversation shifted to the spiritual, and he shared his experience of the "neglected middle."

"I had a classmate in boarding school in Kampala who suffered from 'fits,'" he began. "The young man would yell and destroy things around the school. He talked in a very different voice, which was quite scary. Ten guys couldn't hold him down, because he possessed tremendous strength," he explained (compare to Acts 19, when a man possessed by an evil spirit overpowers "seven sons of Sceva"). Jamal said the boy was possessed by *jin* (the Arabic word for demons). The boy's family eventually removed him from school in order to get help.

It shouldn't be a surprise that someone from the Middle East would know about evil spirits. After all, Daniel (the prophet) was in Persia (Iran) around 530 BC when he had visions. He asked God for help understanding these visions, and God sent the angel Gabriel to explain them. The angel was delayed in responding to Daniel's prayers because *"the prince of the kingdom of Persia (Iran) was standing opposite me for twenty-one days; then behold, Michael, one of the chief princes, came to help me, for I had been left there with the kings of Persia"* (Daniel 10:13). He describes a scene that we don't usually see—spiritual beings fighting for control over people in a region.

After the angel encourages Daniel not to be afraid, he explains that he must return to fight the prince of Persia. He also mentions that the "prince (Satanic angel or messenger) of Greece" will come to Persia. About 200 years later (330 BC), Alexander the Great conquered Persia, bringing his Greek "gods" with him. Alexander practiced Greek polytheism, which meant he sacrificed meat to idols in his gods' temples. Paul later wrote to the church in Corinth, Greece, about what those "gods" are: demons. *"...The things which the Gentiles sacrifice, they sacrifice to demons and not to God..."* (1 Cor 10:20).

"Jin" (spirits or demons) spoke to Mohammed in a Saudi Arabian cave about 600 years after Jesus walked the earth, giving birth to Islam, a potent force battling against Christianity throughout the world even now. Mohammed was initially fearful and reluctant to follow the spirits' commands, but his mother-in-law and wife encouraged him to obey them. And the world was forever changed because of it.

Including Jamal, sitting with me in the front seat of our vehicle.

Winnie at the remains of the Corinth meat market

Modern day spirits

This may seem like ancient history, but people still pine away after these demons! They are carefully rebuilding the pagan temples in Greece, and just before observing the religious season of Lent, many people in Brazil and New Orleans cut loose with Carnival ("celebration of the flesh") and Mardi Gras. They hold parades dedicated to various Greek and Roman gods.

"It's just a fun way to remember mythology," one might argue. Yet, people are deeply affected by those they celebrate, or worship. One of the biggest parades in New Orleans is for Bacchus, the Roman god of wine, agriculture, and fertility (copied from the Greek god Dionysus). At his festivals, "wild women" used to "dance energetically"[5]—something which he still seems to accomplish in New Orleans, where women expose themselves to get trinkets thrown to them during his parades. Debauchery is alive and well in New Orleans, thanks to Bacchus. We even owe the word debauchery to him.

"Wherever I go, one thing everyone agrees on is that the world is in a mess," Pastor Stuart Briscoe shared at a medical missionary conference. "But not everyone agrees why or what to do about it."[6] Paul was clear—it's a mess because of the world, our flesh, and the "prince of the power of the air" (Ephesians 2:2-3). Witchdoctors from Africa and South America, prophets in the Middle East, kings from Europe, and partygoers in the West agree by their actions that the middle spiritual realm is there. It's mostly the intellectuals from the past few hundred years that have neglected this middle.

Responding to the neglected middle

So what? Is it a problem if we neglect the middle? I believe it is. If we are unaware of the adversary, we can't fight. If we deny the spiritual realm around us, God becomes simply a distant, cultural formality. And then it's just a mere step to atheism. Or at least to practical atheism—when we say we believe in God but act as if He's not active in our world.

Scripture shows that Satan can't read our minds and he and his servants aren't everywhere at once. He isn't omniscient or omnipresent. But he has been around for a while, observing human nature, and knows how to plant just the right thoughts to tempt us and pull us away from God. There is a saying in Cuba, which I learned from my father-in-law: "El Diablo sabe mas por Viejo que el Diablo." The devil knows more because he's old than because he's the devil.[7] He doesn't have super knowledge; he's just a keen, immortal student of human nature. He has noticed what tempts us over thousands of years of observation.

He uses that knowledge to mislead us. Satan likes to lie to us. Jesus called him *"the father of lies"* (John 8:44). His primary way of dividing us from "the Father of lights" (James 1:17) and other people is to plant incorrect thoughts.[8] This started with Eve and continues today with you and me. We can resist by knowing the truth, which comes from remaining a constant student of His word. If we are, we recognize the lie when it is dropped into our minds. We can then take captive those thoughts that are not of Christ (2 Cor 10:5). We can refuse to accept them as truth because we know the truth.

On certain nights in South Sudan, we felt a heaviness and tension around us. One of our daughters struggled with irrational fears, such that she wouldn't go alone to the back bathroom in our house. Elizabeth equipped her to speak God's Word, and call out the name of Jesus, knowing that *"the angel of the Lord encamps around those who fear Him"* (Ps 34:7). Praying and speaking the word of God are the actions of swinging the sword of the Spirit, the Word of God. To use the name of Jesus is to restate the authority we have in Him. It is not a magic word, but a word to remind us, and those around us, that we belong to Jesus. This is the practical outworking of the mystery of belonging.

I want our family to be those who have the "white smoke"—the Holy Spirit—surrounding us, that can't be penetrated by the forces from the neglected middle. I want those in the neglected middle to know that we are His property.

Do you believe there really is a neglected middle?

What is the neglected middle? Do you agree that it is neglected?

What do you think of Scripture passages that speak of demons, angels, spiritual forces of darkness, and principalities...?

- Are you prepared to meet its forces?
- Are you in Christ?
- How well are you armed with His Word?
- How accustomed are you to "swinging" His Word in prayer?
- Have you spoken His Word out loud in times of fear? Try it.

Chapter 10

Hard on the Flesh but Good for the Soul

"He has weakened my strength in the way..." (Ps 102:23)

Manny was an imposing presence. At over six feet tall, as many South Sudanese men are, he was unusually muscular for one in that country. When he opened his mouth, there was a hint of a British accent with his crisp English. Manny was our missionary teammate.

"South Sudan is hard on the flesh, but good for the soul," explained Manny (short for Emmanuel). We had only been on the ground for a few weeks, yet I nodded in agreement, thinking of the cultural differences, the heat, and the steep learning curve we had already encountered—all hard on our flesh, and presumably good for our souls.

Manny had authority. He had grown up in South Sudan for his first 8 years, then was taken to Kenya by his mother, who eventually married a British missionary. Manny went to a quality Nairobi school, where he was a local sports star. He progressed to the United Kingdom for university, and played professional basketball there for a time. Now, he was back in his ancestral homeland doing ministry through organized sports for children and youth. He developed "Fly Sports" to give the young men in Yei a forum to work out their energy and physically challenge each other in a way besides fighting in war. War was all they had known. And once their aggression was spent on the football field (soccer), they could better listen to the truth in God's Word and receive discipleship.

However, I had no idea to what depth I would understand his statement. Flesh can mean muscle, body tissue, or another part of our physical existence. But also, our emotional and relational nature. It refers to how I act and react to the world around me. Scripture calls it my sin nature.

The first few years were physically hard, with opening a hospital, building a team, and frequent bouts of diarrhea, typhoid, and malaria.

In the second half of 2013, we took our first home assignment, which had its share of physical hardship. We were to return just after the New Year.

Civil wars

One cold December day, while working in my mentor's clinic in Colorado, I received a phone call with an Australian prefix. It was Dr. Poole, my Australian partner, calling from South Sudan. Civil war had erupted in Juba, the capital city, one week before, and we had been in communication since then. The fighting had spared Yei—thus far.

"We are fine here," he began. "But things have wound down in Yei, and staff and patients seem to be going away into the bush. We are thinking of shutting down for a few weeks."

We were all planning to meet for a conference in Ethiopia a few weeks later, at which time our family would return to Yei, and they would go on leave for a few months. Short-term volunteers were scheduled to cover the hospital while we were all at the conference.

"With the instability, I think we shouldn't have the visitors stay to cover during the conference," he continued. "Are you okay if we temporarily close?"

"Certainly," I responded. "We trust your judgment. Do whatever is needed—you're on the ground."

And so it was that our team met up in Ethiopia, with the hospital in Yei closed. Good thing, too, for during the week of the conference, we received reports from Yei that violence had spread to the city. One tribe was systematically hunting down people from the other tribe, with an estimated 30 killings in Yei during that time. Bodies were washing up on the shores of the Yei River next to our host church. The Bishop told us to delay our re-entry until he deemed it safe again.

As we sought the Lord as to what to do, we were surprised by a new twist—internal differences in our missionary team. As if we were infected by the problems of those we came to serve, we too struggled to agree with one another. Some on the team were offended that we were formally listed as the "Team Leaders" by our mission agency at the conference.

"Who made you the leaders?" asked those that had joined us 16 months earlier. This question seared into our minds and revealed to us how we (wrongly) felt the need for validation from others. (Our Area Leader had appointed us several years before, but never made it very formal. Now, we had a large team of folks from very egalitarian cultures!)

The team would talk about an incident that happened over the previous months, and someone would stop and say to us, "Oh that's right, you weren't here for that, so you wouldn't understand...". To which we felt like responding, "No, we weren't here for that specific incident, but we have been through similar circumstances with different details. And we were away for a very good reason!" Not a holy, mature response, but this is how we felt.

Returning from our first home assignment, to a team of people we had recruited, felt like parents returning to be ignored by a pouty child after being away for a few hours. None of them had ever gone on home assignment, and it felt like they were angry with us for "abandoning" them. I'm not sure they were consciously thinking these things, but in our own insecurity, it *felt like* mutiny on the team.

As we were reeling from these internal civil wars, *and* the news that our city in South Sudan was at war, we felt pressured by our team to go back in and reopen the hospital as soon as possible. They had given "their word" that we would reopen, and they wanted to be sure we understood that. Yet for us, we were struggling to discern if and when the Lord was calling us to step back in there—and the "needs" didn't seem to be part of that decision. There are needs everywhere, so while needs may motivate what we do, they don't steer our call—the when, if, and how of walking it out. And it wasn't an issue of risking life to bring the gospel. They had that seed already.

So, the return to the field was hard on our emotional and relational flesh, and didn't seem very good to our souls at the time either.

Over the coming weeks, we waited in northern Uganda and communicated with the Bishop and staff members. Things calmed in Yei, and we got the green light from him to return. At the end of January 2014, we reopened. No announcement—we just opened—and it was busy immediately, with eleven deliveries in the first five days.

Yei was like a ghost town. Less than half the shops were open. It was hot and dusty, the end of dry season. Because of the fighting, much of the harvest was lost, and there were very few goods or produce in the market. Our diet was limited, especially with regards to fresh produce.

I was the only doctor on the ground, so was glad to have a Family Medicine resident doctor (in training) come from the US for three weeks. He provided some company and manpower to me, which was welcome. Just before he finished, we received our first Egyptian Family Medicine resident, which was really exciting—an Egyptian Christian doctor in her first trip outside her home country to serve another people. However, she was shocked at the lack of development.

"There are no paved roads?!" Rehema exclaimed as we drove from the airstrip. And while she came from southern Egypt where it gets quite hot, she struggled in the heat of South Sudan. We had no path of escape into air conditioning as she was accustomed to. It was definitely hard on her flesh, and she was soon echoing the words of the Israelites—"I want to go back to Egypt!"

After three difficult weeks, Rehema received a call that her brother was in the hospital due to a heart problem. Within a day, she made arrangements to return, and after two days, she was gone. In retrospect, it was good that the Lord had her depart then, for things were about to get a whole lot messier.

Unexpected conversations in surgery

Mary arrived one afternoon in preterm labor, over two months before her due date (31 weeks and 6 days). We discovered she had twins, one of whom was breech and in distress. We took her to Caesarean section, and though they struggled at first, both boys were alive. They required CPAP (pressurized oxygen support), tube feeding, and incubator care to maintain their temperatures. We put umbilical vein lines in them and gave them antibiotics to treat possible infection. They gradually improved, but on their sixth day of life, both boys spiked a high fever. Surprisingly, both tested positive for malaria—congenital malaria, which could have only been passed to them from the placenta before they were born. After treatment for this, they continued to grow and get stronger.

But Mary was not doing well. She recovered slowly, developing swelling in her legs, confusion, and abdominal swelling four days after surgery. A brief look with ultrasound revealed her bladder was obstructed and her kidneys were likely shutting down. After replacing her catheter and draining her bladder, she improved slightly, but on the eighth day after her C-section, she began bleeding from her incision and her blood count dropped. We took her back to the operating room and removed the outer sutures to discover the source of the bleeding.

As it turned out, the bleeding was much deeper than we originally thought, so we had to open her up completely again. Despite being under adequate general anesthesia with ketamine, she was still able to talk. She proceeded to describe what was happening throughout the surgery— using three different languages during the course of the operation.

As we struggled to find the source of the bleeding in order to gain control of it, she kept repeating "Ana bi mutu"—"I will die" in Arabic. These were hardly the words I wanted to hear, as I was worried that I could successfully locate and stop the bleeding.
Moments like this were hard on my flesh. They led me to pray for wisdom from the Holy Spirit, to show me how to deal with an issue greater than my natural abilities.

Gradually, I began to see the problem, gain control of it, and close the damaged areas. Mary then switched to repeating a new phrase over and over— "Dom ma gi kubu"—"the blood isn't pouring out." Her assessment was quite accurate, and made me feel better than her predicting her own death. Perhaps she could sense the blood loss, and knew that blood is life?

As we closed her abdomen, she started in on a new repetition— "Diktor sala ana"—"the doctor fixed me"…again, encouraging me. Then she started going a bit overboard in her appreciation—"Diktor abu tai"—"the doctor is my father"… and "Diktor Rabuna"—"the doctor is God!"

At this point, I had to enter in the conversation, for I recalled what happened to Herod when people compared him to God and he didn't refute what they were saying. So I responded "La, Rabuna gi saidu diktor; bes Yesua Rabuna"—"no, God helps the doctor; only Jesus is God!"

As we closed her skin, she switched to Kakwa (her tribal language) and English, and told us that she was having pain. Our nurse anesthetist was probably distracted by all the conversa

tion and got behind on the anesthesia. So, Mary began asking me to help her—"Diktor loki na."

With the help of my staff, and the patient, I learned my first Kakwa phrase, "Na loki dyo"—I help you. Thanks to the prayers of the patient, her family, many others, and most importantly, the power of our God the Healer, she came through a difficult surgery well, and made it interesting for the operating room staff in the process.

Apparently, when Mary's bladder was enlarged (because of the urinary retention), it pulled away from the uterus and caused fresh bleeding near her incision—an unusual complication. After much prayer, Mary began to recover and was able to nurse her babies for the first time since birth. Little did I know that this surgery was the last one I would be able to perform for many months.

Visual changes

During the time around this operation, I began to notice a blurriness descending like a curtain over the upper inner part of my vision on the right side. I had no pain and nothing had happened to the eye to explain this change. I mentioned it to some of the staff during a procedure one day, and we concurred it was probably just tiredness from lack of sleep. After all, I was the only doctor on site— my colleague, Dr. Poole, was on home assignment and our South Sudanese Medical Officer, Dr. Kiden, was out on maternity leave as she was carrying twins and having considerable problems with vomiting.

Over the next several days, the blurriness didn't go away. I pulled my textbook on eye problems off the shelf, and started narrowing down some diagnostic possibilities. Perhaps it is an optic neuritis, or a retinal problem, or something else, I pondered. I emailed two friends, an optometrist in Texas and an ophthalmologist who specialized in retinal surgery, who was a missionary serving in rural western Kenya (Tenwek Hospital). The email I received back from the optometrist was tentative, concurring somewhat with my self-diagnosis. The next day, Dr. Ben Roberts, the retinal surgeon in Kenya, called me. It was a Friday evening.

"Draw a circle on a piece of paper, and put a dot in the center," he guided me. I did so. "Now focus on the dot and move your fingers in from outside and shade in the area where you can't see them well." As I did this, the concreteness of my issue started to dawn on me. I had shaded in the upper right corner of the paper. I was not just overworked and tired. Something was wrong with my vision.

"Jeff, I think you need to get down here as soon as possible for me to examine you," he said seriously.

"Okay," I replied hesitantly. "Let us check if we could do that…" Elizabeth was at my side during the whole exchange, and she immediately got on the phone with the small airline that had a shuttle flight twice a week into our town in South Sudan. They flew on Tuesdays and Saturdays, taking us to Uganda, and the next flight was less than 12 hours away. She called the cell phone of the single employee that lived locally.

"Doctor is having problems with his eye, and needs to get to Kenya as soon as possible," Elizabeth explained.

"Yes, we have one seat on tomorrow's flight," he reported. Thankful, but struggling with what to do, she quickly booked it. She preferred to come with me, but at the same time didn't want to leave our children in South Sudan without either of their parents. It was March 2014, and civil war had started in South Sudan only three months before. As a second option, someone else might accompany me in case further problems developed. But as there were no other seats, that wouldn't be possible anyway.

We hastily packed a small suitcase, and booked the late night flight I would catch once I reached Entebbe, Uganda. That would take me to Nairobi, Kenya, where I would rest a few hours with a fellow missionary family before starting the five-hour drive upcountry to Tenwek Hospital.

The other issue to grapple with was coverage of the hospital. Dr. Lynn Fogleman was in Yei with the Methodist Church, and had occasionally provided coverage for us. He was mainly doing community health work, so the 24/7 hospital and maternity coverage at *His House of Hope* was not what he was accustomed to, or interested in. However, he graciously agreed to come the next day and step in while we sorted things out.

The next morning, Elizabeth and I parted at the airstrip with a sense of dread. Which was worse: me traveling two countries away by myself with failing vision in one eye, for possible eye surgery, or leaving my wife and eight children in a town that had only recently become safe to re-enter? Yet we had a peace that this is what we needed to do. Perhaps it would be a minor problem that Dr. Roberts could diagnose and treat, and I would be back in less than a week.

Once travel was underway, the course of events was in motion, and I wondered if we had overreacted. I felt helplessly caught in a freakish series of mishaps. I noticed small spots floating across my vision and worsening blurriness as I sat in the airport waiting for the next leg of my journey, which at least reassured me that there truly was a problem in my eye.

Seriously, God? I thought. Why this, why now? I was the only missionary doctor keeping this hospital open. Why would this happen, to me, just then? We had barely reopened the hospital after the team evacuated three months before. Perhaps I had believed the patient, Mary, a little? Was I thinking too highly of myself, like Herod did? Or was Satan having a conversation with God about me, like he did about Job? "Sure, things are going well for him, but let me afflict him and weaken him at just the point where he is 'doing' so much good, and then see how he reacts! He will despair, not hope in You!"

I arrived into Nairobi late Saturday night and our friends sent a driver they knew to bring me to their home. The Byerlys, friends from our sending agency, welcomed me and gave me a bed in which to sleep for the brief, remaining night. There was still a five-hour drive upcountry to Tenwek Hospital and Dr. Roberts, and traveling at night wasn't a good idea. Early in the morning, the driver returned and we departed. We climbed up out of Nairobi until the escarpment that sloped steeply into the Great Rift Valley. As we wound our way down the two-lane road that clings to the edge of the escarpment, the blurriness in my right eye became even more noticeable. I closed my eyes and surrendered the whole crazy situation to the Lord—what else could we do? Words from the Lutheran Liturgy of my upbringing rang back to me, "Lord, to whom shall we go? You have the words of eternal life." (Astute students of the Bible may note that those words are not original to the Lutherans, but actually come from John chapter 6—a fact I discovered in my college days, when I started reading the Bible for myself...)

I arrived at Tenwek on Sunday afternoon, and the Roberts family ushered me into their home.

"Drop your bags, and let's go up to the eye unit to see what's going on," Ben said like a man on a mission.

He, together with a Samaritan's Purse Fellow (a missionary doctor on a two-year program), examined my right eye under the slit lamp and then with a high-powered light and magnifying lens.

"You have a retinal detachment of about a fourth of the back of your eye," he explained. "It is almost, but not quite, to the fovea centralis (the central point of vision)—so that is a positive point. You have lattice degeneration, which leads to a tear in the retina, and allows fluid to enter behind. The retina then 'peels' away as does paint from a wall if it gets wet."

"So, what do we need to do?" I asked.

"We need to do surgery, today. Now. I'll call and assemble a team to operate."

I felt a churn in the bottom of my gut, like you get when cresting the top of a large roller coaster—knowing that you are committed to a path that you can't alter. Pain was inevitable and I had to surrender to that—knowing that God was in control of it. I sensed He would keep me—not from physical suffering, but that He would at least keep my soul. I called Elizabeth and told her what we would need to do. She prayed a lot in those days, and held everything together. She carried the family and me. She was being stretched to depend on the Lord in ways she didn't want to—not being with her husband as he underwent surgery in another country; in Africa, nonetheless.

"We'll do it under local anesthesia," Dr. Roberts explained. "I usually do that because it is safer. Our eye unit is not close to the main surgical theatre, so I worry about complications if you were under general anesthesia." That sounded very rational and most secure. What that meant was that he would inject numbing and paralyzing medication below my eyeball, through the soft space behind my lower eyelid! Then, I would be awake and need to remain perfectly still on the operating table as he inserted several trochars (large needles through which instruments are passed) into the white of my eye. My eye was paralyzed, but I could still move the rest of my body.

I managed to remain still. I was thankful for the presence of the Holy Spirit that day, particularly for the self-control that He gives to us that let Him. I wasn't brave—I just knew I had to do this, and any other option was worse. Dr. Roberts kindly mentioned that I was as stoic as his Kenyan patients, undergoing major eye surgery simply under local anesthesia. I wondered if they were so tough because they, like me at that moment, didn't really have any choice to be anything other than that.

On that day, I wished I hadn't gone to medical school. Or paid attention in anatomy class. I was more than awake—my senses were heightened by the extremity of my circumstances, and I could understand each step of the operation that he was doing on me. I could sense the vibration of the machine as it suctioned out my vitreous (the gel that fills the eyeball). Simultaneously, the remaining vision in that eye went black. It wasn't painful until the point at which he used the laser to burn the retina to the back of eye—"tacking" it back down where it had detached. The retina is like a sheet of nerves, an extension of the brain really, and that type of central pain wasn't blocked by the local injection. After replacing the retina, they filled my eye with saline (IV fluids) and a "gas bubble" to hold the retina in place until it sealed. The surgery finished, and the pain set in as the numbing medication wore off.

They put me in the guesthouse. I would need to keep my face down for 1-2 weeks, so the gas bubble remained at the back of my eye, against the retina. I was trapped in Kenya without my family, to recover from surgery. Dr. Roberts and the Fellow came to check on me late that night, looking concerned.

"There's not usually this much swelling and pain," Ben began. "Most of the time, we don't remove the bandage this early, but we need to check what's going on." As they removed it, I could tell they didn't like what they saw. "There's bleeding into and around the eye. It's stopped now, but this is uncommon. I'll talk to my mentor about this more tomorrow."

Thus began a long few weeks—sleep was hard to come by, as I had to sleep on my face but without pressure on my right eye. The Roberts family lent me an iPod on which to listen to worship music and sermons, which greatly distracted me from the pain and isolation. During the second week, I could walk around a bit more, as long as I kept my face to the ground. I was able to attend the medical lectures with the Kenyan and other African doctors in training. This was a refreshing experience in the midst of a harsh time.

He rechecked my eye almost daily, to see if the gas bubble was reduced enough for me to travel by air (there was concern that pressure changes in the airplane could lead to serious complications). Finally, almost two weeks later, he cleared me to travel. Because of the bleeding that had occurred, I could not see with my right eye. I would need to return for a second surgery to wash out the blood. Before I left, he checked my left eye and found a retinal tear in this, the "good" eye. There was a hole, but no detachment yet. He quickly lasered the defect to seal it off. Neither of us had expected to find something in the other eye, so I didn't have any pain meds on board. He noticed my expression of great discomfort and commented, "I guess we could have at least given you some Tylenol before!"

I reached the airport on the shores of Lake Victoria in Uganda just before midnight, where I would board the small plane to return to South Sudan at eight in the morning. It was pouring rain, my eye was hurting, and I was tired from the five-hour drive to Nairobi and subsequent flight to Uganda. To leave the airport I would have to pay over $100 for visa, taxi, room, and end up getting just a few hours of sleep. Unfortunately, there was no one from the airline there at the time, so they couldn't check me through to the "transit lounge." Immigration almost forced me to leave, but I pleaded with them to let me stay in the seats outside the transit area. They finally consented, so there I sat on a hard plastic chair, with a still swollen right eye, with flying insects of all varieties visiting me through the door that opened onto the tarmac.

Reaching home was a warm relief. Elizabeth and I had never been separated this long in our twenty years of marriage, much less for reasons of me having a life-altering surgery. Meanwhile, she had been maneuvering coverage for the mission hospital, and still parenting and schooling the eight children in a war-torn country. Eva, then almost twelve, read aloud to me as I recovered, as even reading was painful for me. It was a precious time of connection, and good to get caught up on the teenage fiction I had missed growing up—Nancy Drew mysteries!

While I was lying on my face in Kenya, Elizabeth had been finding doctors to keep the hospital open. She sent countless emails, engaging the missions community worldwide through Pioneers, CMDA (Christian Medical Dental Association), and missions-focused residencies such as In His IMAGE and Via Christi. Dr. Lynn Fogelman covered for the first week. Despite usually doing community health outreach, he willingly stepped in on short-notice to see patients in the hospital and perform C-sections.

The second week, Dr. Kiden, our South Sudanese Medical Officer, came off of maternity leave. She was nearly 30 weeks pregnant with twins and suffering from severe vomiting (hyperemesis gravidarum). The Clinical Officers, nurses, and midwives took care of much of the work, but if a C-section was needed, they would give the patient *and* Dr. Kiden an intravenous fluid bolus, so she could stand up long enough to complete the operation. By the third week, a missionary doctor preparing to move to India was able to make the trip. Dr. Teubl arrived to the compound after over thirty hours of travel, dropped his bag in our house, and said, "Point me to the hospital—I'm ready to see patients!"

The following week, Dr. Marc Carrigan and his family, who were considering moving to South Sudan, came for a two-week visit. He was able and willing to step in and do the work that was needed. There were also several South Sudanese Medical Officers who came from the government hospital and the Juba Teaching Hospital to complete a rotation. Ten midwife students "happened" to be on rotation at the time. Our Clinical Officers took on more responsibility. These young professionals would remain beyond our time. Despite me being the only doctor at the time of losing my sight, the Lord kept *His House of Hope* open throughout, until Dr. Poole and family could return. The needs were endless, but the Lord could handle it.

When I was able to begin some light work in the hospital again, I was surprised to see Mary and her twin boys still there. It seemed like ages had passed since I performed the surgery to repair the bleeding behind her bladder—my last surgery done with binocular vision.

After nearly a month in the hospital, Mary and her sons, Innocent and Logan (the latter named for our son), went home healthy.

Return to Kenya: Surgery #2

Elizabeth and I agonized how to go about having my second surgery. It was a "simple" wash-out. Dr. Roberts expected it to take less than half an hour. Dr. Carrigan had been in Yei for several days, and bravely offered to carry the ship. Our missionary nurse, Kitty, would stay with the children. Elizabeth couldn't bear me having another surgery without her being there with me. Yet, neither of us was excited about leaving our eight children, even with people we trusted, in a country with a smoldering civil war.

Jeff and Dr. Teubl review an X-Ray

We chartered a small plane with African Inland Mission (AIM), in order to fly directly from Yei to western Kenya, thereby saving 3-4 days of travel time and reducing the time we would have to be away from the children. Jonathan Koski was our pilot, taking us from Yei to Arua, Uganda, then past snowcapped Mt. Elgin in eastern Uganda, to Eldoret, Kenya. Finally, we landed at a small crop-dusting airstrip called Farmland, near Tenwek Hospital. We hoped to have the surgery the next day, and return two to three days after leaving.

Once at the hospital, Dr. Roberts ordered some pre-operative labs, since I had bled during the first surgery. They revealed a mild abnormality in my clotting ability. Suddenly, the brakes went on. I had a consult with the Internal Medicine specialist, who referred me to a hematologist (blood specialist) in Nairobi.

The next morning, we were on the five-hour drive to Nairobi again, and by noon, we were seated in a plush office in a high-rise medical complex near the city center. Many of the other patients were Muslim women, in full garb—as the doctor herself was a Muslim woman.

"We will send your blood off for further testing in South Africa," she gently explained. "But I understand you need to have this surgery quickly, and can't wait for a week to get the results back. So, I think we should give you some clotting factors prior to the surgery." Fresh-frozen plasma (FFP) was a component of blood given to replace deficient factors and help one's blood clot effectively.

"Where can we get FFP?" I asked.

"Oh, it is available through the national blood bank system. I can have them send some units from the Kericho Blood Bank—it's only an hour from Tenwek."

So it was. We returned to Tenwek later that night, and the units of FFP were there waiting. We were astounded at such efficiency! The next morning, they prepped me for surgery. As the first unit went into the vein of my right arm, I felt an intense burning along the course and divisions of the veins. The nurse stopped the infusion, slowed the rate, and retried. The same thing happened. They tried the second unit, and there was no such reaction. Another unit was also given after that one, and the surgery proceeded.

Dr. Roberts washed the blood out of my eye, and I could actually see a bit! Everything had a reddish hue, which he explained was due to the posterior capsule of my lens being stained with the blood that had been in my eye for a month.

"It should decrease over time, or else they will open it up later when they do your cataract surgery," he calmly explained.

"My what?!" I responded.

"Oh, most people who have complications like this end up with a cataract within a short time—six months or a year."

The news just kept getting better. And little did we know that more "good" news was coming.

What we found back in Yei

We eagerly boarded the small plane with the pilot Jonathan, ready to get back to our kids. We had called him the day before to let him know we were ready to go. After a brief stop in Eldoret, we flew straight for Yei. In the small 5-seater Cessna 206, Jonathan radioed the AIM base in Nairobi for a weather report on Yei.

"None of our contacts in Yei are responding," they reported to him. "Do your passengers have someone there we can call?" Elizabeth looked in her phone and gave him the number of our compound director, Mr. Mourice. Jonathan got on the radio again and passed this information back to the base. They called Mr. Mourice, who was on his way to the airport to pick us up. He told them there was a thunderstorm a ways off, but around Yei it was still clear. We landed well, and Mr. Mourice drove us the 9 miles back to our home. Such was the messiness of air travel in rural East Africa.

Kitty had mentioned Winnie had a case of malaria, but was under treatment now and was improving. Entering our home, we saw Winnie, pale and lying on the floor. Usually she would have popped up and run to greet us—but she didn't. Elizabeth was immediately concerned. She was on the third day of anti-malarial treatment, but was still getting occasional fevers and didn't want to eat. Elizabeth noted that she needed fluids.

Dr. Carrigan came over to look at her with me. Kitty started intravenous fluids, and we retested her blood for malaria. Negative. Over the next few days, her fevers started increasing, coming higher each time, seemingly about every 24-30 hours. Her stomach began paining her more, she had headache, and she wouldn't eat. When the fever came on suddenly, she had intense rigors—shaking chills that racked her little body and made her cry out for help to Mommy and Daddy. It was heart-wrenching, seeing her suffer so much. We had added broad-spectrum antibiotics by this time, but she didn't seem to be responding.

We prayed and cried out to the Lord for help. I got on the phone with AIM Air and tentatively booked a medical evacuation flight for the next day. But she was worsening quickly, with temperatures up to 105-106 degrees Fahrenheit. I feared that by the time we traveled to a larger hospital, obtained lab tests, waited for results, and established her care in a new place, it would be too late. During these times, I would carry her to a cool bath to reduce her fever—forgetting my eye surgery just 5 days earlier. I conversed with the Lord. Please save our daughter... I don't care if I ever see out of my right eye again—my sight is a small thing. Please show us this mercy. I wasn't bargaining with God; I was simply expressing to Him what I valued most.

Elizabeth had her own conversation with the Lord, in which she released Winnie to Him. She went all the way to envisioning where she would bury her—in the back yard of the house under the tree. Yet I can still trust You, even if that happens. You are enough, she said to Him.

Dr. Carrigan and I went to the books and put our heads together. The most likely possibility was bacterial infection that caused a cyclical fever and was not covered by the antibiotics with which we were treating her. We narrowed it down to a resistant Salmonella typhi infection (which causes typhoid, or enteric fever), or a rickettsial infection such as tularemia, which could be transmitted by cats or rabbits. Winnie loved holding cats and bunnies, and we later found out she had been scratched by one of them a few weeks earlier.
With our limited medication supply, the only option to cover these was intravenous chloramphenicol. This medication is no longer available in the US, as in rare cases it can cause the blood cells to drop dangerously low. We checked her blood counts again, and cautiously started the drug.

The next morning, Elizabeth remembers awakening to hear the death wail of a woman at the hospital, across our back fence. The woman's young child had just died. She looked over at Winnie, in the bed with us, on an IV. Just then, Winnie sat up and asked for something to eat. Her body was cool to touch, and the brightness had returned to her eyes! We thanked the Lord for showing us this mercy. We didn't deserve it any more than the woman who had just lost her child.

Later that morning, the vision in my right eye suddenly and completely turned red. I figured I had bled into my eye again. We were in no shape to travel immediately. I called Dr. Roberts, who agreed that we could wait for a few weeks, until we were scheduled to go to Kenya again for a previously planned conference.

We felt awful about the "vision trip" the Carrigans had. He assumed the weight of a busy mission hospital and rarely saw his family, while they all witnessed us nearly lose our daughter, as I struggled through surgeries and the loss of my vision. We weren't surprised, and couldn't blame them, for choosing another place to serve. The Lord had allowed them to walk through the worst few weeks of our lives in Yei. Yet He must have had His reasons, for He was still sovereign, even after all these years.

Back to Kenya: Surgery #3

Winnie recovered completely, and several weeks later, we departed for Kenya as a family. We had planned a holiday before the crazy events of the previous few months. It turned out that Dr. Roberts and his family would be passing through Nairobi on the same day as we would be transferring at the airport. (Yep, God was still sovereign...) Elizabeth and the children made their way through immigration and on to our next gate, while I diverted to the parking lot.

We stood next to his vehicle while a Muslim man kneeled on his prayer mat in the parking lot, praying to the east. Then, Ben donned his headlamp and brought out his powerful lenses to again examine my right eye. We both expected that he would see blood in the eye again. But we were wrong.

"Your retina has completely detached," he said gravely.

We had precious few minutes to process this information and decide on a plan. "When do we need to deal with it?" I asked. My family was already inside the terminal, waiting by the gate for our next flight, and we didn't have Kenyan SIM cards for our phones, so I couldn't reach Elizabeth. Dr. Roberts was about to leave with his family for a conference as well.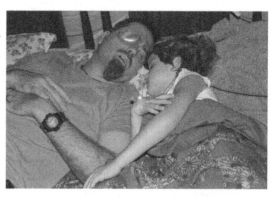

"The sooner the better," he replied.

"Would a week or two make a difference?" I clarified.

"At this point, probably not. We could delay until you and I get back. I'll need to put silicone oil in your eye after we replace the retina this time, and it will stay for six months."

We prayed, and parted ways. I delivered the news to Elizabeth—another surgery, another change of plans. We went ahead with our time of rest and play in Mombasa, in which we swam in the Indian Ocean and ate some good seafood. However, the place we had rented was infested with bugs, and the community wasn't very welcoming to new guests. Elizabeth and several of the kids were riddled with bites.

Dejected, Elizabeth and I went out one day to get some food, walking on a dirt road in the rain in order to find a tuk-tuk (three-wheeled taxi). We were struggling with what to do about our housing situation, when a friendly American man wheeled around and pulled up next to us.

"Want a ride?" he asked. His large Boerboel dog (South African Mastiff) peered out of the back window of his SUV. Normally we don't accept rides from total strangers with huge dogs, but we strangely felt at peace with it.

"Hop in!" he encouraged. We did. It turned out that he and his wife were missionaries who lived nearby. We told him the woes of our current rental situation. "Well, you can stay in our guesthouse—we don't have any groups coming in the next few weeks, and we have a pool and air conditioning!"

We moved later that day, and it was an incredibly restful experience in the midst of a burdensome time.

There were lighter moments, at least in retrospect. I accompanied our newfound friend to the supermarket to get some needed supplies. Upon exiting the store, several men sprung up from the side of his vehicle as we approached, and ran away. We did a walk-around inspection, but nothing seemed obviously awry. Driving off, things seemed fine, and we began talking in a more relaxed fashion again. As he slowed for a speed hump, both of our gazes were simultaneously drawn to the sight of his left rear wheel continuing on down the road, detached and separate from us! We retrieved the wheel, which the men had obviously been after, and we were fine, other than being short a few lug nuts. I mean that literally, though I suppose many missionaries are probably short a few lug nuts in the metaphorical sense, or we wouldn't be following Jesus so far from the relative "safety net" of our passport country!

Back at Tenwek, the surgery went well, other than discovering that there are few pain medications I can take. Ibuprofen gave me a stomach ulcer when I was young, so they gave me paracetamol (like Tylenol) and tramadol. Vomiting after eye surgery is a big no-no. As it turns out, tramadol makes me vomit. So, no more tramadol. They dug up a dose of an injectable narcotic pain medication, which helped me sleep the night after surgery, though the injection site was sore for days after.

With oil in my eye, there were fewer precautions. It would need to be removed six months later. I recovered fairly quickly, but the oil distorted the vision severely, and already a cataract was forming. I was depressed, thinking I likely couldn't operate again—certainly not for a long while.

I was sharing this with Dr. Joy Draper, one of the obstetricians at Tenwek, and she said, "I don't see why you can't still operate. Your brain will adjust." I was heartened by her encouragement.

We returned to Yei, and I was able to gradually step back into duties. The team and hospital found a groove of shared responsibility, teaching, and growth.

As we made plans for the next surgery, we learned that Dr. Roberts would be away during those months. The South African church that had cared for us during our holiday there offered to host and connect us with a good retinal surgeon. But Mr. Mourice, our Kenyan compound director, encouraged us to return to the US for my next round of surgeries. "Go back to your home, not mine, for your surgery!" We agreed and felt peace with his advice, so we made plans. The challenge, and part of our hesitancy, was the cost. We would need about $16,000 for this unplanned and unbudgeted trip back to the US. We put this request out, and a doctor with whom I had trained, but hadn't been in contact with for years, gifted us $15,000. Others gave as well, and we again had a front row seat to see the Lord provide.

A Storehouse and a Hole: Pastor John's dream

Pastor John had been asked to leave the ministry of Harvesters, for reasons we never fully understood. His wife still attended antenatal care and had already delivered one of their children at *His House of Hope*. I hadn't talked to him in over a year, and he wasn't aware of anything we had been through. Out of the blue, he called me one day about a month before we were to leave for the US.

"I had a dream about your family, and I want to tell you about it," Pastor John said somewhat timidly (which was unusual for this "short" Dinka man of only 6 feet 3 inches height).

Elizabeth and I were able to walk to their house two days later. He related that he had a dream about us back in November of 2011. In the dream, he saw a large storehouse filled with seeds of many types, which represented blessings. From that, he had gathered that we were truly sent by God.

Then several nights before he called us, he had a dream in which he was walking through a forest and found two girls from the orphanage, talking and laughing.

"There was a hole nearby with people in it, including Doctor," Pastor John began. "His left knee was bandaged and there was something over it to apply medicine. Doctor was discouraged and told me that you were going back to the US—and that Elizabeth's uncle had bought you a house. Then Elizabeth came over to where we were talking and was saying 'How could this be the right thing to do? God has more for us here.' She went on, challenging Jeff not to be discouraged."

"I then woke up—it was 3:30 in the morning—and starting praying earnestly for you all. I had not thought or prayed for you or anyone else in the ministry for over a year (since he was asked to leave the ministry). But I feared being 'pfunished' by God if I did not share this dream with you," he explained.

He didn't have our cell phone number, but sought it from someone else and called us. He did not know that I had gone blind in my right eye, or anything that was happening in the ministry. There was no advantage to him in telling us about this, other than obeying the Lord. He felt there might be discouragement from relationships or physical difficulties that we were facing, but didn't know what they were.

I don't know all the reasons the Lord gave this dream to Pastor John, but it was an encouraging moment of connection with him, someone with whom we weren't particularly close. We were encouraged that the Lord spoke to Pastor John about our situation, and that he obeyed and sought us out. The Lord was active and aware of what we were walking through, and used one of His children to remind us of His attention.

Hope or Despair?

"To be or not to be?" is not the question.

"Hope or despair?"—that is the question.

Why do bad things happen to good people? Also not the question. There are no "good" people, no people "worthy" of only good in life. Rather, the question is "why do good things happen to bad people?" Why do drug dealers drive the nicest cars? Why do pimps have the best clothes? Why do cutthroat business people relax in first-class on the airplane, while the missionaries cram themselves into economy seats? Why does God send rain on the crops of farmers that don't pay their immigrant workers a fair wage? Why does God show mercy even to broken, messed-up missionaries?

It seems to be borne out in Scripture that God allows, and sometimes even causes, difficult things in our lives. He allows the natural consequences of our sinful choices, the brokenness of the world system, and at times, Satan and his servants to produce pain in our experience, even though we are mostly doing right at that moment. Yet, God is good—He defines good. He equals good. And He is looking to produce in us glory—glory that far outweighs the suffering we are walking through now (2 Cor 4:17).

Regardless of what one believes about the origin of pain and suffering, what matters is how we respond. Satan would have us despair. God wants nothing more than for us to trust Him and choose hope in spite of our circumstances.

When we returned to the US in December 2014, my eye was scarred. It had almost no pressure. The renowned eye surgeon to whom we were referred nearly refused to see me because of the outbreak of Ebola virus that year. He read a report that suggested Ebola was in South Sudan, so he called to tell us he would need to report me to the CDC. I would be placed in quarantine for 21 days before he would be able to see me.

"But I just left there, and we had no Ebola," I countered. "And my partner is still there, emailing me every day. I would have heard if it came since we left!" We were devastated. We had traveled around the world for this surgery.

"I have to do my own research," he insisted. We ended our phone conversation, and I looked up the article he mentioned. There had been Ebola in South Sudan. In another area, in 2007, there were 17 suspected cases. Ten of them turned out to be measles. It never became an epidemic.

He called back later, to apologize. He had contacted public health officials in Colorado Springs who confirmed we were safe. It was a tense and awkward beginning to our doctor-doctor and doctor-patient relationship. As we found out, he was very cautious and prone to realism. And he was a very good retinal surgeon.

"I give us a 40% chance of saving your eye," said the surgeon. He told us frankly that useful vision was unlikely—he was only talking about preserving my natural eye. When we told the children, Hazel said she really hoped I didn't end up with a glass eye, because that was gross and would give her nightmares!

The surgery was painless, because I was knocked out—for which I was very grateful. Praise God for general anesthesia. The recovery, however, was extremely painful. The surgeon had placed a silicone band (a scleral buckle) around the white of my eye and cinched it down to give an hourglass shape to my eye. Several weeks later, my eye began maintaining its pressure again. No glass eye! I was really glad, for Hazel's sake. A cataract surgery and another laser treatment followed.

I ended up with a small amount of vision in the right eye—distorted, like a funny house mirror. People's heads look small, their bodies distorted. I see the world like Frodo (from Lord of the Rings) did when he put on the ring (though I haven't spotted any ring wraiths yet). Everything has an orange, misty hue (at least I think so—I'm also color blind). There are a few places in my vision where I can read large letters. Unfortunately, the images of my right eye aren't lined up with the left, so I also have double vision, like I am constantly seeing the reflection of something off a glass window. My peripheral vision is severely limited, and I no longer have 3-D vision. My brain must perceive depth in other ways, through shadowing or relative size. The problems in my eye range from barely noticeable to very distracting and wearisome, to times when a deep pain starts behind the eye and bores into my head.

It is then that I become a pirate. I cover it with a patch—especially when traveling, as it helps with dizziness, and lets people in a busy airport know that I don't see much on my right side. My kids also encourage me to put it on when we are going through security, because it seems to throw them off a bit, so they don't hassle us as much!

Good for the Soul

Faithful people come and speak great words of encouragement to us, and pray that God would heal my eye completely. I believe He could. Some might suggest that my faith is not enough. But then, what about Paul—was his faith not enough?

As I have asked God, the Holy Spirit reminded me of a passage in His Word—that this was to be a thorn in my body, a scar that is for my good and His glory. Through it, He reminds me that His grace is enough for me each day. I am still able to perform surgery, drive a car, play with my kids (though my ping pong skills have suffered), love my wife (though I still have a lot of room for improvement), and provide for my family. I can still write, speak, read, teach, and care for patients. He gives me what I need to do the works He has prepared for me, though I don't feel as physically confident as I once did. I am forced to depend on Him more and more.

> "...there was given me a thorn in the flesh, a messenger of Satan to beat me—to keep me from exalting myself! Concerning this I implored the Lord three times that it might leave me. And He has said to me, 'My grace is sufficient for you, for power is perfected in weakness.'" (2 Corinthians 12:7b-9, NASB)

Obedience to God changes us, and not always for the better in our physical and emotional parts. The discord amongst our team was often more difficult to bear than the physical wounds. Most of these relationships have been healed through conversation, prayer, and forgiveness, but some remain scarred or cut off.

The physical scars are real. If we had lived in the US when my retina detached, I would have been able to access a retinal surgeon more quickly. With a healthy Western diet, my eye probably wouldn't have bled. Winnie wouldn't have contracted a serious bacterial infection that almost took her life. And there were months of relational rifts that were often more painful than the physical traumas.

We still carry these physical and emotional scars. I wear an eye patch as I write these lines. We have shocks of panic, post-traumatic stress, whenever Winnie spikes a fever or complains of stomach pain. She still struggles with vague abdominal problems on and off, possibly because of her previous issues. My heart aches as the children recall playing with friends that they will likely never see again, partly due to the pride of their parents (us and them).

We are not the same as when we started this journey, and those changes often don't feel good to our flesh. In fact, we are *"always carrying about in the body the dying of Jesus, so that the life of Jesus also may be manifested in our body"* (2 Cor 4:10).

At the end of the Lord of the Rings trilogy, Frodo and his companions return to their beloved home in the Shire, after nearly dying to complete their great task. They look around at those carrying on life as if nothing had happened, and they look at one another in a moment of realization, seeming to think—we will never fully fit in here, because we are different now. Frodo carried a scar from the enemy, from which he never fully recovered. He wasn't the same, and his home was never like it once was— for him, at least.

God was chipping away at our pride. True, we had started a mission hospital, but we were not indispensable. Through the team brought by the Lord, the hospital continued to grow and thrive during my incapacity. God was more concerned with our sanctification and His glory than any works we might have done. He was conforming, chipping, and chiseling us into the image of His Son through the mess He allowed in our lives. The process was palpably painful at times.

He may not keep us physically and emotionally unstained, but He always does what is good for our soul. He will **keep** *your soul. (Ps 121:7b, emphasis mine)*

"The Lord will rescue me from every evil deed, and will bring me safely to His heavenly kingdom; to Him be the glory forever and ever." (2 Tim 4:18)

Do you believe God works all things for your individual good (Rom 8:28)?

If we understand that God is speaking to the Church as a whole ("those who love Him"), such that my suffering may only result in good for others in the Church, how does this change your understanding of how He might be working good in "all things"?

1 Peter 4:1-2 (NASB) says, *"Therefore, since Christ has suffered in the flesh, arm yourselves also with the same purpose, because he who has suffered in the flesh has ceased from sin, so as to live the rest of the time in the flesh no longer for the lusts of men, but for the will of God."* God's objective is that sin would cease to have power over us, and that we would desire to live for His will ("good for the soul"). **How might God call you to intentionally put yourself in situations where suffering in the flesh is very likely to happen?**

Chapter 11
Home Assignment Blues: *Seriously, God?!*

Home Assignment is an unexpectedly messy time in the life of a missionary. It is understood by most, including missionaries early in their careers, to be a time of rest, recuperation, and restoration. Six months to a year "off" of work every 2-4 years to relax, eat good food, and be "home" once again, supported by understanding friends and family! A well-deserved break to put one's feet up and recount stories of God's faithfulness on the mission field. In the past and in some circles still, Home Assignment was called Home Leave or Furlough, a leave of absence granted as a "sanity check." It conjures up images of a wonderful time of renewal.

These lofty expectations are often met by difficult realities. "Home" no longer feels like home. Friends and family can't understand the world in which the missionary has been living. They may try to listen, but after thirty seconds, their eyes become glazed over, because they don't have a "hook" on which to hang what they are hearing—experiences with which to relate. The food is good for a while, but the missionary's body is no longer accustomed to the rich diet, so he feels ill, gains weight, and new health problems spring up. And relax? Often the missionaries don't own a home, so they don't ever feel settled. They must be on the road for weeks or months at a time to meet with supporters and share with churches. Suddenly it is stressful to live in a place that no longer feels like home, while the work to which God has called them goes on without them, or not, far away.

The missionary is burdened by the work back on the mission field. She may receive reports of the work from her teammates, and cringe at how they are dealing with the problems that have come up. The team may perceive she is on one big vacation, inadvertently (or intentionally) heaping guilt on her by communicating how overwhelmed they are by the work, furthering the uneasiness she feels.

Re-entry stress is real.

We arrived back for our first home assignment with such misconceptions. After two years of living in the bush, with little variation in diet, and constant medical work and cultural adjustment, we were ready to be home and to rest. But of course, we needed and wanted to go report to the individuals and churches who had made it possible for us to be there. Our supporters were spread over 23 states, including Alaska and Canada (okay, I know that Canada is not a state…), and our first mistake was to try to hit them all.

We embarked on a 3-½ month, 16,000 mile, 40 state tour in our church's 15-passenger van and our cargo trailer. As per our usual family economic fortune of buying high and selling low, the price of gasoline had just crested at over $4 per gallon. Getting less than 10 miles to the gallon, we trekked from Colorado to Oklahoma, Texas, Louisiana, Alabama, and on to Florida. Furthering our poor gas mileage, the air conditioning was on most of the time, since we were traveling in the hottest areas during the summer—which seemed to be our pattern. We are slow learners.

We connected with our sending agency and other missionaries in a debrief week. We shared our own stories and heard those of others—it was important to listen to what God had done in the lives of others and step back to see His work in ours. We also connected with the Finance department, where we revised our budget. In our eagerness to leave for the field, we had chosen a minimalist budget, which left us struggling to pay for visas, travel, and living expenses on the field. We needed to raise half again as much as we had before leaving for the field. How would we do this?

A Front Row Seat to God's Faithfulness

While there we also met up with Elizabeth's childhood friend Tabby. She had spontaneously started supporting us during our first term. We heard how she had started attending church again, felt convicted to be giving, and started sending support for us through Pioneers every two weeks. The amazing part was the timing—she had started giving just as another family had to drop their support due to a family crisis that almost ended in divorce.

We no longer owned a travel trailer, and hotels are expensive for 10 people. In many places, we could stay with friends or churches. Some nights, however, we didn't have either. As we made our way up the East Coast after leaving Florida, Elizabeth "cold-called" a large church in Savannah, Georgia. Within an hour, they had several options—we could stay with a family from the church or stay in the band room at the Christian school attached to the church. We stayed on the floor at the church, but a man gave us money and recommended a great breakfast place—delicious pancakes! We were most encouraged at the readiness and willingness of the Body of Christ.

On one leg of the trip, we drove through eight states in one day. Granted, they were the small ones—leaving Virginia, on to Maryland, Delaware, New Jersey, New York, Connecticut, Massachusetts, and into New Hampshire. Another time, Elizabeth drove on through the night, completing a leg from Milwaukee, Wisconsin, stopping at Mt. Rushmore, South Dakota before sleeping in Wyoming. We were hustling then so we could reach the wedding of a missionary in British Columbia, Canada!

We made our way down the West Coast: Vancouver Island, family in Seattle, on to San Francisco (fun parking the van and trailer in the city…), Los Angeles, and back through the desert Southwest. We spent some precious time with missionary friends who serve in Malaysia, who happened to be back with family in New Mexico. From there, we returned north to Colorado. We were spent.

Finally, we could be in one place for a few months! The family who had rented our home had vacated, so we were able to be in our own place for a few months. I worked part-time for my mentor, Dr. Schmucker. Several weeks after arriving back home, Elizabeth and I flew to Baltimore so I could present about the work at *His House of Hope* at a Global Health conference. While there, Elizabeth had a brief, severe headache, but we didn't think much more about it at the time. We returned to Colorado.

One evening, a headache assailed Elizabeth. Sudden onset, worst headache of her life. It didn't respond to medications we had at home. She met the "red flag" criteria of a headache—there were concerns about something more serious going on. We headed into our local hospital emergency room. The doc gave her some medication, which reduced the pain, and after a brief evaluation he released her. Her blood pressure was moderately elevated, presumably due to the pain she was having.

In the middle of the night, the headache returned with a vengeance—worse than the first time. This time, she and I climbed into the car and drove the 55 miles to Pueblo, the next major city. I had worked as an ER doctor myself, but when it came to my own family, I didn't want to make the diagnosis. Unconsciously, I would avoid going down certain diagnostic paths that were too scary to consider. If there was another doctor available, I wanted him or her to evaluate. Many times in South Sudan I was on my own in diagnosing my family, but in the US, I was glad to rely on others.

The ER doctor ordered a CT scan of her brain, which was normal. Everything checked out fine, but her blood pressure was even higher than the previous day.

"I'm thinking the headache is because of the high blood pressure, not that her blood pressure is elevated because of her headache," the doctor said. "Let's treat her for hypertension and see if the headache improves."

Once she was on treatment, the blood pressure stayed down and the headaches went away. At age 43, Elizabeth had followed her mother's genes and developed high blood pressure. A new diagnosis on our first Home Assignment.

The next shock was the bill, as the invoice for the two ER visits was equal to 1-2 months of running the entire hospital in South Sudan ($15,000)! It was jolting to us. But God provided—through having decent insurance, thanks to the wisdom of our sending agency, and through the opportunity to work a few shifts in the hospital. He also provided the budget we needed to return to South Sudan, through increases in giving and new support from a few churches and individuals. We were privileged to have a front row seat to God's faithfulness, such as we saw with one church in the small town of

Las Animas, Colorado. They ramped up their giving to a level that only a few, much larger congregations were managing.

As we prepared to return to South Sudan at the end of 2013, we received news that civil war had broken out in the capitol city. A week later, the team had to close the hospital and evacuate. It was a messy return from a messy Home Assignment.

Hobbled on Home Assignment

When our second Home Assignment rolled around, we had more realistic expectations. We would not hit every state and see every supporter! We saw my family in Washington and Alaska as we flew into the US via Seattle. We enjoyed reconnecting with a few close friends, and the kids joined in a "Rodeo Bible Camp" run by one of our faithful churches, Valley Cowboy Church.

I was the camp doctor. Fortunately, there were few injuries, and I learned that most rodeo types are tough enough that they rarely seek medical care, even when the steer they are wrestling knocks out their front teeth! The speaker for the week was a horse trainer (a real life "horse whisperer"). He explained that sometimes a horse had to be "hobbled," in which two of his legs were tied together so he couldn't bolt. The more strong-willed horses could only be trained if this were done.

In June 2016, we embarked on a modest, 6-week journey of "just" eleven states. We still hadn't learned to travel the southern states in the cooler months, so we once again headed to sunny Florida in July, when it resembled a steam bath. Thankfully, the price of gas had fallen to $2.38 per gallon.

We had an encouraging time at a retreat in Oklahoma, reconnecting with other missions-minded doctors from In His IMAGE, my residency training program. We left on Saturday night and drove the 5 hours to Mt. Pleasant, Texas in the dark, so we could be at Calvary Chapel the next morning.

After church, Elizabeth went with some of the girls to get supplies to make lunch for 24 people (we were staying with the DeLisi family, the very ones who had initially asked us to help plan the hospital in South Sudan). As she was walking in shoes with a slight rise of the heel, in the flat, paved parking lot of Brookshire's grocery store, her right foot rolled under her and bent backwards. Several of the kids saw it from the waiting van.

"Oh my gosh! Your mom fell," exclaimed Corban, one of the DeLisis. "She can't get up! Call your dad! Call my dad!" (Both of us dads are doctors.) The store manager came out and helped Elizabeth get up, since most of the kids were stuck under the groceries in the van. She was in excruciating pain and couldn't put weight on her foot. Lillie called me on the phone.

"Mom just broke her foot!" she declared. Being known to exaggerate, and hoping that was the case this time, I fought back the adrenaline and calmly told her that Dr. DeLisi and I would evaluate her when they got back to the house.

It was bad. She was in a lot of pain, and it was obviously not just a sprain. Lillie hadn't exaggerated. Dr. DeLisi and I organized to take her down to the small, rural hospital where he worked in the midst of our Sunday afternoon. We found an X-Ray tech in the hall, who quickly shot pictures. What we saw was not good; 3 broken bones in the middle of her foot, with possible tearing of the ligaments in the middle of her foot (a Lis-Franc fracture, which typically only happens when someone falls from a horse and gets one foot caught in the stirrup). He sent a picture of the X-Ray to an orthopedic surgeon friend, who gave instructions.

Six weeks of non-weight-bearing. Then six weeks more in a cast boot. And we were less than a week into our six-week driving trip, with thousands of miles to go. As it was her right foot, there was no way she could drive. Every bit of driving would be on me, but my right eye got tired and became painful with long periods of driving. We were hobbled, like an unruly horse being broken by a kind but firm trainer.

Finding a wheelchair in rural Texas on a Sunday evening proved to be more difficult than we expected. Finally, we located one at an obscure store we vaguely remembered hearing about—Wal-Mart.

After learning how to stow the chair behind the back seat of the 15-passenger van, we were back on the road. In New Orleans, our dear friend Donna arranged for an electric scooter, which made longer walks more feasible for Elizabeth.

With only one driver, we couldn't travel as far each day. So as I drove, Elizabeth secured places for us to stay each step along the way—such as a Catholic convent in Tallahassee and the parents of a Pioneers missionary we had just met at our debrief time. It was messy being hobbled, but in the process we saw the beautiful mystery of the Body of Christ caring for us. We had a front row seat to God's faithfulness.

Arrows at a homeschool Mom's heart

The next stop on our southern summer tour was our debrief at Pioneers. They had hired a new educational consultant, and she offered to conduct standardized testing for our kids. The previous 2 ½ years had been rough—blindness, near-death illness, unexpected trip back to the US for further eye surgeries, and worsening conflict in South Sudan. Even during the week of debrief, our team had to evacuate again due to increased fighting around Yei. Needless to say, there had been a lot of distractions to their schooling. And, we had realized that we needed to switch math curricula, as they weren't tracking with the one we'd been using. We needed to have the children tested, so we agreed to have it done there, as long as they didn't miss any of the debrief times, sharing their stories with the other missionary kids.

Upon arrival, we learned that they would need to miss some of the debrief time to do the testing.

"But, the other kids will be missing also, so they won't be alone," the consultant assured us.

Test day came. It was to be the first day of the debrief and connect week. We had left South Sudan in April, been home for several weeks, and traveling the rest of the time up until July. They hadn't touched schoolwork for months, and we had abandoned the math curriculum in search of a new one. The kids sat in a large, air-conditioned conference room next to the director's office, while she administered the tests. Most of our kids had never taken a standardized test, and those that had, hadn't done so during the previous 5 years on the field.

"When you are done, you can go back to your session," she explained to the children.

The next day, we met with the educational consultant and our member care representative. She slid the tests across the table to Elizabeth, seated in a wheelchair.

"I don't know what to say," she began with a pained expression on her face. "Let's not even look at these."

She went on to explain that several of our children had done very poorly on the testing, and she was concerned that there was a serious learning problem in a few of them. She was worried that we were limiting their possibilities for the future.

"I'm not sure this one will ever be able to attend college," she said gravely, speaking of one of our older children.

For a homeschooling mother committed to her children, it was devastating. Like arrows at her heart.

After we returned home, she sent a lengthy email with 9 recommendations, which included having one of our children evaluated by a Pediatric Neurologist, delaying our return to the field until the kids demonstrated academic improvement, complying with the educational laws of Florida and Colorado, and that we the parents would be "strongly committed to improving education for their children."

I wrote back to our Member Care representative and the educational consultant. How would they measure our "commitment"? Rather, we felt it was important to simply retest the kids in a better environment, once they were back in the school mode, with some test-taking preparation (like most public schoolchildren), before making any firm decisions. We would also renew our enrollment with the homeschool association in Colorado. We were thankful that Pioneers agreed with our plan and didn't insist on all of the consultant's requirements.

Several months later, the kids retested, and all passed with at least what was expected for the state of Colorado. The one she was concerned about being "ruined" for college immediately enrolled in a community college course, passed the entrance exam, and finished second in her class amongst older students. As we found a groove in some new curricula, the kids started accelerating by leaps and bounds. The whole testing and scrutiny left a sour taste in our mouths, however. We wished we had simply waited to test them until we were back home.

Why was this time of "rest" so messy?

Herding cats

Speaking of tests, I next had to recertify with the American Board of Family Medicine—a 600+ question, one-day exam to demonstrate I still knew what I should know as a family doctor in the US. Elizabeth and I went to a weeklong prep course to help catch me up on the latest research and practice guidelines.

During the conference, Elizabeth ended up on the phone with an angry team member back in South Sudan, after our Area and Regional leaders asked us, the Team Leaders, to tell the last few single missionaries still in Yei that it was time to evacuate. The situation had deteriorated, all those with families had left, and most of the hospital staff had fled. The international security advisor for Pioneers said "enough"—they needed to get out. But they refused, and this strong-willed missionary was angry that we were directing them to leave.

A week later, the Area Leaders visited Yei, and relaxed the orders. The singles could remain. After several weeks, however, things worsened, and the singles finally chose to leave. Later, one of them reflected that she didn't realize how bad things had become there until she got out. This is called the "frog in the kettle" phenomenon in security circles. If you put a frog in a pot of water and turn the heat up ever so slowly, the frog won't notice until it has been boiled alive.

It is said that leading others can be like herding cats. Cats don't like to be led anywhere. Leading missionaries, who by nature are usually strong-willed, called by God, and sometimes overly determined to persevere in their service, was like herding wild cats. And we still hadn't figured it out.

Home assignment was messy and certainly not restful.

We are not essential

Most of the population of more than 150,000 in Yei ran to northern Uganda by December 2016, the very month we planned to return from our second home assignment. The elders of our home church, together with Pioneers, concurred that we should delay our return until we knew where we would return. Would the evacuation be just a few months, or would it drag on for years? No one knew. So we waited.

I once asked our Member Care advisor about the length of Home Assignment.

"We plan for a certain length of time, but in our twenty years on the field, we never once had a Home Assignment that occurred when we expected or lasted as long as intended," Dan explained. "Visa delays, illnesses, changes in our team... all these messed up our plans."

By May 2017, it was clear that the South Sudanese were not returning any time soon. But we felt we needed to return where they were to discern the next steps for *His House of Hope*, reconnect with staff, and put our finger on the pulse of the South Sudanese people again. So it was that we relocated to Moyo, northern Uganda that month.

Home Assignment was much messier than we anticipated. It wasn't restful. True, we did reconnect with friends, family, and supporters, and we stepped out of the near-boiling pot of water long enough to look objectively at our place of service. Most importantly, Home Assignment showed us that we were not essential to the work. God would use us, yes, but He could take care of advancing His kingdom in South Sudan even if we weren't there. And perhaps that advancement required the radically messy situation that was developing in South Sudan.

Home Assignment taught us to depend even more on His strength, to trust His grand maneuvers in the world, even as He hobbled us in both physical and emotional ways.

What do you think is the purpose of Home Assignment?

In what ways should a missionary be 'essential' to the work they are doing? In what ways should he or she *not* be 'essential'?

Chapter 12

A COG in the Wheel: *The Mystery of Belonging*

cog (n.)—1) a tooth on a gear (or cogwheel), fitted into a slot in a gearwheel; 2) a person who plays a minor part in a large organization or activity

When the Deputy Minister of Health was in Yei for a visit to the Evangelical Presbyterian Church of South Sudan (EPC) health facilities, Bishop Taban made sure that Dr. Poole and I were there for the big welcoming event. We made the three mile trip through the teak forest to the EPC compound, which was situated on the banks of the Yei River. Outside the large, open-sided meeting hall with metal roof, the Bishop spotted Elizabeth and I, then walked briskly toward us.

"I have someone I want you to meet," he said. He grabbed my relatively small, white hand in his enormous, black hand, as we strode purposefully through the crowd. I still wasn't used to this—grown men holding hands in public. It was a sign of acceptance and friendship, but it still felt awkward. Elizabeth and I, on the other hand, couldn't hold hands in public. That was not considered appropriate. Cultural differences are often profound and the outward expressions reversed like this.

The Bishop introduced me to the current County Commissioner, and suggested to him that I could give him some medical advice on his chronically swollen legs. I did the best I could briefly, in a public setting, and encouraged him to come by the clinic so we could more properly evaluate him.

The evening ceremony began, with Dr. Poole and I seated on stage right, along with many dignitaries. The "big men" gave speeches, the choir sang, and Bishop got up to speak. At one point in his address, he highlighted the good deeds of the church.

"I want His Excellency the Deputy Minister to know that EPC has brought 3 containers of medical supplies free of charge for the good of the people of South Sudan. EPC has also brought these 2 doctors, from America and Australia," he detailed. Dr. Poole and I gave each other knowing glances and smiles. It struck me then that we were like pawns of the church, listed right after the containers, as if we were goods. It didn't really bother me, but checked me. What was wrong with being a pawn of the indigenous church? Wasn't I called to be a servant of the church?

The Bishop was using us to bring light on the church and a good name to the followers of Jesus. He was also using us to endear EPC to the government and establish a Memorandum of Understanding (MOU) with the Ministry of Health. An MOU would grease the wheels of getting much needed supplies and equipment into the country, without paying exorbitant taxes. This would empower us to take care of more patients, better. So, we were okay with being pawns of the Bishop.

Were we playing chess?! Were we the pieces?!

A week later, walking back to the hospital on a hot afternoon, an image dropped into my mind: *a set of interlocking* cogwheels, *turning each other and spreading out infinitely in every direction.* I'm not the type that gets "visions," but perhaps that's what this was. I felt like I was one of those cogwheels, playing a small but important part in the greater work of God. Some of the cogwheels were larger, some smaller. I realized that each one drove the others, and they still others. I also saw that if one stopped or broke, it impacted the others.

The picture encouraged me. It was easy to develop the feeling that everything depended on me, forgetting the many others that supported me. We often felt discouraged by the lack of visible impact, medically and spiritually. Who were these other cogwheels? And the image was not particularly inspiring, but rather like something out of the industrial revolution, conjuring up images of grey skies, acid rain, and billowing smoke stacks from early American factories.

The Lord had been teaching me that my acceptance and value didn't come from what I accomplished (such as setting up a mission hospital), but simply because He chose me and made me His child. I was a child of God. I belonged to Him, He belonged to me, and believers belonged to each other because we were the Body of Christ. The cogwheels must be believers—members of the kingdom of God. We were all *cogs*. Not very glamorous, unless I understood *cog* to be an acronym for *Child Of God*.

I am valuable because I am a child of God. As are all those who have followed Him. All of us together were children of God fulfilling the purposes for which He created us. **Not glamorous, but glorious.**

Medical work: part of church planting? Proclamation or Presence?

On our survey trip in 2007, we met the Area Leaders with Pioneers, Peter and Kim Johnstone, as we were considering if we should come under a sending agency. We wrestled with the question of whether we "fit" with the mission of Pioneers—to mobilize teams to glorify God among unreached peoples by initiating church planting movements in partnership with local churches.

"How is starting a hospital and helping with an orphanage part of church planting?" we asked them.

"Church planting is a long process and involves many different types of work in the local church," Peter replied. You absolutely fit within the church planting movement.

With that encouragement, we joined.

Traditional church planting focuses on proclamation of the gospel. We usually think of proclamation as speaking or preaching. Colossians 1:24-25 is sometimes translated as Paul stating, *"that I might fully carry out the preaching of the word of God"* (NASB), but a more literal translation reads *"that I might make full the word of God."* He writes this immediately after saying that he rejoices in his sufferings on behalf of the church, which is part of *"filling up what is lacking in Christ's afflictions."* This astounds me! What could Christ lack?! My understanding is that as we suffer with and help those who are suffering, we make Jesus (the Word) "full" or visible since

He is no longer in the world physically. This is the ministry of the presence of Christ.

I believe we are all called to both proclaim Christ with our words and be the physical presence of Christ. To be the presence of Christ involves showing compassion as He did, thereby proclaiming with our actions. Healing was integral to the ministry of Christ. As we provide healthcare, we are the presence of Christ, yet even then we are called to proclaim with our words the Christ whom we follow. We are all called to proclaim and be His presence, but each of us can't do both fully—we need each other.

Healthcare is integral to church planting, because physical health is central in people's lives. If we plant a church that is not relevant to the context and fails to address the crises that people face, they won't come to the church when they are really in trouble—they will resort to their old ways.[1] The church we plant will drift into syncretism.

Early in our time in South Sudan, we witnessed some who attended church on Sunday go for "prayers" in the village when illness came. "Prayers" meant they were calling the witchdoctor for tribal rituals to solve their core needs. In this primitive area with staggeringly poor health statistics, healthcare was an immense practical issue. Having a hospital connected to the church gave those that wanted to follow Jesus a viable, Biblical option, to come for medical treatment combined with prayer to the one true God. It also connected the dots for those who didn't know about Jesus. They witnessed followers of God caring for their physical bodies.

Paul is the icon of church planting to the unreached. In Romans 15:20, he wrote that "...I aspired to preach (proclaim) the gospel, not where Christ was already named, so that I would not build on another man's foundation;" but soon after, he talks of his upcoming relief work among the Jewish Christians. He wasn't just a church planter according to the standard definition. He also followed up with struggling churches, did a lot of writing, and raised funds for relief work. He was the presence of Christ and he proclaimed Christ. There are many facets to the process of launching a church and helping it to maturity.

The Church is called to care for the whole person: spiritual, emotional, and physical. If we plant a church without demonstrating this, we may communicate that God is only concerned with the spirit, and leaves people alone to fend for their emotional and physical health needs. We model an incomplete church with a limited view of the Lord. We fall into the Gnostic error again, showing that the spirit is separate from the mind and body. The truth is that He is Lord of our whole lives. Paul knew this truth.

The question of church planting and medical work often resurfaced, and we saw the answer played out in the life of another Paul.

Abini Paul

In the early months after our arrival, Paul approached me after church. Seated in an old metal wheelchair, his legs were spastic, often shaking uncontrollably as he tried to make it through the worship time. Often he had to leave early because of difficulties controlling his bladder. He came about once or twice a month, and didn't do much else. His home was three-quarters of a mile from Harvesters, across dirt paths. If it rained, he couldn't make it in his chair designed only for smooth, hard surfaces. Before he had a wheelchair, boys from the orphanage brought him in a wheelbarrow.

"Can you help my legs?" he asked in broken English.

"Uh, well, why don't you come to the clinic tomorrow," I reluctantly stammered. I had no idea what I could offer this man. Did he expect me to get him walking again? We were there to start a women's and children's hospital, and here was a male paraplegic. This was not the plan.

Fortunately, Elizabeth was listening better than I.

"Perhaps Paul is the person of peace who will open up relationships in the community," she wisely counseled. I still had my doubts, especially in my medical knowledge. I was not a neurologist.

I met with him and learned that he had contracted tuberculosis about ten years before, and the mycobacteria had attacked his spine, destroying one of his vertebrae. This was known as Pott's disease. When the bone in his back collapsed, it damaged his spinal cord, leading to his paralysis. His leg muscles were tight, and any attempt to stretch them led to a revolt of rhythmic spasms.

I sent an email to Royce, my physical therapist friend from Swink, Colorado. He sent a treatment plan for Paul, which we put into motion. We helped Paul out of his chair onto an old mattress on the floor of the one-room clinic, and began gently stretching his legs and back. It was stifling in the little clinic, and the work wasn't very pleasant. I wasn't very optimistic (I grew up in Seattle and blame my tendency toward pessimism on the 21 years of cloudy weather I endured).

As we stretched, we counted to 30, to 60, all in Arabic. Paul taught me to count, which is very important in Juba Arabic, as the names of the days of the week and months are based on numbers. Later, when we started doing antenatal care and deliveries, this proved essential, as I needed to find out the date of the patient's last period to determine the due date. He also brought long lists of carefully written words for me to learn. He was my first language helper. If nothing else, he was blessed by the opportunity to give to me, and I was certainly blessed by the help learning the language.

But he did get better. His spasticity decreased, and he reported that he could sense when his bladder was full. When we transferred him to the floor and back to his chair, he was able to assist and bear some of his weight.

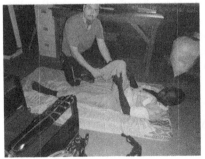

After several months of this, our first supply container arrived, from Samaritan's Purse - World Medical Mission. We had given them guidelines of what we needed, but the warehouse manager told me that they would fill it with other things that might be useful.

"We don't ship air!" he said boldly.

At the back of the container, we discovered six large boxes labeled "PET." Was this some kind of joke? Or mistake? We opened one, and discovered the "PET" was a personal energy transporter. Still, we didn't understand what it was exactly, as it was in many pieces, with a bag of tools and bolts.

I called the students James and Aaron to our house to help me put one together. When it was done, before us stood a hand trike, with thick, solid rubber wheels made for muddy, uneven roads, and a cargo area behind the seat. We presented it to Paul, and it revolutionized his life.

Suddenly, Paul could make it to church in half the time, using half the energy, even after a heavy rain. He started coming to the mid-week prayer time in the local language and participating in other activities around the community.

Once the hospital opened, he and several others from the church began going to the hospital to talk and pray with patients several times a week. He had the gift of intercessory prayer. After my eye problems began, Paul came to our front verandah to pray with me multiple times. When he prayed, his eyes were shut tight and his face tense with fervor. His prayer was an intense, staccato of rapid-fire Arabic, clean and distinct, filled with meaning (as much as I could catch!). He prayed with earnestness that I have seen in few others, and he encouraged me deeply.

But Paul still struggled. As he got more active, he developed sores from the time he spent in the hand trike. On some days, I was inwardly annoyed when Paul showed up with yet another problem. He would catch me in the hallway as I was rushing to the labor ward, where half a dozen women were in labor. One would likely need a C-section. And we had 60-70 patients to see in antenatal clinic. He felt like a distraction to the "real work" of the hospital. Thankfully, it wasn't all up to me. *The team, and God, made sure I didn't interfere with His work.*

Kitty, the missionary nurse, had experience in wound care, so she and Katherine worked faithfully to deal with his ulcers, though they never fully healed. The hand trike wore down, and parts started failing. Chris Low, a missionary jack-of-all-trades, welded and fashioned new parts to keep him rolling.

At first, it seemed that Paul prayed to enable the medical work that we were doing at the hospital. As time went on, I realized that we were treating him so he could do the work of prayer, and glorify God. If we did nothing more than enable those like Paul to do the work of the church, we obeyed and completed the work He sent us to do.

So many *cogs* in the wheel, all playing a part in accomplishing the work. **And the real work was prayer.**

Betti was a 24-year-old woman previously treated in Juba and Kampala for an invasive molar pregnancy, a type of cancer of the uterus, with possible spread of cancerous cells to her lungs. We started treatment with methotrexate, a chemotherapy drug. Her mother was disturbing the other patients at night by wailing and praying loudly, so we consulted our South Sudanese pastor.

Pastor Hillary and Paul came to talk and pray with Betti and her mother. The patient confessed to submitting herself to three abortions, and consulting a witchdoctor after her husband secretly divorced her. She had hidden all of this from her family, and was overcome with guilt and shame. She knew she might die, and was afraid because of her sin.

That day, Betti "aglibu geliba bitoo le Yesua"—turned her heart to Jesus. She repented and turned from darkness to light.

Several days later, Paul stopped by and prayed with her. It was a powerful thing to watch the local church in action, getting at the spiritual disease while we attempted to treat her physical disease. And, seeing the pastor train and equip members of the Body, like Paul, to continue the task of the Church.

As her treatment progressed, her white blood counts began to drop dangerously low, and an overwhelming pneumonia ravaged her body. She remained near death for several days, on oxygen, antibiotics, and propped up to sleep. In the last few days of her life, Pastor Hillary, two Egyptian doctors in training, and I gathered around her to pray in Arabic.

So many *cogs* in the wheel, working together to usher a saint into glory.

As I looked at Betti, I had the distinct feeling that while she had only been a follower of Jesus for several days, she would likely soon know Him far better than I—as she would see Him face to face.

Betti died on Nov 8, 2014. At the very same moment, two emergency cases arrived: undiagnosed twins presenting with a footling breech and a young mother in labor with fetal distress. We needed to do simultaneous Caesarean sections. A visiting surgical team delivered the twins while we scrambled to set up the second operating room to deliver the baby in distress. All of the babies were born alive and healthy.

I left the hospital after the last Caesarean, the teams having completed five C-sections, producing seven healthy babies in 24 hours. I passed by Betti's ward. The family was not doing the loud, hopeless wailing typical after a death, but instead was grieving as those with hope. Betti had died reconciled to God. They quietly covered her with a pink embroidered sheet—her story, at least on this earth, complete.

We were a medical *cog* in the wheel, supporting the Church and giving her a way to meet the serious medical needs around her. God was already at work in the Church, and we were mainly there to fan the flame of the local believers such as Abini Paul.

African Theologians

I was intrigued to hear local church leaders engage their people in God's Word. The illustrations were drastically different, like Pastor Hillary describing the awfulness of sin. In some villages, he detailed, if someone killed another person, they would tie the victim's dead body on the back of the perpetrator. It would remain there until it began to rot. Worms would begin eating the dead body, and burrow into the flesh of the guilty one carrying the corpse. The Sunday morning service was graphic, but the people were captivated by the vivid description of the seriousness of sin.

When a missionary spoke, our analogies often missed the mark. Speaking about Elijah and the prophets of Baal, an American pastor preached about our "mountaintop experience" and being "down in the valley." He was met with a lot of blank stares, as mountaintops are symbolic of problems or are the places of demon worship (as they also were in Elijah's time). Valleys are seen as good, fertile places. The opposite of our Western ideas. For this reason, we tried to leave the preaching to Pastor Hillary, and pray for him instead.

If I did teach or preach, I consulted the Africa Bible Commentary, a single volume commentary written and edited entirely by African theologians. Pastor Rumrill, from our small Colorado church, recommended it to me before we moved to Africa. He used it not out of need to speak to an African congregation, but simply because he found the authors gave such unique insights into Scripture.

In the foreword of the Africa Bible Commentary, the late British theologian John Stott states that it is "a publishing landmark...its foundation is biblical, its perspective African, and its approach to controversial questions balanced. I intend to use it myself in order to gain African insights into the Word of God. Indeed, I hope it will have a worldwide readership."[2]

Many sub-cultures in East Africa are quite similar to those of the Bible, giving them an advantage over Westerners in "reading between the lines" of Scripture. They often understand what was left unsaid by the writers. Most African theologians have practical experience engaging with spiritual warfare, poverty, suffering, war, and death. They have experiential knowledge of walking with the Holy Spirit and allowing Him to work in the lives of the Church.

Pastor Hillary, our pastor in Yei, South Sudan

Pastor Jimmy, our Ugandan pastor during our last few years in East Africa, breathed much new insight into how we understood God's Word. When he shared from the story of Mary and Martha, I realized how I as a Westerner was quite sympathetic to "type A" Martha, because her busy personality was valued in our culture. But this personality is not necessarily valued by Jesus. Pastor Jimmy pointed out that people followed Mary to Jesus, but there is no record of others following Martha to Him (Luke 10:38-42, John 11).

There is now a movement in the global theological community that the Majority World or Global South (Latin America, Asia, and Sub-Saharan Africa) should contribute substantially and uniquely to the Church's understanding of Scripture and the deeper realities of God. We experienced this first hand at our area conferences with Pioneers, where our teachers were largely African theologians.

Ben was a fellow Pioneers missionary from the US, working on his doctoral dissertation at a Kenyan theological college. He taught university and masters-level students in addition to being taught by African professors. God used Ben to connect this rich reservoir of knowledgeable church leaders with Pioneers. Having sat at the feet of these instructors, I would recommend that Westerners consider going to the Majority, non-Western world to pursue theological education.

Another effect of Ben doing missions on a student visa was enabling the church to send out its own. The East African church was looking for a vehicle through which to send missionaries to the rest of the world, and Pioneers provided such a framework. As of this writing, a mobilization office has formed and is preparing to send out cross-cultural workers from East Africa to the world.

Sadly, some Westerners still hold the misconception that the Majority World lacks theological depth. "We from the West bring the theological knowledge, while those in Africa provide the zeal and strength to get the Great Commission done," commented one older British missionary, to a room containing multiple Africans with doctorates and books to their names.

I replied to him that I saw quite the opposite. Increasingly, we encountered short-term workers from America who had lots of zeal but very little theological depth, while we were surrounded by a wealth of wisdom right there—our African brothers and sisters.

We were grateful to learn more about the Lord and His Word from these African theologians, and I hope I can study more under them.

A niche for our cog

As medical missionaries, what was our part in church planting? We stumbled across at least one niche. The Islamic government of Khartoum had terrorized the local indigenous church since the 1950's. This left a lot of emotional baggage. It was difficult for people in the local church to see those who had dropped bombs on them as a mission field, as ones who needed God's love and forgiveness. As expatriates, we didn't have their history.

I befriended Sharif, a shop owner in Yei who came from the Darfur region of Sudan. We verbally exchanged our names and phone

numbers in Arabic, entering them into our phones. I showed him my phone to confirm the spelling of his name. He shrugged "I don't know" and smiled at what I had written. He entered my name as he heard it into his phone, and showed me the entry—all in Arabic script. I did likewise—shrugged and smiled! After several invitations, he came to consult about his back

Pastor Jimmy (left), our pastor from Moyo, Uganda with Pastor Tilton, our pastor from New Orleans

problems. He was a towering African man, dark skin contrasted by his flowing white Arab garments and traditional decorative cap. It was our hope that the compassion they received at the hospital would provide an inroads to the Muslim community.

An Eritrean Muslim man brought his wife to Bet Eman having high blood pressure, prolonged seizures, and in labor. She had eclampsia, a dangerous condition in pregnancy. I could hardly reach the patient because of the seven family members crowding around the delivery bed as she repeatedly convulsed violently. We managed to communicate our need to take her for C-section and they consented. Despite a difficult surgery, she and the baby survived and recovered well. During her weeklong recovery, the father told me of a conversation with his friend.

"I told my friend, 'You must come to Bet Eman,' but he said he couldn't because it was a Christian hospital and they wouldn't treat Muslims. So I said to him, 'No, you can come! They treat everyone!'"

His report encouraged me. That is what we hoped for. He later had us over to his family's hotel in Yei, including a traditional Eritrean coffee ceremony. We were excited about what the Lord was doing to develop relationships in this community, and I was excited to drink good, strong coffee! I had a few Arabic Bibles on my shelf in hopes of beginning a "discovery Bible study" with these businessmen.

Our non-medical missionary teammates began a unique way of developing relationships with the Pakistani Muslim shop owners—playing cricket on Sunday afternoons! As American blokes, they had to first learn the rules from our Aussie mates. Soon they were being invited into homes for meals and celebrations after the cricket matches.

Sadly, the civil war disrupted most of these budding relationships, and we never saw the "fruit." Perhaps God will still use those interactions as part of bringing others to Himself.

Mobilizing Medical Missionaries from the Muslim World

Another niche surfaced at Bet Eman. A missionary doctor in southern Egypt was training Egyptian doctors in the specialty of Family Medicine. They were struggling to get the young doctors enough hands-on experience in obstetrics and pediatrics. Through common friends, he contacted me and we agreed to have his resident doctors come to us for 3 months of training in these disciplines.

Most of the young Egyptian healthcare professionals had never been out of Egypt. It was a big step of faith for them to leave the comfort and familiarity of Egypt and come to rugged South Sudan without paved roads or air conditioning. "Sam" was one young physician who came. He not only gained valuable medical experience, but he was also challenged to trust God more than he ever had before. He was stretched physically and emotionally, and witnessed the struggles that the South Sudanese faced every day. As a young doctor from a predominantly Muslim nation, Sam has the potential to quietly enter the Arab world as a medical missionary in ways that a white Westerner never could. Perhaps our niche was to raise up those like Sam to go and make disciples at the "ends of the earth" where we weren't able.

We were privileged to see the reality that mission work is changing. No longer is it "the West to the rest." Missionaries are now springing up from everywhere, to everywhere.

A difficult richness: multicultural teams

We were there to make disciples. We all agreed on this "Great Commission" set out so clearly by Jesus (Matt 28: 19-20). But to be known as disciples of Jesus, He himself said we must love one another (John 13:35). In this country wracked by decades of civil war, the locals needed to see that the missionaries cared for one another. If we couldn't figure out how to get along, we didn't have anything to offer them.

The "Yei Team" of Pioneers missionaries was reminiscent of the "A-Team" of the 1980's action television series. Only instead of "Mr. T" we had Dr. Fairy and Dr. Fool! Well, we weren't as exciting as the "A-team," but we did bring different gifts, personalities, and cultures into the mix, making team-building something we had to work on intentionally.

Initially, we thought our like-mindedness would carry us through our differences. After all, we were Western medical professionals with a heart for discipleship, quality medical work, doing ministry as families, caring for orphans, and supporting the local church. But within the very close community that we formed, our differences seemed to grow like a nagging tumor.

There were philosophical ministry differences. We had different views on leadership; some liked more structure, while others wanted things loose and equal. How should we walk out servant leadership in a culture that expected a great "power distance" between the leader and followers? If we were too "servant-like" in our leadership, our staff might discount us as weak and ineffectual. Some missionaries leaned towards idealism, others toward realism, or even pessimism. How much should we trust our local staff? As we encountered various trials in the ministry, these differences rubbed and grated against each other, as if shaving the dirt-clad skin off of a cassava root.

We underestimated the differences between our various Western worldviews—Australian, New Zealand, and American. It seemed silly to be reading about Australian culture while serving in the tropics of South Sudan, but that's exactly what our Area Leader suggested we do. Becoming students of one another proved to be essential to loving one another.

And while there were cultural differences, within each culture there were great personality differences. We struggled for three years. Finally, at one of our area retreats, we asked for help from our sending base. They took us through a "Clock Walk," in which we enacted how our different personality types engaged in a team decision. It was eye opening to see several members begin talking immediately and quickly move on to logistical issues. Others remained quiet for a long time, still processing the reasons and many possible outcomes of the decision. We learned that some needed to be purposefully quiet and listen, while we as a team needed to seek out the thoughts of the quieter ones. We returned to Yei with a renewed effort to understand one another better.

Life on a multi-cultural team was messy. But the richness of it was a foretaste of the kingdom of God's mystery. And it was worth it.

Pilots & Peacemakers

Part of our role in church planting was enabling other missionaries to stay on the field and be a *cog* in the wheel of His kingdom. When a pilot developed increased asthma problems, his license to fly was jeopardized. I changed his medications, and after a few weeks, he was breathing easily again. Things went both ways, though. He was the very same pilot who had flown Elizabeth and I to Kenya for my second eye surgery. He had helped us continue in our time of need.

Shelvis and Nancy arrived to Yei within months of us. They were both ordained pastors from the US. Shelvis was an exuberant, encouraging guy with a history of playing professional (American) football. His wife Nancy was energetically compassionate, skilled at asking just the right questions to unearth a person's trauma history. Their mission work was in the area of reconciliation and peace building, something essential to a country coming out of a lifetime of war.

Shelvis and I occasionally got together to talk and pray, once trying out the rumored espresso machine at an Ethiopian bakery in town. It was almost too good to believe!

No, it *was* too good to believe.

"It's spoiled," the man behind the pastry counter explained about the espresso machine sitting idly by. Meanwhile, the baked goods behind the glass lost their appeal when we saw the multitude of bugs sampling them ahead of us. We settled for a soda and walked on down the road.

We later jubilated with Shelvis and Nancy as they shared the news of their first pregnancy. Elizabeth and I were also nervous. Not only had I seen harrowing complications of childbirth in my patients, Elizabeth had experienced difficulties with several of her own births.

"We are so excited for you!" we began. "When are you planning to head back to the US?" we inquired, hoping they wouldn't push it too late.

"In November sometime," they said.

We were relieved. She would be on the plane before she was 34 weeks. Or so we thought.

When October 2012 rolled around, Nancy was 33 weeks along in her pregnancy—still 7 weeks from her due date. They were scheduled to fly to the US a few days later. Our family had just returned from the holiday in which Given fell and broke her head.

It was Saturday, and I was on call.

The hospital had been open for six months and hadn't had any preterm babies yet. I was dealing with an elderly woman who was actively dying when Elizabeth called.

"Nancy is here, and you'd better come see her now," she began urgently. "She has 'the look.'" Young doctors learn to diagnose labor, but Elizabeth had been

Aussie and American missionary kids: messy fun together!

around enough to recognize the real thing with a glance.

I promptly made my way to the operating theatre, where the staff had taken her for privacy. She was in full-blown preterm labor, and despite medications and fluids, there was no stopping her. After only 45 minutes, Nancy delivered a baby boy. The first preterm baby born at Bet Eman was also the first American citizen born in the new country of South Sudan.

Our missionary team scrambled to set up "bubble CPAP" (continuous positive airway pressure) for the first time. I had seen it done at other mission hospitals, and missionary nurse Katherine worked out the details. We cut one half of an oxygen tube and placed it a few inches under water in a cup, while clamping the other cut portion. The oxygen flowed from the concentrator through the other half of the tubing, into baby's tiny nostrils, with more pressure than usual.

This would keep his not-yet-fully mature airways open. We started intravenous fluids and antibiotics and began the complicated process of transferring a premature neonate by air to Nairobi. More than 36 hours later, the neonatal transport team took him away to continue his care.

Jordan Eman, as he was named, did well and is now a healthy boy. His middle name is the Arabic word for *faith*, after the hospital where he was born. The story of his birth was even featured in a special segment on CNN. He later returned to South Sudan with his parents, and our children became his favorite babysitters (and he, their favorite "babysittee"!).[3]

Shelvis and Nancy further developed the *Reconcile Peace Institute*, a 3-month course for community leaders from the many tribes of South Sudan. As Shelvis became aware of the hospital's need for blood donors, he tried to get his students to donate.

Few would. To most tribes, blood is life, and to share blood with someone outside the tribe was unheard of. Dr. Poole, Shelvis, and I put our heads together and saw opportunity. Dr. Poole and I alternated sharing at their devotion time, looking at how the blood of Christ has reconciled us and broken down the dividing wall of hostility.

> *"But now in Christ Jesus you who formerly were far off have been brought near by the* **blood** *of Christ. For He Himself is our* **peace**, *who made both groups into one and broke down the barrier of the dividing wall"* (Eph 2:13-14).

We shared how we had seen a Dinka man give his blood to save the life of a Kakwa woman. A Bari woman could give hers to save a Nuer. Australian blood could be given to a South Sudanese child (provided we matched the blood types!). The very tribes that fought had the same blood. We might look different on the outside, but the lifeblood in each of us could help another. We challenged them to take a practical step of reconciliation, and give blood. Some gave. Others declined, often for fear of a positive screening test for hepatitis or HIV.

We were fortunate to be *cogs* in the wheel of God's kingdom with the likes of Shelvis and Nancy. They continued to be great encouragers of us over the years, especially as both they and we were forced to leave our lives and ministries in Yei.

Years later, after we had both relocated to northern Uganda, they came to live with our children for one week. They did this to enable Elizabeth and I to return to the US so we could surprise her parents with our presence at their 50th wedding anniversary—a very important milestone, especially given her Cuban heritage and the Latino importance of the *familia*. It was almost unthinkable

for us to leave all our children in rural Africa while we flew around the world, visited for 3 days, and returned exactly one week after we left. Had they not unanimously offered from a sense of calling from the Lord, we never would have considered doing such a trip away from our kids. Shelvis and Nancy not only took care of our children, they immersed them in fun activities and poured God's Word into them. More than we could have ever hoped for. It was the Body of Christ at work again.

The local church

We were pawns of the local church. But, we were willing pawns. Servants. We were *cogs*, children of God, in the wheel of His kingdom.

"I do my share on behalf of His body, which is the church..." (Col 1:24)

The Bishop was our local authority and protection. The government would have had a hard time kicking us out, because we were an extension of the local church. We submitted to his leadership, and he didn't interfere with the details of the medical work. He intermittently hinted at the vision he had for the hospital, and after counsel with others, we sought to walk that out if possible.

There were times of hurt and strain in our relationship with the Bishop, and our vastly different cultures made for misunderstandings at times. Yet there was love for one another and for the God we served. After he and his wife adopted a young South Sudanese boy, he regularly brought his family for care at *His House of Hope*.

More than all the activities we did, the Lord wanted us to love one another, to be one, to love His Church. This applied to us as missionaries with respect to the local church, and with our fellow missionaries. We were not all the same; we each had our own, unique role to play in His kingdom. We are a body, and we can't accomplish the mission of the Church without each other.

God doesn't *need* our service; He *wants* our **fellowship—with Him and one another**. He wants us to **belong**, to Him and to each other. *The Church is the method God has chosen to reveal His mystery of belonging to the world.*

"To me... this grace was given... to bring to light what is the administration of the **mystery**... *so that the manifold wisdom of God* **might now be made known through the church**" *(Eph 3:8-10)*

As messy as it is, we must never abandon the Church as we carry out mission work, whether it is the church that sent us, the church with whom we work, or the church we are trying to plant. For some reason, fully known only to God, He chose the Church to display His wisdom and glory to the world. And we need all of us, broken as we are, to show His magnificence for the nations to see.

How do you feel when you read that God "chose the Church to display His wisdom and glory to the world"?

What is your "niche" in the Global Church?

How is Jesus calling you to function in His Body?

Chapter 13
Abscess of the Soul: *Pride, Power and Control*

I felt like I was learning the Juba Arabic language pretty well after nine months of living in South Sudan. As I confidently strode through the hospital, I even tried a little humor. They laughed! Wow—they say humor is an advanced part of language acquisition, and here I was less than a year into learning, cracking jokes! I felt good about myself. Maybe I had the gift of tongues after all…

As I leaned over to examine the next patient, my name badge dangled between us. The photo caught my eye as it spun around. It was that of one of our cleaners—an African woman! I must have grabbed her ID card instead of mine from the holder near the door. They weren't laughing at my jokes—they were laughing at me, wearing someone else's picture. I was the "kawaja" (foreigner), and God checked me when I started to think more highly of myself than I ought.

Much of the messiness of missions buds from our own sinful tendencies. The pressures of the mission field often squeezed out the pride, power, and control issues from the depths of those called to difficult places. It was a mystery to me that God chose to work through broken people like us.

I noticed a disturbing trend in myself as the hospital began to grow and find success. When I did something well, I felt overly good about myself. Okay, I was prideful. I had learned from an early age that my accomplishments gained me approval from others. And through my years in church and professional training, I had learned the fine art of calling attention to my deeds yet appearing humble, because that is socially (and spiritually)
more acceptable.

I had learned it so well that I often fooled myself.

People helped me along the way. They were very impressed that my wife and I were "giving it all up" to help people that had great needs. And we were even taking all of our children! We tried to deflect these comments, but deep inside we tended to agree with them and were glad they noticed our sacrifice. Many missionaries catch this disease and arrive to the field with the attitude of "well, aren't these people lucky that I'm here finally?!" As we begin ministry, our delusions are fortified—people do seem to need us, and for that matter, so does God! We feel that we are indispensable. If we step away, our patients will begin dying. If we aren't there to preach and teach, those that die will have never heard the good news. "Pride is the delusion that God, if he exists, is awfully lucky I've shown up and should mind his p's and q's lest I change my mind"[1]

The problem was, when things didn't go well—as they often didn't—I slipped into despair. My world was rocked. Maybe I didn't have what it took. Maybe I wasn't called by God to be there. I was on a roller coaster of unhealthy emotions, and my accomplishments (or lack thereof) kept ratcheting my rickety car up the next incline of track. "The twin of pride is despair...the lie that God, if he exists, is too inept or distracted or apathetic to even notice us, let alone come to our aid."[2]

Pride results from reliance on human ability amidst the gift of successful outcomes. Despair comes from reliance on human ability amidst overwhelmingly difficult circumstances. If pride and despair are twins, their mother is the delusion of self-reliance.

Pride is like an abscess.

We treated a lot of abscesses in South Sudan. The constant heat, seasonal rains, and lack of freezing made for soil that was rich in microbes. The bacteria had already received abundant life from Jesus the Creator.

Any little scratch could turn into a raging infection overnight.

An abscess is an infection that is "walled off" from the body to prevent the bacteria from taking over the whole organism. Some call it a "pus pocket," and it is filled with a mixture of bacteria, decaying cells, and immune cells from the body. If it is near the skin, it is red, warm, and painful; in this location, it is easy to identify and expel the infection. The worst abscesses, however, are those deep in the tissue and hardly noticeable. One can barely detect a faint bulge of the skin and there is slight tenderness if one presses deeply.

Draining an abscess is messy, painful, and anesthetics don't help, because the pH (acidity) of the abscess prevents the medicine from working. It must be released surgically, and when opened, it stinks up the whole room. It was foul, yet in a visceral way, it was one of the most satisfying treatments we did—to forcibly expel disease, wash it out, and allow the healing process to begin. If the infection had been there long, the doctor had to probe the abscess with a metal instrument to break up the small pockets within the abscess. Very painful. And necessary. I know because I inflicted this crucial pain on many patients. And then I became one myself.

I developed an abscess on the back of my neck just as Dr. Poole arrived in South Sudan with his family. I was ill with typhoid at the same time. I was a mess.

After he settled in, I asked to go under his knife. Dr. Poole tried to numb the area, and then stabbed into the red, inflamed area on the back of my neck with the scalpel blade. The pain in that location was excruciating—perhaps because it was so close to my spinal cord! He moved the small metal hemostat around in the newly created cavity as I hugged a pillow and clenched the edge of the mahogany dining table. The room began to spin and a warm wave of nausea crested in me. He washed the wound with saline and began packing it with antibacterial gauze. Every time he changed the packing during the following week, it was like a hot iron probing inside. I had newfound respect for the patients I had treated.

Pride was like an abscess in South Sudan. Those in power set up their own little kingdoms. If one tribe injured another, the victimized tribe was sure to retaliate, to defend their honor (the "noble" face of pride). Pride was endemic there, having a stronghold over the people, even spreading to churches and mission groups. Easy-going, egalitarian Westerners arrived, casually claiming to be there to humbly serve and having "no agenda." When someone described himself as being humble, it meant he wanted to *appear* humble. Perhaps he hoped to convince you (and himself), contrary to your perception of him. *If humility is genuine, others see it, and there is no need to say it.*

Many missionaries succumbed to the wiles of pride, as if there was a special on this particular sin at the local supermarket. It was a deal too good for most of us to resist—we bought in.

When others joined the team, it was great to finally share in the work with them. They brought new ideas, fresh energy, and capacity to carry the physical and emotional load of running a hospital. But I noticed resentment rise in me when our staff praised the new missionaries.

"Dr. Poole is such a great teacher!" exclaimed our lab tech, Frazer. "He is the best. It is so good that he has come." Rather than rejoicing with him, I found my flesh offended at the comments, as if his happiness about Dr. Poole meant he didn't appreciate me. I was so sadly selfish and prideful.

Then there were the "new ideas" that our teammates brought. Often, they weren't new; they were concepts that we ourselves had tried to introduce, only to be shot down. The new folks would present the same ideas, and the leadership readily accepted them.

I knew I had a deep abscess of pride in me, but wasn't sure how to deal with it. As I read through 1 Corinthians, I stumbled across two surgical instruments the Lord wanted to wield on me, *that God would test our work* and *I was not to judge others' motives.*

First, the fact that God would test each of our "work" by fire and only that which was based on Christ would last. I didn't need to compare and compete with my teammates. God would test what we did, and He would decide if it was done on the basis of Jesus or not. Each of us was responsible to Him alone for what we did. My concern was that what I did came from the foundation of my relationship with Him. Truly, it was God's work, and our work as a team—I couldn't claim anything as mine.

*What then is Apollos? And what is Paul? Servants through whom you believed, even as the Lord gave opportunity to each one. I planted, Apollos watered, but **God was causing the growth**. So then neither the one who plants nor the one who waters is anything, but **God who causes the growth**. Now he who plants and he who waters are one but each* *will receive his own reward according to his own labor...* **But each man must be careful how he builds on it**. *For no man can lay a foundation other than the one which is laid, which is Jesus Christ... Each man's work will become evident; for the day will show it because it is to be revealed with fire, and* **the fire itself will test the quality of each man's work** *(1 Cor 3:5-13, NASB; emphasis mine).*

We had planted, and others were watering. We were one, on the same team. Dr. Poole was my Apollos. Through His Word, God realigned me. It was God who caused the growth, and each of our work would be tested, as to whether it was based on Christ.

Secondly, I was not to judge another person's motives. On a cross-cultural team, this was a real temptation, especially when the other person's words or actions seemed to me to demonstrate pride or selfishness. The Lord was showing me that I could never truly know another's motives, and besides, it wasn't my business—it was between that one and God. If my brother or sister was engaging in outward, sinful behavior, then it was my duty to confront them. *"But actually, I wrote to you not to associate with any so-called brother if he is an immoral person... Do you not judge those who are within the church?" (1 Cor 5:11-12).*

But if I just suspected wrong motives, I needed to leave it alone.

Therefore do not go on passing judgment before the time, but wait until the Lord comes who will both bring to light the things hidden in the darkness and disclose the motives of men's hearts; and then each man's praise will come to him from God (1 Cor 4:5).

I felt the vise grip of pride and despair loosen as I attempted to daily walk out these truths with the Holy Spirit's reminding.

But His greatest tool to produce humility is affliction. *"He leads the afflicted (or humble) in justice, and He teaches the afflicted (or humble) His way"* (Psalm 25:9, NASB). The Hebrew word in this passage can be translated as either humble or afflicted, indicating how closely tied they are. Truly humble people have walked through affliction and been broken. We're not there yet, but through the loss of sight, broken relationships that we can't fix, and crushed hopes, He is gradually leading us to a deeper dependence on Him, while chipping away at the illusion of pride.

Pride, Power & Control in Ministry

Pride easily infected many of us in South Sudan. It was endemic in the culture. There was almost a palpable vibe in the air that bred it. Why was this?

I believe it was a combination of individual sin, societal patterns, and spiritual forces at work. A spiritual stronghold grows when Satan plays on particular sin patterns that have developed over many centuries within a culture. He and his demonic forces plant thoughts, encouraging those sin patterns in the residents— including foreigners. The thoughts give birth to sin and thwart many good plans. And then we are shocked that we ourselves are falling into the same bad patterns as those we came to serve.

We came to South Sudan in 2011 with visions of not only opening the hospital, but also of contributing to the health of the orphans on the compound. At an early staff meeting, the orphanage nurse commented on the increase in cases of malaria amongst the children. They all slept under mosquito nets, as was recommended. A few moments later, another staff shared about the older children doing extra evening studying.

"Where are they studying at night?" I asked. Up until that point, I had been mostly silent.

"In the dining hall, where there are lights powered by the generator," the orphanage director explained.

"I think their late-night studying is increasing their malaria exposure," I observed. The dining hall had a roof but was completely open on the sides. "Is there another way we can allow them to study where they aren't in the open air next to a light, getting so many mosquito bites?"

We didn't solve the problem then, but I did discover a new problem! I soon learned that the orphanage staff didn't appreciate my input. They were offended by my suggestions, as perhaps what they had been doing had had negative effects on the children. Was that pride on their part? I'm not sure of what was going on inside them, but pride and desire for power often manifested as control. Who controlled certain activities? Who had the power to shut down a program? Was it pride on my part to think that I could speak into the educational and health challenges they faced, after we'd been there only a few months? Unwittingly, I had flagged these issues of power and control.

Power and control ran both ways. When we traveled to Kenya to learn from other mission hospitals, one of the ministry leaders decided to utilize the hospital lab supplies to test all the orphans for HIV. We received an email that all of the test supplies were gone, unwittingly disrupting our careful planning and ordering of supplies, which had to be brought in from Uganda. Unfortunately, the nurse who performed the tests didn't conduct them properly, and there were many false-positives. For over a year, we were under the mistaken belief that several of the children had HIV. When we finally retested the orphans, with lab techs using the correct protocols, none were found to have HIV.

We were angry that this ministry leader had stepped into the medical arm of the ministry, which we had understood to be our responsibility. The board discussed it and backed us on this situation. That non-medical leader should not have conducted medical tests using hospital supplies. Issues of power and control permeated life on the field.

"So, when do you think you and Mama Elizabeth are going to take over?" asked the founder of the ministry casually. It was difficult to tell if she was fishing for our willingness or asking out of fear.

"Never," I said simply. We had no interest in being in charge of the orphanage, school, church, and the hospital. We understood our role to be about bettering the health of the community, which included the people in all of those areas.

After several more clashes over advice about the orphans, the leadership verbalized their feelings more clearly.

"The orphanage is not your area," we were told. We were confused. We thought they wanted us to contribute to the health and well-being of the orphans, not simply put up a hospital. We had a heart to prevent disease, not just react to it. Besides, the children at the orphanage were becoming our children's friends, and we hated to see them sick.

The hospital and our home were built on the other side of the south fence of the orphanage. In one meeting, a comment was made to us to "stay on your side of the fence." This phrase became symbolic of our relationship with the ministry as a whole from that point onwards. Saddened, but unsure what else to do, we pulled back, put our heads down, and plodded on with the development of the hospital and staff.

There were many crossover issues, however. Food for the hospital patients and staff was prepared at the central kitchen by cooks paid from the hospital budget. The main guard for the orphanage supervised the hospital guards also. The staff all compared salaries, which led to discord. The orphanage staff complained that the children from the orphanage shouldn't have to wait to be seen at the hospital, whereas we felt the obligation to take care of emergency cases first, whether from the orphanage or the community.

We continued to dialogue about these problems. I was thankful that the others on our team had more patience than I to carefully work out new systems such as seeing the orphans early in the morning before the clinic rush began. The system would work well for a while, but over time the orphanage personnel would fail to bring them at the appointed time, or we would be short-staffed, and it would no longer function as it was meant. The issue would again be brought up in a meeting. Increasingly, we felt a lack of trust from the leadership.

Christopher and Georgia came to help at the orphanage, but their job description wasn't clear at the beginning. He was direct, blunt, and had a strong personality. Our families became fast friends. He and I met weekly with a few other male missionaries to share and pray together. After six months, the missionary leading the compound stepped down and left Yei. Christopher was the clear choice to replace him, and the board called on him to do just that.

Power does strange things to people.

In a leadership meeting, our African pastor and compound director commented on plans for dealing with a certain situation. From their body language, I sensed they were saying, "Don't do it," though they didn't come out and say so. I was learning that their cultural value of preserving the relationship and honoring us (as their patrons or benefactors) made it difficult for them to contradict us in a formal setting. I confirmed this after the meeting in a more informal discussion where they felt the freedom to speak their minds.

I reviewed the meeting with Christopher. He was convinced that they loved the idea, and listened only briefly to my interpretation and follow up conversation. He thought the suggested plan of action was good, and since they didn't disagree in the meeting, he would proceed. Power was affecting him. Since he had the authority, he felt that his interpretation was correct.

Scovia was an orphan girl who was thought to be seventeen years old. She began having times of depression alternating with periods of being agitated and unable to sleep. During her times of agitation, she became increasingly violent, slapping some of the other children. Scovia was not a small girl—she was nearly six feet tall, and strong.

She most likely had bipolar disorder with psychosis. One night, she became irrational. The orphanage staffs were unable to control her. She was having what is called a psychotic episode, and they called the hospital staff to intervene. Dr. Poole was covering at that time, and it took nurses, doctor, and several guards to subdue her enough to administer an injection of chlorpromazine (an antipsychotic sedative like Haldol). They kept her in one of the spare guest rooms at the orphanage, with a guard watching the entrance. In the morning, she was better, and after a brief stay at St. Bakhita, the mental health ward run by the Catholic church, she was started on preventive medications.

Unfortunately, she secretly refused to take them, spitting them out after feigning to accept them. After a few months, she again had a break. This time, she came to our family home and started screaming for me. She pushed her way past our guard and threw herself on the floor of our storeroom. Half of the guard staff helped me get her over to the hospital, and we managed to calm her down. She was kept in a clinic room with a guard posted outside.

In the morning, she was gone! She had climbed out of the window and snuck past the guard, making her way back to her dormitory at the orphanage. We again sent her to St. Bakhita, but she escaped from there as well, as they could not keep patients against their will.

We met as a leadership team, after consultation with the extended family. It was decided to send her to the national mental health hospital in Kampala, Uganda. One of the missionaries accompanied her and oversaw the admission process. It seemed satisfactory. They could keep her safe and provide some different medications and counseling options. I asked that the psychiatrist contact me to come up with a discharge plan prior to sending her back. As the receiving medical director, I would be responsible for her care, and for the safety of the hundreds of children on the compound—missionary, staff, and orphan children.

The challenge was what to do with her when she was released. There are no institutions to care for the mentally ill. In most cultures of East Africa, the mentally unwell wander the streets, easily identified by bare feet, shredded clothes (or no clothes), and "that look" in their eyes. The residents of town tolerate them, and occasionally give them a small amount of money, food, or water. And so they live.

Scovia was not at this level, however. Mr. Mourice, our Kenyan compound director, talked with the Bishop, and they discovered there were family members who could, and should, receive her back... especially since she was at least nineteen years old! I was in hearty agreement, as the hospital was not equipped to manage her with the other patients we had, and I felt her presence was a jeopardy to the other children. I expressed my feelings to Christopher.

"As medical director of the hospital, who will end up taking care of her, I feel it's not best to have her come back to the orphanage," I explained. I thought it was a no-brainer that she was not fit to be at Harvesters any longer.

"Well, Harvesters will decide that. We have a plan to make sure she takes her meds and follows up with St. Bakhita, and we are going to work that plan," he countered.

"We already tried that plan, and it didn't work. I am saying we cannot and will not treat an adult psychiatric patient, which is what she is, at *His House of Hope* anymore," I responded.

"Yes, you will, if Harvesters says so. It is Harvester's hospital, so you have to do what they say!" said Christopher.

I was stunned. "Actually, doctors don't like to be told how to practice medicine. That is crossing the line. I can't have Harvesters practice medicine through my license," I finished.

When I returned home, Elizabeth called me into our room.

"Lillie and two of the girls from the orphanage just shared that Scovia held a knife at Lillie's throat and threatened her a few months ago. Lillie was too scared to say anything, because the others said Scovia would end up in a mental hospital, which is a bad place. So they all kept quiet!" she explained. "But now that she has been in the mental hospital, and might return here, they decided they needed to come forth." Scovia had pushed Lillie against the wall in the pyat (dining hall) and put a knife to her throat. Several girls witnessed it, and Scovia suddenly laughed and pulled back from Lillie, saying she was joking. Lillie was shaken.

We shared this news with the Harvesters leadership, along with our now definite stance that she should not return to the orphanage. Elizabeth and I looked at each other in agreement—we could not stay at Harvesters if they chose to bring Scovia back.

We waited for nearly week as the decisions were made. In the end, Mr. Mourice and the Bishop put pressure on the family to receive her back. They eventually did. Scovia was not allowed back on the compound, though we were shocked to see her show up twice at church. She didn't cause any problems, but many of the children were nervous.

I know there was pride in me during this time, and I sensed pride in Christopher. The outward issues of power and control were great in the ministry. Christopher and the organization were clinging to power and control, even in the area I thought had been delegated to me. And even when the safety of my own children was at stake. It was a messy problem.

Yet, the abscess was not completely exposed. It would later be incised, probed, and drained even more.

The best scheme

Pride is the best scheme to debilitate a believer, because it starts inside him and his flesh walls it off, making it difficult to diagnose and treat. It is an abscess. An abscess that leads to broken relationships, disunity, and disruption of carrying out the Great Commission.

Paul and Timothy were "...not ignorant of his schemes" (2 Cor 2:11), speaking of Satan's attempts to divide believers by pride and unforgiveness, as was happening in the early church at Corinth. The reality is that we all need each other. No one is complete. The Church is a Body. The abscess of pride can eat away at the unity God desires for the Body.

God began dealing with my pride through my physical problems, forcing me to depend on others and let others step into their gifting. Our team challenges improved after I went blind, as Dr. Poole and I divided areas of leadership based on our interests, gifts, and passions. The truth was, Elizabeth and I couldn't have gone on long without teammates coming alongside. The result was so much better when the missionary team and staff were empowered. When pride was confronted and God was allowed to drain its abscess, Satan's schemes did not succeed.

Rather, it was then that we were given a glimpse into the mystery of the Church showing His glory.

The Great Commission, the Great Command, and the Great Conflict

It is sad to note that the most common cause of a missionary leaving the field early is the inability to get along with other missionaries. Our sending agency told us this statistic before we left for the field, but we never thought it would threaten us! We were very wrong. Most of this great conflict stems from pride, power, and control. God's objective is to root out my pride, selfishness, and lack of faith.

The missionary life (really, the Christian life) is all about the progressive sanctification of the child of God. It can't be anything else, for every missionary is somewhere on the journey to being conformed to the image of Christ. We are a mess. And we must continually allow Him to make us more like Him if we have any hope of getting along with one another.

This is discipleship.

Missionaries love to talk about the Great Commission. The Great Commission is to make disciples. If we focus mostly on making disciples and fail to attend to our own growth in Christ, we may drift away from regularly following Jesus. And how can we invite others to follow someone that we ourselves are not consistently following?

The mark of a disciple is found in the Great Command: to love one another. We are known as His disciples by how we love one another (John 13:35). It is no coincidence that the greatest source of messiness, the great conflict on the mission field, is how missionaries, or Christians anywhere, love one another. Or rather, how they don't love each other well. Missionaries live or die by this, thrive on the field or leave the field prematurely because of this. It shouldn't surprise us, though. The central prayer of Jesus before ascending into the heavens was that His disciples would love one another and be united.

"By this all men will know that you are My disciples, if you have love for one another" (John 13:35).

"…that they may all be one; even as You, Father, are in Me and I in You, that they also may be in Us, so that the world may believe that You sent Me" (John 17:21).

Jesus knew we would struggle with pride, power, and control. He knew we'd be messy. That's why He prayed in this way. Even so, He chose us—the Church, His Body, His followers, His disciples— to present the mystery of redemption to the world.

How have you seen pride at work in you?

How much time and energy should be devoted to working on relationships in a missionary team? Several days a week? One night a week? One day per month?

Chapter 14
Stripped Away

In the West, most houses have glass windows. In South Sudan, there are usually iron bars on the windows and doors. After the riot at Bet Eman, the locals urged us to put up a fence around the hospital and orphanage. Some of the missionaries didn't want to do this, however.

"We don't want to cut ourselves off from the community. We want to communicate openness," they said.

"But there is no way to control the flow of who is coming and going at the hospital, and we just had a riot," we replied. "And if you look around the community, anyone who has the ability to do so puts up a wall or fence." We even picked up from the locals that they thought we were foolish to not have a barrier around the compound.

Eventually, the local wisdom prevailed. While recovering from eye surgery, our daughter Eva helped me measure the distance around the hospital grounds and vocational school, with a tape measure. Adam and the labor crew from Harvesters constructed one mile of chain-link fence around the compound, and the guards thanked us for making their job doable.

A Norwegian aid group was actively removing land mines around Yei. On the way back from the airstrip one day, bringing a visitor to Harvesters, the police stopped traffic. We looked around and suddenly heard a loud explosion. They had just detonated a mine that was found on the grounds of a secondary school in the midst of town. It had been used to house Arab prisoners in 1997, after the southern Sudanese recaptured Yei from the Khartoum government. Another time, traffic was blocked on the main road when a grenade was discovered buried in the dirt near the entrance to Reconcile—the peace-building ministry where our friends Shelvis and Nancy worked. There was a sad irony to it.

After the civil war started in December 2013, we increasingly heard unusual, explosive sounds. One Sunday morning, Logan walked outside and heard the sharp retort of multiple gunshots in the near distance. He paused and looked at the guard. The guard looked back at him with a concerned expression, but offered no words of explanation. Logan turned on his heel and went back inside.

One evening in the middle of 2015, after reading to the kids, Elizabeth suddenly declared to the whole family, "If you ever hear gunshots close to the house, crawl on your knees to the back hallway where there are no windows—that is the safest place in the house." She later shared she felt compelled by the Holy Spirit to share that just then. Needless to say, the children struggled a bit going to sleep that night!

A few short days later, at 9:30 PM, two series of three gunshots rang out very nearby, from somewhere on our compound. We didn't initially know what was going on, but our three middle children who were still awake did just as Elizabeth had instructed the night before. There was an armed robbery of the main house on the compound. No one was shot, but several were struck and injured, and the family who lived in that home was emotionally traumatized. It was the family of Christopher and Georgia.

Thereafter, we were often on edge, and there would be a surge of adrenaline when we heard any such sounds. Our children began to differentiate between the sounds they heard.

"That was a land mine... that was heavy artillery... that was just thunder... that was a gunshot... that was an elephant fruit hitting the metal roof of the storage container..." the discussions would go.

As we look back, we were "frogs in the kettle." If one puts a frog in a kettle of water, and slowly turns up the heat, the frog doesn't notice the rising heat until the water is boiling. Then it's too late. He is cooked. We talked of this analogy often as we tried to reason objectively about security decisions. The problem was that we are subjective beings, and this was now our home. Most days, it wasn't so bad, and we really didn't want to uproot our whole life and work. We had a "risk assessment / contingency plan" in place by then, yet when tripwires were crossed, it was unclear how to respond. When should we pull the plug and leave?

Perhaps when we felt the need to purchase an AK-47 to keep in the house, just in case a thug took out our guard, we should have noticed that the temperature in the kettle had risen a little too high. We often wondered if this would be the day we would need to hide out (or "shelter in place") or leave the country suddenly. The house was even carefully stocked with food to last for weeks. We kept a "go-bag" with important items and documents in case we had to evacuate within hours.

We had to say bye-bye to the illusion of safety. In the West, we feel we are safer than we actually are. Driving on the freeways is riskier than we believe it to be. Random acts of violence, road rage, and shootings at schools and other public places shock and surprise us—but should they? We feel more comfortable where we grew up because it's what we consider normal, not because it's necessarily safer.

Living in another culture, with different, more obvious risks, our illusion of safety was shattered. The reality that our lives here are short was brought right before our eyes. It sharpened our focus on making the most of the time we had. Each day might be our last in South Sudan, or our last on this earth. What really mattered? And was I doing what really mattered? Shouldn't we live with this reality before us always?

The civil war raged and began to center in on Yei. We remained until our scheduled leave was to begin in April 2016, when Dr. Poole and his family returned. From hot, dry South Sudan we stepped off the plane to the cold, green wetness of early Spring in Alaska and Washington. It was a refreshing balm to be with believing family, out of the kettle that South Sudan had become.

One month into our much-needed home assignment, we heard about Dr. Veronika. News reports mentioned what had happened to the nun we knew and worked with in Yei.

Dr. Veronika was a delightful, 60-year-old Slovakian nun. When I first heard of her, I wasn't sure of her medical training, as the local people often referred to any foreign medical personnel as "Doctor." But in fact, she was a medical doctor, having worked in Africa for nearly three decades. While in West Africa, she had done full-spectrum hospital work including C-sections and surgeries. She was in charge of St. Bakhita, the clinic and hospital run by the Catholic Church in Yei. They provided general medical care as well as mental health services.

We met after a Ministry of Health coordination meeting for Yei County. In the poorly lit conference room, she hurried over to me, wearing a big smile so typical of her nature.

"We are planning to open a Maternity Ward and start delivering babies," she began excitedly in her Eastern European accent. "But we want to coordinate with *His House of Hope* and bring any complicated cases to you. We have an ambulance. We also want to adapt your medical record forms so it will be easier to work together on these patients."

I was greatly encouraged by her forethought and desire to be synergistic. Too often, we medical missionaries tend to operate in "silos" of our own, isolated from others doing similar work. True to her word, they developed antenatal forms based on ours, which made transfers nearly seamless. Elizabeth, all the children, and I attended the opening ceremony of the new Maternity Ward, celebrating with them our common efforts to provide safe deliveries for the women and babies of South Sudan.

Dr. Veronika or one of the other nuns drove the ambulance, bringing multiple patients to us every week. It felt right to work together. On the front lines of the mission field, denominationalism seemed ridiculous.

One May night in 2016, Dr. Veronika drove the ambulance to *His House of Hope* twice, in the dark, with women struggling in labor. Both women eventually delivered healthy babies. After leaving the second patient at our hospital, she began the 4-mile drive back to the Catholic Church. At around 2 AM, seven armed soldiers stopped her at a makeshift checkpoint, less than a kilometer from the hospital. They ordered her to get out of the ambulance, filled the vehicle with bullets, and then shot her several times in the abdomen.

Someone transported her back to *His House of Hope*. Dr. Poole was on duty, and thanks to the grace of God, Dr. Lo Alcorn, an Irish surgeon, was still working with us, being only a month after Timothy fell from the mango tree and died. They performed emergent surgery and repaired the injuries to her bowels. The bullets had not damaged any major blood vessels, or she might have bled out immediately. Over the next day, however, she developed high fevers despite aggressive treatment with antibiotics. She had sepsis, an overwhelming infection in her bloodstream.

The team worked with church leaders to transport her to Nairobi emergently. After two days in the hospital there, she died.

Her body was brought back to Yei, where the Catholic Church buried her. The priests and leaders expressed their forgiveness to those who had killed her. The community leaders of Yei expressed their outrage at the men who did it.

A month later, a bullet fell through the roof of our staff housing and one of our nurses brought the bullet to Dr. Poole. The team evacuated temporarily due to increasing violence in Yei. We were all deeply troubled at the loss of Dr. Veronika. In the past, we'd had discussions on our team about whether or not the locals would harm us. We were missionaries, doctors and nurses, here to serve them. Surely they had at least a little respect for that. But after her death, any remnants of idealism were gone. If they would kill her, a missionary doctor, a nun, an older woman in a habit, here to sacrificially care for the people, against whom would they not lash out? It was a crude, painful reminder of the horrible, sinful, messy world in which we live.

We struggled with fury that her life was cut short in this harsh, violent way. Many nights, Elizabeth awoke, deeply troubled at her death. The Lord reminded her that "precious in the sight of the Lord is the death of His faithful servants" (Ps 116:15). This too is a mystery, that the death of a glorious one like Dr. Veronika is precious in His sight.

We plan to see Dr. Veronika again, in glory. She was a saint. A holy one. One who displayed the mystery of Christ in her, the hope of glory. Perhaps she'll even be given the title of "Saint" in the Catholic Church. I checked; she meets all their requirements, save one—that a miracle be attributed to her. But I would guess that the two mamas who rode in her ambulance that night would vouch for her.

Death was a part of *life* in South Sudan. As a doctor coming from the West, I rarely had a patient die that was not older or with a chronic illness. In South Sudan, we routinely lost mothers, babies, and children, despite giving the best care that we could manage in that setting. My expectation of having successful outcomes for most patients had been stripped away.

In the West, we do everything possible to escape the reality of physical death. We spend tens of thousands of dollars on intensive care to eek out a few more days or weeks of life. My mentor in Colorado since 2002, Dr. Schmucker, mused about this reality as we worked together during our last home assignment, which was also the last months I spent with him on this earth.

"How much could you do in South Sudan for what we spend in a week on one patient in the ICU?" he queried. Truthfully, we could probably run the entire hospital for six months or more.

Over the years before we left for South Sudan, he and I worked together to bring many lives into the world in southeastern Colorado. He would usually suggest to the new mother what she should name her child, as we finished the C-section. "'Jeffrey Lee' sounds good to me," he would hint, combining my first name and his middle name. I can't recall any takers. So, when a mama in South Sudan asked me to name her twin boy and girl, I couldn't resist calling them "Lee" and "Elaine" (after his wife).

Dr. Schmucker had an eternal perspective. He had survived cancer over thirty years before and suffered two heart attacks in the previous 5 years.

"I'm living on borrowed time," he would comment.

During that home assignment, I worked more regularly with him. He developed a persistent cough that didn't respond to antibiotics. I believe he knew his time was coming to a close. Many mornings in the clinic, he coughed and struggled to breath. So how did he respond? He told a joke.

"There was a man in the Old West who developed a severe cough due to pneumonia that wouldn't go away. He eventually died. As they were carrying his casket up the hill to the cemetery in the back of a horse-drawn cart, the horse stumbled and the wooden box fell out of the cart, slid down the hill, all the way into town, until it finally bumped into the drug store and the lid popped off. The man sat up and asked the druggist, 'Do you have anything to stop this coffin (coughin')?!'"

During our last few months together, he continued to work, but occasionally stepped into a back room of the clinic to put himself on oxygen. In May 2017, he was diagnosed with lung cancer, just as we prepared to return overseas. I called him a few months later from East Africa, and thanked him for investing in my training and life over the years. He loved our family and cared for me as a young physician. But more than that, he treated me like a son. My father had died one year after I started practicing in Colorado, and Dr. Schmucker once stopped by to check the oil in our van prior to us leaving for an unexpected trip—something a father would do. Because he poured himself out for me professionally, I had the skills needed to provide medical care in South Sudan.

During that final phone conversation, he paused to ask about how my eye was doing. As he was nearing death from lung cancer. He closed the call by speaking the Aaronic blessing over me— something he would randomly do over the years, often as we closed up after performing a C-section, bringing new life into the world.

'The Lord bless you, and keep you; the Lord make His face shine on you, and be gracious to you; the Lord lift up His countenance on you, and give you peace' (Numbers 6:24-26).

Several weeks later, he died. Dr. Schmucker didn't fear death because he knew he would soon see Jesus and be with Him for eternity.

With so much effort being spent on the physical, temporary, seen things of this world, many Westerners don't have much left to emphasize eternity. We also neglect the middle realm where spiritual beings affect our daily lives. However, in places like South Sudan, we didn't have to convince people of the existence of God, the spirit world, or the importance of eternal issues. They mainly wanted to know if He was more powerful than the other spirits and if He could cover their shame.

The Abscess Resurfaces

During our home assignment, we found ourselves again defending ourselves and explaining the hospital vision to the board. They felt the hospital had grown too big, and that we were spending too much time and energy teaching our staff and caring for people from the community. They had wanted a small, excellent hospital to care primarily for the 155 orphans. They felt we had strayed from the vision. Looking back at our written statement of vision and mission from 2008, we were carrying out our five-year objectives, only slightly ahead of schedule. We agreed that the growth felt fast and the work had gotten big. But the Lord had provided, and we had listened to those on the ground and to each other as we put together our strategic plans each year.

The work had grown out of the board's control. We had gained experience that gave us authority in this area of the ministry. Undoubtedly, there were ways in which my pride had festered, though it had been tempered by the afflictions of illness, failure, and blindness along the way. The leaders were threatened, and we were growing weary of the battle to defend this very difficult work. The abscess of pride, power, and control was still there, under the surface, threatening to burst forth.

In South Sudan, the local staff had fled the country to the relative safety of temporary refugee camps in northern Uganda. Several missionaries remained, and two were in a local grocery store when a gunfight broke out in the street. They ducked behind the counter with the shop owner. The time had come. The team evacuated in late 2016.

We were scheduled to return in December, but to what? The hospital was closed, and the security situation in Yei was abysmal. It was clearly not safe to return. One missionary who remained after our team had left wrote that "things in Yei are fine. Yesterday, a helicopter gunship attacked a group of rebels 2 miles south of town…". Things were obviously not *fine* in Yei; this missionary was a frog in the kettle, very close to boiling. He also left a few short weeks later.

Very few locals had stayed around. We wrestled with what to do, and our home church elders stood with us as we together decided to delay our return. Our member care support with Pioneers commiserated with us that in his many years on the field, he and his wife never had a home assignment go a "standard" length.

We connected with other missionaries who had begun to establish a presence in northern Uganda, moving with the South Sudanese people. With each passing week, and each horrific story of the brutality happening in the areas we used to call home, it became apparent that peace and return to safety in South Sudan would be a long time in coming.

Nonetheless, it was difficult to know what was true and what was media hype. We felt we had to get back on the ground in East Africa to put our fingers on the pulse of the situation. The next challenge, however, was finding a place for our family of ten to stay in an area being flooded by hundreds of thousands of refugees and a wave of aid workers coming to help with the chaos.

Through word of mouth, we met a missionary couple based in northern Uganda through email. They would allow us to stay on their compound for several weeks while we decided where to live and what to do, as we discerned the way forward with *His House of Hope*. So, it was with this very flimsy plan that we returned to East

Africa, and found ourselves in Moyo District, northern Uganda— only five miles from the border of South Sudan.

Our children were mourning the loss of their home in Yei, our dog, friends in South Sudan, and life as they knew it. During our second term, we had been given a Bull Mastiff by missionaries who were leaving the field. "Jezzie," short for "Jezebel" (named for the wicked Biblical queen whose life was finished off by dogs, ironically—see 2 Kings 9:35-36), had been a great companion.

"She's so ugly, she's cute!" our younger girls would say. Jezzie was extremely loyal and gentle with our family and a trusted few others.

She was also great protection, thwarting several robberies and the attempted murder of a pastor seeking refuge on our compound during the worst of the civil war. She slept in the concrete room under the water tower during the day, and we'd let her out in the evening. She spent time playing with the kids in the yard and inside the house. Just before locking up for the night, we'd say, "Time to go to work, Jezzie!" and out she'd trot to join the night guard. Our guards bonded with her also, calling her the gafir ma arba kuraa (guard with four legs)!

During our home assignment, when it became apparent that we could not return immediately to South Sudan, Hazel, then age 10, asked the first question: "What will happen to Jezzie?"

We didn't know what would happen to her, but our Kenyan compound director had seen her value, and used his own funds to get more food sent from Uganda. Upon our return to Uganda, we coordinated sending food for a while, and then other missionaries took over her care.

In the midst of this painful time of transition, realizing we would not return anytime soon to South Sudan and Jezzie, our friends Paul and Shawna had given us a one-year-old white standard poodle. He was white, looked odd, and we knew he would stick out when we returned to East Africa. What else could we name him but Kawaja (white foreigner)? He was a balm to the raw souls of our children as they dealt with the loss of the life they knew in South Sudan. Kawaja accompanied us on the return journey, and helped with this transition for the children.

I connected with Medical Teams International, a Christian relief agency who had been tasked with caring for the hundreds of thousands of refugees spread across several sprawling camps in northern Uganda. They were also committed to improving the health of the host community, which was the Ma'di tribe in Moyo District. As such, they "loaned" a few of us doctors to the Ugandan Ministry of Health District Hospital to help them cope with the increased number of patients pouring in.

We prayed that we could find a home that would be safe and large enough for our family, as we prepared to be there for up to six months. We looked at several that were too small, dark, or not secure. As Elizabeth and I made our way, each on the back of a boda, to one more rental house, I asked the Lord for one thing—that we could look out over the land and not be trapped in a hole. The next place we were shown was a skeleton of a house. No generator, no power, no city water, completely unfurnished, and overgrown with grass above our waists. But it had enough space, was secure, and best of all, in response to my small request of the Lord, looked out over a small valley to the north, only three miles from the border with South Sudan. We immediately knew it was the place, and struck a deal with the landlady, a Ugandan living in the United Kingdom. It took much effort, but we were able to get it back into a functioning home, and she was very supportive of the improvements we sought to make.

I was assigned to the Pediatric Ward as the attending, with anywhere from 15 to 40 patients on which to round. A newly graduated Ugandan Medical Officer did daily rounds, and I supervised him.

I struggled through a rudimentary medical history in Ma'di, the local language we were trying to learn. I was comforted when I encountered a South Sudanese patient and could easily converse with them in Juba Arabic. Together, we started a monthly clinic to preventively treat children with chronic anemia, who kept returning for transfusions, especially when they contracted malaria.

The kids enjoyed the land around the home, as we planted a garden and raised goats, pigs, and chickens. For the first time in our missionary career, we were in the community surrounded by local neighbors. Our girls took their goats out to graze alongside the neighbors and their goats. Still, we longed for our home and life in South Sudan.

Once a week on Fridays, I made the trek down to the refugee camp with two of my older girls, Lillian and Eva. By then, Lillian had her Certified Nursing Assistant license, and was allowed to volunteer with the nursing staff. When Eva turned sixteen, she was approved to observe the midwives. It was a bumpy, at times harrowing, ride as we plunged down the rocky hillside on hastily constructed roads to the old Ma'di hunting grounds along the Nile. We passed scrubby trees and large rocks, until we had a clear view of the River Nile, winding its way lazily past the settlements along its bank in the early morning sun. It was horribly dusty in dry season and treacherously muddy in wet season. At times, the way was blocked by trucks or buses tipped on their sides, after failing to navigate the slick, curvy roads.

This vast area was transformed to a new town where there had previously been nothing. New communities sprung up with small dukas (shops), rudimentary health centers constructed out of plastic tarps and tree poles cut by hand, and tukuls (mud huts) just the same as back in South Sudan. In fact, practically the entire town and county of Kajo-Keji, South Sudan had picked up and moved across the border into Uganda, forty miles south of where it had once been located.

Our driver collected us from our home at seven in the morning, with the first hint of light in the day, and we returned about twelve hours later just as the sun set on the other side of the horizon. They were long, exhausting, and fascinating days in the refugee camp.

"Feel," the old Sudanese man said, grasping my hand and moving it to a series of grotesque scars on his right flank.

"He wants you to 'feel' his injury," said the Ugandan clinical officer with whom I was seeing patients in the Health Center under a tent. But after exchanging further conversation with the patient, in Juba Arabic, I realized he was saying "fil," the word for elephant. He had survived an attack from the world's largest land mammal. It was no wonder he had post-traumatic arthritis of his right hip.

Yet, we hoped this was just a temporary role, and that within six months we could re-open *His House of Hope* and return to our home in Yei.

Elizabeth and I each took a day trip by plane into Yei in July 2017, to check on the possibility of reopening the work. We went separately as we didn't want to risk losing both of our lives and leaving our children complete orphans without either parent. We were stunned to see no movement on the roads. Yei was cut off from the rest of the region. It was only accessible by plane. I met briefly with the Bishop, during a week of optimism that things were getting better in South Sudan, though by the following week the situation worsened again.

It pained us greatly to see the empty hospital buildings, a few people whom we knew, and our home in disrepair. The trees around the house had sprung up another ten feet and there were guards camped outside our home that we had never known. It had been fifteen months since we left, expecting we would be back six months later, and being there was disorienting and disturbing. We were there, but alone and not to stay.

It felt "off." Everything seemed wrong. An odor of mold and dust clung to the inside of the dimly lit house. Worse than that, there was a pervasive spiritual feeling of evil that had temporarily won, seeming to mock me. Fear and violence had emptied the hospital compound that once served to bring life into the world, bring back children that were on the brink of death, and most of all, enabled teaching about medical care and Jesus.

We hastily gathered a few belongings and hurried back to the airstrip where the pilot nervously waited with the plane. I had never felt so strongly the feeling that I didn't want to be doing what I found myself doing. This situation was not supposed to happen. Nevertheless, we had to get out before dark, as it wasn't safe at night. Bringing items back from our home in Yei surprisingly didn't help our longing to return; they rather served to remind us of the lost relationships, hopes, and possibilities that we thought still lay ahead.

Back in Uganda, Elizabeth and I formulated what would be necessary to reopen. First and foremost, we needed to be on the same page as the board of directors, with their trust and support. Reopening in this new climate would be more difficult than opening in a time of peace. Security, commerce, staffing, food supply, and finances were just some of the issues we faced.

Bet Eman – His House of Hope Hospital sits sadly devoid of people, with new lab building (R) nearly finished, on our "bye-bye" trip, 2017

During the pause created by the war, the executive director came to our home in northern Uganda. We reflected on the challenges over the years and came up with three options. The first, in which the board agreed with the vision as laid out in 2008, and would support us in continuing to carry this out. The second option, if they didn't like the vision or how we were walking it out, was to part ways amicably. The third option, if they felt the work was good, but too much for them to oversee, was to create a separate non-profit to govern the hospital alone—or "spin it" to another organization. We had talked of this third option for some time, as a way to reduce the crossover conflicts. Running a hospital had many requirements that a school, church, or orphanage didn't face. It was becoming confusing.

We ended our discussion with the director agreeing that we were open to other options, but these were three possible outcomes we could see.

Less than two months later, the board met. We had a scheduled time to call in from Uganda and talk with the board on the second day of their meeting. We asked the director to share the notes from our meeting ahead of time, so we could have a more productive discussion. We awoke to an email on the morning of our scheduled meeting, saying that the call would not be necessary. The board couldn't construct any way to give us the "autonomy" we needed. We hadn't requested autonomy, but rather, delegated authority and trust. They said they were sad to make the decision, but they felt we should "pursue other ministry opportunities."

After ten years of service, we were dismissed by an email and one follow up call from the same director. There was no opportunity for further discussion with the Board. We felt misrepresented and misunderstood. All that we had poured our lives into for a decade, and the life that our eight children had known and loved, was suddenly cut off. We felt confusion, anger, pain, and sadness like a death. A death of what could have been.

The method of dismissal was another symptom of the power and control issues within the ministry. From the lips of one who served alongside us in the ministry for that decade, "there have always been issues of power and control in this organization."

All had been stripped away. The strongholds of power and control within the ministry were the very same that had a choke hold on the country we longed to serve. This issue was between them and the Lord. Elizabeth and I were left facing our own struggles.

Probing the loculations

Ten years of our lives, our home in South Sudan, almost all that our children knew, were no longer open to us. Closed. There were friends we wouldn't see anymore, parts of our lives that would only be memories now. It was painful to realize that we would never see the completion of the half-finished buildings, set up a new lab, or continue teaching and doing research. Each time a former staff member called to ask when the hospital would open again, it was like having a scab ripped off again.

Only when our role in the ministry was stripped away did we realize how much we looked to our accomplishments to validate ourselves. God was probing the loculations— those deep, walled-off pockets of infection in me—of pride. Over the following year, He and I had many conversations about my pain and my misplaced search for value. He wanted me to rest in His pleasure of me, not on my works. When I trusted in what I did, I rode the roller coaster of pride and despair. He wanted me to be rooted in Him alone, so my successes and failures didn't send me hurtling into pride or despair. My strength and power were to come from Him alone.

I struggled with the "unfinished" work in South Sudan. Dan, with Pioneers member care, gave me a helpful nugget of truth from Scripture during this time. As I bemoaned the work that was yet to be done there, he reminded me of the parable of the sower.

"Even the most fertile soil still had a finite limit. You had an idea of how much you wanted to accomplish, but the Lord had specific, limited work that He intended for *you* to do, and *perhaps that is finished.*"

Our last term on the field was largely about the Lord breaking up these pockets of pride, starting to heal us from the inside out. It was a messy process emotionally, but pointed to the mystery of Christ in us, the hope of glory. He had greater things in mind for us. He wanted us to be made whole and truly well, to be in Him, and know that *belonging to Him* was more important than *any work we could do for Him.* As painfully messy as this experience was, we now know that He had our very best as His aim.

How have you experienced something of value being stripped away?

How did you respond?

How do you think the Lord was working on you?

Chapter 15
Mechanical Messes & Mystery Managers

Mission work is messy. It almost never looks the way the missionary expects it should. A counselor in East Africa reported that most missionaries struggling with emotional issues complained that they weren't engaged in the work they had planned. When asked further, they were doing good work, advancing the kingdom of God—it just wasn't the particular work they had anticipated. It had turned out different, messier, than they had anticipated. This was certainly true of us as we continued life in northern Uganda. As we submitted to the mess, we began to see glimmers of the mysteries along the way. We were privileged to have a small part in managing these together with the Lord.

Through the generosity of churches and individuals, we had purchased a brand-new Toyota Landcruiser six months before we left South Sudan for our home assignment, fully expecting to return. It still smelled and drove like new. Upon our return to northern Uganda in 2017, the roads were unsafe in South Sudan and few people dared drive them. We clung to hope that arrangements would be made for a military convoy to drive it out of the country to us. However, someone in the ministry in South Sudan laid claim to the vehicle, and thwarted those efforts. If we had brought it to Uganda, it would have cost us a third of the value of the vehicle in taxes, or we'd have to drive back to the South Sudanese border to re-register it once a month (where they were actively fighting). It was a mess any way we looked at it. We never saw the Landcruiser again.

Thankfully, the ministry that had just fired us did at least buy the vehicle from us, enabling us to look for something to drive in Uganda. We ended up purchasing two older vehicles. They were fairly good vehicles, but had been driven on rough roads for twenty years and not been maintained well. We were fixing something every few weeks.

Over time, our small green Toyota RAV-4 required new tires, radiator, luggage rack, battery, front and rear suspension, shocks, air conditioning pump and condenser, electrical systems, engine gasket, and various other parts. It was difficult to find a trustworthy, competent mechanic in our rural area of Uganda. They *worked on* cars, but rarely "fixed" them. We had to make the four-hour drive to Arua for any substantial work. It was often a frustrating mess, but over time we saw God working His mysteries into the lives of those who needed Him, through these very messes.

Jamal was the younger son of a respected Iranian Muslim family. He and his older brother ran a quality garage in Arua, handed down to them by their father, who was now quite elderly. Their grandfather had come to the region during the British colonial days, and served as governor of the region in the early to mid 1900's. We heard about Jamal from another missionary. After another mechanic worked on an issue, the same problem recurred just as we tried to leave Arua. Jamal came to where we were staying and was able to solve it.

A short while later, we had another mechanical mess, and Jamal shared that he would be in Moyo that week, as part of their business involved selling automotive fluids to various parts stores. He arrived one evening, diagnosed the problem, and asked me to pick him early the next morning when the parts store opened, to acquire the needed component. He hopped in the car, and we made our way to the parts store, which was, not surprisingly, not yet open (opening times were rather flexible). We began talking about things of faith as we sat in my vehicle in the cool African morning air. Undisturbed time, in a safe environment. I asked about his beliefs, and he asked about mine.

"How are you ever sure you have been good enough that you will get into heaven?" I asked him.

"We don't, we just do our best to follow Muhammed, and hope that Allah will be pleased," he responded.

"Wow, that's a heavy burden. We rely on Jesus to be our advocate before God, as we know our good will never outweigh our bad, nor will a perfect God ever be pleased by our mix of good and bad," I shared.

"Yes, Muhammed is like that for us too," he came back quickly, though without much certainty.

He shared about his experience with a classmate in school who had been demon-possessed. We dialogued. Then, the parts store opened, he found the part we needed, and he fixed our car. He returned to Arua later that day. Our mechanical problem led to a conversation about salvation. I didn't like the mess, but I liked that God opened the way for His mystery to be shared.

Stranded in Hostile Territory

Yumbe District sat directly between Arua and Moyo Districts. While Moyo had a long history of Catholic influence, Yumbe was over 95% Muslim, and fairly hostile to outsiders and Christians. When we first arrived in Uganda, we considered living there, as it was truly an unreached area, with few believers, and almost no self-replicating churches. Another missionary had taken me to Yumbe, where a man met us, and then drove me alone to a small home. The modest building sat along a dusty road amongst overhanging trees several miles out of town. It was there that I secretly met with an older Ugandan Christian.

I was quietly invited into their front room, where the wise, gray-haired man and his wife visited with me. They had a deep, sober joy about them. They were inexplicably at peace, though memories of suffering were visibly close at hand. We discussed what it would mean for our family to live in the district. He was very concerned, as two missionaries had been martyred there just ten years earlier, and he and the few other believers felt responsible for their deaths.

"We weren't careful enough," he explained. "They lived too far out, and we didn't keep a close watch on things with them." Apparently, Pakistani "missionaries" had paid some locals to kill them. "But if you lived closer in to town, or on the church compound north of town, I think it could work."

As we explored these options, however, there just simply weren't any houses available, due to the huge refugee crisis in the region. Through these circumstances and other ways, the Lord led us to settle in Moyo. Yet with each trip to and from Arua, we found ourselves driving through the heart of this district, praying as we went—for our physical safety and for their eternal spiritual safety.

One hot day during dry season, I was travelling back from Arua with Logan, Given, and Winnie. Jamal had just done some maintenance on the RAV-4 while we were there. We were passing through a sparsely populated area of Yumbe, ready to be home. It was over 100 degrees Fahrenheit. Suddenly, a cloud of steam billowed from under the hood, escaping around its edges. I pulled over, and cautiously opened the hood. Keep in mind that I know little and have no practical skills in terms of repairing vehicles. Fortunately, the problem was obvious—the radiator hose had detached from the radiator and coolant was pouring out.

After I waited quite a while for the parts to cool down enough to touch (which didn't happen quickly in the midday sun of equatorial Africa), I managed to reattach and tighten the hose in place. I called Jamal to let him know the problem we were facing. Without hesitation, he said that he was on his way, even though we were about two hours from Arua at this point. He said to continue on carefully if we could. We used our remaining drinking water to refill the radiator, and slowly resumed our journey.

With each hill, however, the temperature rose dangerously high, and cooled off a bit with the downhills. We stopped to buy all the water we could afford in a small village, and kept going, inching along the hilly terrain as the day waned on. One of the girls confessed to me years later that she kept some of her drinking water aside because she was afraid of being thirsty.

We rolled the windows down and turned on the heat to draw heat off the engine. We were very uncomfortable. Darkness fell as we crossed into Moyo District. Cell phones worked only at certain points along the way, but I had managed to contact Elizabeth at one of these places, so she was making her way to us as well. Finally, we met her just as Jamal and his crew arrived, at the roadside in the pitch dark of night in an African forest.

They quickly diagnosed the problem—a pump that circulated the coolant through the engine had failed. They managed a temporary fix, and took the car slowly back to Arua that same night, arriving after two in the morning. We were grateful to be home, and thankful for Jamal and his team. They repaired the RAV-4 over the next few days and drove it back to us.

Our relationship with Jamal and his crew illustrated the paradoxical mission 'non-strategy' which has been described as *Jesus' theology of mission—to go in need of those He was to reach.*[1] We were in northern Uganda, dependent on the very ones with whom we hoped to communicate the good news of Jesus, to fix our car. Jesus showed up at a well without something to draw water, and asked the Samaritan woman for a drink of water. His admission of need created a space for dialogue, which led to a discussion about much deeper issues (see John 4). Jesus showed up at the seashore, needing a boat from which to address the crowd, and asked Peter to borrow his. Then Jesus invited Peter to follow Him into a radically new relationship with Himself, and everything changed for him (see Luke 5). We showed up in Moyo, Uganda without transportation, bought an old vehicle, and were thrust into dependence on our mechanics. Dialogue and discussions about Jesus ensued—part of His messy, mysterious 'non-strategy' of missions.

The Mess Opens the Way

During an unplanned Sunday trip to take a young missionary to Arua, we started hearing a funny rattle in the engine. It still ran okay, so after stopping to inspect, we continued on the 100-mile journey, over half of which was on dirt roads. I took the car to Jamal.

Jamal listened to the engine and looked at the exhaust color as he revved the accelerator. "You need an engine overhaul. The crankshaft and bearings are worn and the whole engine could seize up on you suddenly," he reported matter-of-factly.

"What?!" I responded in disbelief. The car hadn't seemed that bad, and we had to get back to Moyo and fly out 2 days later. This was not the time for major work. "Can it wait? Could we make it back home safely and do it later?"

"You might… about 50% chance. But I wouldn't recommend it," he replied. I knew I didn't want to be stuck on the road again. Once was enough!

We went ahead with the repair. As I talked with Jamal, I learned that his father was in the hospital. He had fallen the night before, apparently from a stroke, and broken his hip. The family was trying to decide if they should move him to Kampala or have surgery there in Arua. I asked a few questions about his condition.

"I'd be happy to help answer any questions for you and your family," I offered. Just then, his brother came up and heard us talking. The brothers had recently parted ways within the family business, and there were tensions between them.

"Yes, please, can you come with me to see him at the hospital?" said Rajav, Jamal's brother.

"That would be really great if you could do that, Doctor," Jamal added.

Logan and Winnie had come with me, and I left them safely at a restaurant near the hospital after ordering food. Rajav took me to the small hospital where his father was being treated. It was a relatively new, clean clinic with a few inpatient rooms.

I entered and saw his father, a distinguished grey-haired Iranian man, lying still on his left side. Several middle-aged men, probably cousins I thought, stood around the edges of the room. His mother was resting on a second bed in the room, dressed in colorful silk garments and her head wrapped with a cloth. I greeted them all, and began reviewing the chart and X-Rays. He had memory loss, high blood pressure, and a badly broken hip. He needed a CT scan of his brain, good pre-operative care, hip surgery, and good post-operative care. He was at risk for clots or an extension of the stroke.

He was able to answer some of my questions, and his wife completed some missing details. I gave them my assessment and answered their questions. Before leaving, I asked if I could pray with them.

"Yes, please," replied the matriarch of the family. And so I did, in Jesus' name.

I had left on the trip irritated that we had to make the unexpected 8-hour round trip journey, then grew more annoyed when the engine started making unusual sounds, and became downright frustrated when I learned we needed an engine overhaul! What a mess. But as I left the hospital room, I was overwhelmed by the fact that God uses the mess to bring us in contact with those who need to know His mystery of redemption. I was focusing on the messes in which we kept finding ourselves, but He was teaching me that we are first and foremost managers of His mystery.

Our repeated car repairs brought us in contact with this family, and this time, at a crucial moment in their lives. Sadly, he passed away a few weeks later, and other missionaries in the area attended the funeral and continued to love them.

The "what for" of the Mess

We live in a messy world, filled with suffering. We know it's a result of sin, which has damaged creation, strained interactions with others, and severed our original relationship with the Creator. But is there purpose in it?

The mess causes us to spin around in a fruitless attempt to control our surroundings. The Kiswahili word for foreigner, the equivalent of kawaja, is mzungu, which literally means "one who spins around." This is likely how early cross-cultural workers appeared to the indigenous East Africans, spinning around, trying to control the mess!

The mess breaks us. It brings us to the end of ourselves, where we fall at His feet and trust in Him. We learn to rely on Him, not ourselves. It has the good potential to crush the Western idols of self-sufficiency and individualism. We realize we can't control the world in which we live, and that we need others to help us. We see that we are merely broken vessels.

Kintsugi ("golden joinery") is the ancient Japanese form of art that began as a repair method. The craftsman takes a broken piece of pottery and joins the shards together using a lacquer containing powdered gold, bringing glints of beauty in the otherwise unsightly fractures. The end result, in the hand of a master artist, is a piece more glorious than the original ceramic bowl. It highlights the scars rather than ignoring them. The focus is on the artwork of the master, not on the broken pottery itself.[2]

"But we have this treasure in earthen vessels, so that the surpassing greatness of the power will be of God and not from ourselves" (2 Cor 4:7).

When we live in the mess, we learn that we can rely wholly on His grace. When others see broken people such as us following Jesus, they see that they can come to God just as they are. But when a Christian tries to appear "perfect," others can be led to think they must approach God with something good in themselves.

God uses the mess to mold the missionary. To discipline us. To sanctify us and make us like Him. "…He disciplines us for our good, so that we may share His holiness. All discipline for the moment seems not to be joyful, but sorrowful; yet to those who have been trained by it, afterwards it yields the peaceful fruit of righteousness" (Heb 12:10b-11).

By using broken people in a messy world, God leaves little room for us to try to steal the glory for ourselves. The messiness never goes away, but God can handle it, and works in spite of and through the mess. We are called to be *"servants of Christ and managers of the mysteries of God" (1 Cor 4:1, CSB).*

How do we manage these great mysteries? We must engage with the mess, press on, and pray (more on this process in the final chapter). Sometimes, we are privileged to see a bit of the mystery.

The Mystery: Christ

Several months after Jamal and Rajav's father died, our car began having problems again. Logan, Winnie, and I made the 4-hour drive to Arua, Uganda again to see our mechanics. Winnie happily visited her Scottish friend, Amalie, while Logan and I hunkered down for long day at the mechanic's shop. It was no mystery to Winnie that our mechanical messes meant more time with her friend!

We sat outside under a large tree on old, hard wooden chairs as we waited for Jamal to repair the car. We were used to this routine by now. Logan brought his guitar, while I prepared medical lectures for the staff at the refugee camps. This time, however, Rajav came up and asked if we would join him and his wife for lunch in their home. We readily accepted! Not only were we glad for the opportunity to talk with them, but we loved Persian food!

"I am always seeing you and your children sitting under the tree waiting for your car, and I wanted to invite you in, but was afraid you wouldn't want to come," said Rajav's wife, Salima. During lunch, the conversation shifted to how the family was doing after the death of the patriarch, Rajav and Jamal's father.

"It's hard. The children ask when they will see Baba again, and we tell them we will all be together again in heaven—if they are good," Salima explained.

"How do you see it, in your beliefs?" Rajav asked of me.

I was cautious, as they were still emotionally raw, grieving their father. To suggest directly that he was not in heaven could shut down conversation and relationship.

"Well, we believe that none of us will ever be good enough to stand before a perfect, holy God, and that's why Jesus sacrificed Himself for us." I put my fork inside my cup of water, using an example taught to us by a dear friend and pastor, Ron Finch. "If we are 'in' Christ, like this fork is inside this cup, then God only sees Christ's righteousness, not our sin, and we can live with God eternally."

"Yes, that is how it is for us with Mohammed. If we follow the prophet, he will help us when we face Allah in judgment," replied Rajav.

Given the moment, we didn't enter a debate about the differences between Mohammed and Jesus. In such dialogues, we differ when it comes to the truth of Jesus as the only way to eternal life. Christ is the great mystery of God, and without the Holy Spirit, a person won't be convinced of the necessity of Jesus in his or her life.

We continue to pray for Rajav and family, that one day they might turn to Jesus as the Truth, so *"that their hearts may be encouraged, having been knit together in love, and attaining to all the wealth that comes from the full assurance of understanding, resulting in a true knowledge of God's mystery, that is, Christ Himself"* (Col 2:2, NASB, emphasis mine).

How do you respond to the messes in your life?

How might God be asking you to manage His mysteries amidst these messes?

Chapter 16:
Discipleship Revisited in the Mess

We found ourselves doing life in Uganda, but it wasn't what we intended. We were without the hospital we came to start, the work we envisioned, and the home we had forged in South Sudan. These elements were stripped away, but there were still relationships.

Bond was a friend to Logan and our girls since our first trip to Yei in 2007. He was one of the brightest students at Harvesters school and orphanage, and one of the few orphans with neither father nor mother living.

He was raised in a hilly valley near Ombasi, a village southwest of Yei and close to the border with the Democratic Republic of Congo. His father died in the war and his mother died several years after he was born, while delivering another child. Bond went to his maternal grandmother, where he was relatively safe, but had little in terms of food and no possibility of going to school. Children without living parents usually received the few family resources after the children most closely related. It was a "Cinderella" syndrome. Looming over him also was the unpaid bride price, or dowry. Bond's father had not finished paying the dowry for Bond's mother, so Bond was prohibited from meeting any of his father's family (because his father hadn't completely paid for the "property" of his mother and Bond, their offspring). Culturally, he would one day need to seek them out if he wanted to get married. Without his father's family, he was without a cultural identity.

Logan (age 4) with Bond (age 13), 2007

One of Bond's maternal uncles remembered him when he heard of an orphanage and school in Yei—Harvesters. He and 7-year-old

Bond walked the 20 miles to the orphanage where he had secured a place for him. Bond recalls that his legs were so swollen after that journey that he couldn't get up for nearly a month.

Bond worked hard in school and excelled. When we arrived in 2011, he helped transform our plot of land from the crude pasture it once was to a lush oasis. There was no shade and no privacy, as we lived 50 meters from the hospital with only a chain link fence between us. People peered in our yard as they waited to be seen.

Given (L) and Winnie (R) in front of our bare front yard, 2011

The same front yard, transformed in terms of vegetation, but devoid of people, 2017

As I recounted in an earlier chapter, he planted umbrella trees that would later become shade, and "living fence" around the perimeter— a toxic, succulent plant that became a thick privacy barrier that was alive. He sacrificed in doing so; the sap caused his eyes to burn horribly. I later heard it is known to cause cancer, so we pray this one-time exposure won't have lasting effects. When we returned to our home for the last time six years later, the trees and plants were providing complete shade and privacy just as intended.

He was intelligent because he read a lot and asked many questions. He perceived problems in the ministry, and his questioning sometimes turned into challenging those in authority, which didn't go so well for him. He left for his final two years of secondary school in Uganda in 2013, on shaky terms with the leadership of Harvesters.

He did well in his first year in school, and made a trip into Yei over Christmas 2013 to see his extended family. During those weeks, violence erupted in Yei. Bond hid in his uncle's tukul, near the army barracks where shootings had started and spread over the town. Bodies washed up on the shores of the Yei River. He didn't know if he'd get out.

The next day, the shooting diminished.

"Get out now," his uncle directed him. "Take my bicycle and ride to Ombasi." Bond was frightened, but left immediately, without any of his belongings. Miraculously, he made it out of town and rode the twenty miles back to his village in the hills. Several days later, he risked the trip back and so returned to Uganda.

We met up with him shortly after this harrowing time, in January 2014, as we awaited our return to Yei, and he was just starting his final year of secondary school in Arua. He was traumatized by his experience, and feeling hurt by the accusations made against him by staff at Harvesters. He never mentioned this to us at that time, however, as it was too fresh and painful.

We weren't sure where he was in terms of his faith, and whether there was some truth to what others were saying about him. But, we had him and other students over for a meal and talked with them. They were "launching" into their adult years, without much family on which to fall back.

He finished secondary school as the top student in one of the best schools in that part of Uganda—ahead of hundreds of other students, Ugandan and South Sudanese, who had much more stability in their lives. He went on to secure a spot in Law School at Makerere University in Kampala, the "Harvard of East Africa." He was the only South Sudanese student in the school.

On break from school in July 2015, Harvesters had him teach the younger students in Terakeka, South Sudan—north of Juba. Once again, he found himself in the wrong place at the wrong time. Fighting broke out in the capital city, and nearly a thousand people were killed. His only exit from South Sudan led him directly through Juba.

When there was a lull in the fighting, he was given money for transport and school fees, and he began the risky journey back to law school in Uganda. Along the way, he saw soldiers by the roadside. Rather, he saw boys dressed as soldiers, soldiers who were thin, thirsty, and hungry. He gave several of them money for food and water and proceeded on to Juba. There he met up with other students also trying to make their way out of the country. Word had it that President Musevini of Uganda was sending the Ugandan military to escort their citizens out of South Sudan. Bond secured transport at an exorbitant price, using his last bit of money.

They traveled in military and private convoy, thousands of vehicles fleeing on the only stretch of paved road in the whole country. Every few miles, there was carnage, with burned out cars and heaps of dead bodies openly displayed along the roadside. The procession crept along slowly, making the 60-mile journey to the border last almost 12 hours, and allowing the smells of death to permeate the stifling vehicle.

He finally reached Kampala and began his next year of law school, though without any of the funds sent with him. Somehow, he made it through the year.

When we returned to northern Uganda in May 2017, we reached out to Bond. His plan for his school break was to stay in his youth hostel. It wasn't safe for him to return to Yei, as the roads were impassable, not to mention the fact that one of his uncles was a known rebel army leader. He feared for his life if he were to go back in. We were in the process of mourning and discerning if we would ever be able to return to Yei and reopen *His House of Hope*.

After clearing it with Harvesters leadership, we invited him to come work for us, cleaning up our compound in Moyo during his break. It had been several years since we had been around him, and we weren't sure how he was doing in terms of his character. He was honest about the difficulties with Harvesters, but was working through his feelings and trying not to become bitter or turn from following Jesus. Despite the damage in relationships, he was thankful to God for providing him opportunities—through the means of Harvesters.

We had almost finished guest quarters adjacent to our home back at Harvesters in South Sudan, when it was cut short by civil war. We never returned to complete that space which would have housed visiting doctors in training, and allow for closer discipleship with them. It was yet another sad, unfinished mess that resulted from war and broken relationships.

However, we had a few thousand dollars remaining in that project account. Because construction costs were so much less in Uganda, we were able to build a small "boys quarters" on our compound. This space allowed Bond, and others during our time there, to live close to us. It provided a space so discipleship could happen. God redeemed this little mess as well, though it didn't look like I had hoped it would, and I still struggle when I see pictures of the other nearly-finished building. We don't mourn the building; we feel the loss of the work that would have occurred with people in those spaces.

Bond asked to study Scripture, so we began a weekly men's Bible study with him, Logan, and several Ugandan men. Our kids loved having big brother Bond around, and he provided them a point of connection back to the life we no longer had in Yei.

Over the following year, he came back to Moyo several times, and whenever we were in Kampala, we joined him for worship at Watoto Church and shared a meal together. Our relationship with him was one of discipleship that spanned eleven years of the turbulent life of an orphan becoming a lawyer. We saw that he was wrestling with how to live out his faith in the unique place he found himself—a South Sudanese man becoming a lawyer from of one of the best law schools in East Africa. He did an internship with a top law firm in Kampala, prior to his final year in school, and graduated from law school later. He eventually passed the bar and began seeking opportunities to gain experience as a new lawyer in Uganda.

His hope is to return to South Sudan to help develop and write policies for the still struggling young nation. He also dreams of returning to the family land in the hills around Ombasi to grow crops such as coffee, providing jobs to those in the village. He wants to study Mandarin, as he is aware that the nation of China has its hand in the pot of South Sudan's resources (which are many).

At the direction of Mama Elizabeth after church one day, he re-joined a cell group (small group Bible study) with Watoto Church, as we know intentional fellowship such as this gives him the best chance to continue growing in his faith.

As of May 2022, Bond was temporarily back in Juba, South Sudan, working for the United Nations. His work was to support the National Ministry of Justice in implementing a segment of the then current peace agreement—the very mission he hoped to engage in. He returned to his usual job with a law firm in Kampala.

We continue to pray for him as he grows professionally and spiritually. He has the potential to be an agent of great, beneficial change in South Sudan and Uganda. But we also know that power and money have the potential to be agents of devastating change in ones character and walk with Jesus. He is growing, and we pray the Lord keeps him as he treads a difficult course.

Dr. Kiden

Bond, Logan, and Jeff, Kampala 2018

After covering for me when I went blind, Dr. Kiden Annet delivered twins. Joshua and Caleb were beautiful, and Joshua was diagnosed with Down's syndrome. Joshua struggled with respiratory infections, and despite prompt treatment, he died of pneumonia at 8 months of age, even with the best care our hospital staff could provide.

Dr. Kiden continued to learn and grow at *His House of Hope*. She was a Medical Officer (Resident Doctor) who was hungry to learn, gain experience, and faithfully serve at the hospital until the last of our missionary team evacuated. She was not interested in staying once the rest of the staff and missionaries left. Her surgical skill was quite good; by the time we parted ways, she was much more confident and efficient, whereas I was a bit more cautious seeing as I had lost vision in one eye!

Dr. Kiden headed to Kenya with her husband and children, eventually landing at Maua Mission Hospital along with Kitty, one of our missionary nurses. After working at Bet Eman, which focused on the health of women and children, she felt drawn to get additional training in Obstetrics & Gynecology. She was assigned to the Maternity Department at Maua while she waited for a training program to become available. Once she does so, she will be one of the few OB-Gyn consultants in South Sudan.

We had the privilege of seeing her in Kenya in October 2018. She had just been appointed as the Medical Officer in Charge. It was unusual for this level of responsibility to be given to a foreigner, a South Sudanese, or a woman. She was all of these. She was given

Dr. Kiden holding Caleb

charge of more than 20 medical staff including Clinical Officers, Medical Officers, and consultants—some of whom had more training than her, and most of whom were Kenyan. The hospital was struggling due to declining patient numbers, and the Board asked her to find the problems and take corrective actions.

"I don't feel equipped to do this," she confided to us during our visit. "But I will give it my level best. I don't have much hope, but when I am taking care of the patient in front of me, it gives my heart joy, and I will keep on doing so as long as I can."

And she was giving it her level best. One of the nights during our stay, she led a 4-hour meeting with the clinicians, listening to their thoughts, grievances, and possible solutions. This was after starting morning report at 8 AM, giving us a tour, rounding with the interns, and performing a difficult repeat C-section. She planned to do such meetings once a week for the following many weeks.

Stopping by her home late at night after her lengthy meeting, we saw part of the mystery of who she is: her husband, Robert. When we arrived, he was dressed in a blue Adidas jacket, with a hat on (it is relatively cold there at an elevation of 6,000 feet). He was in the kitchen washing dishes. This may not sound unusual to those of us from the West, but for a South Sudanese man, and one who is finishing his Master's thesis in International Education at the University of Oslo (Norway), it is extremely unheard of!

"When my mother came and saw him doing work in the kitchen, she was really disturbed! But, I couldn't be doing what I am doing without him," Kiden later said. "God has been so good to me, giving him to me as a husband. He does whatever it takes so that our children can have a good education and I can progress in my profession."

I asked him about his thesis. He had done research in the refugee settlement just across the River Nile from where we had been working in northern Uganda. He discovered that the ideal of "education as a right" for South Sudanese refugees was far from reality. Even for the host population in Uganda, it was not a right. School fees were always a barrier for the poor.

Kiden had grown up as a refugee in Uganda. "I don't want our children to grow up as refugees," she explained. Robert affirmed that, noting that Heritage ("Harry"), Joy, and Caleb (the surviving twin, born at Bet Eman) were finally established in school. They were learning Kiswahili and beginning to progress in their studies again, after several years of disruption from the war in South Sudan. It was good to see them unified in their thinking with a long-range plan of what was best for them and their children. This was not a self-interested plan, though. God willing, their efforts will one day enable them to be integral parts of healing the nation of South Sudan. We prayed together to begin and end our short time together, and lamented that we couldn't share more of life together.

"I always thought we would all be back at *His House of Hope* again together someday," Kiden confessed. "But I guess not. The Lord knows." It was a mysterious mess as we looked back on our time in Yei.

We left many empty buildings in South Sudan. They were vehicles for delivering medical care, spiritual healing, and teaching truths of medicine and faith. Some buildings were left unfinished, like the new laboratory that would have opened up microbiological diagnosis in the region, to greatly increase our quality of care. It would have allowed for our students and interns to conduct original research. All that suddenly halted when the team evacuated.

Yet if we accomplished nothing else during our time in South Sudan than encouraging ones such as Dr. Kiden to practice medicine to the glory of God, that was enough. She demonstrated the love of Christ as she cared for women and children in South Sudan. If the Lord wills, she will be there far longer than we ever could have been. She is another of the glorious ones we had the privilege of working alongside, one who was glorious because Jesus was in her, setting her apart for Him. We are eager to see what Jesus does in and through her in the years to come.

Aaron O. and James L.

Aaron and James were junior high students when we first visited Yei in 2007. Aaron was slender, serious, and smooth-shaven. He was always respectful and asked many detailed, in-depth questions. He lived near Harvesters with his older brother, and they had no living parents, so the ministry had taken him under their wing to provide schooling and guidance for him, as they did for the children actually living in the orphanage. James L. was kind, gentle, and humble. He lived in the orphanage, and like Aaron, excelled in maths and science, through a moderate amount of raw talent and heap of hard work.

When we returned in 2011 to live at Harvesters full-time, James and Aaron approached me.

"Can we meet with you regularly to have you tutor us in science?" they asked with trepidation. I responded affirmatively, with trepidation of my own, as I had seen their chemistry curriculum, and it scared me. I hadn't done that level of detailed chemistry since I was an undergraduate, 20 years earlier. As it turned out, we talked more about the intersection of science and faith, how one didn't need to pitch out faith in the "light" of science. Rather, faith put light on science. Our times morphed into discipleship, delving into deeper issues of faith.

James and Aaron helped me build the hand trike that enabled Abini Paul to be a force of prayer in the hospital and community. They became translators in the hospital once it was functioning, opening my understanding to the woman's description of the wizard that harassed her overnight in the hospital, and protecting me and our Kenyan mechanic during the riot.

In 2015, they left for Clinical Officer school in Kenya, and found themselves doing clinical rotations under the tutelage of Dr. Kiden at the end of their courses. We had the privilege of visiting them during their final months in 2018, as they worked alongside Dr. Kiden, just before their graduation.

They hadn't been home for three years due to the fighting, and struggled to be accepted into Kenyan internships. After graduation, they returned to Yei to await the start of their internships in Kenya. While there, Abini Paul got very sick. James and Aaron went to his home to assess his state and help transport him to the government hospital, but he was already seriously ill. He became septic from the chronic wound on his back, and died.

(L to R) James L., Jeff, and Aaron, 2015

After their internships, Aaron and James made their way back to South Sudan, working in small clinics in Juba and Yei while *His House of Hope* remained closed during the ongoing, smoldering civil war. James was in a serious boda (motorcycle) accident, and nearly died of complications. Gradually, he recovered, and we recently communicated about that time. "God has been great in my

James and Aaron at graduation from Clinical Officer School, Kenya 2018

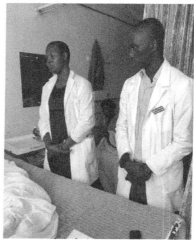

Dr. Kiden on teaching rounds with Aaron, Maua Methodist Hospital, 2018

life and one thing I learned from him and especially when I was sick after my accident, is to trust and to have faith in him and in doing so, I saw his provisions and care for my life when I didn't expect it. Truly his goodness, favour and grace has always been in my life and this has given me so much confidence to trust him more and to be more obedient to his word. But God is so, so good. How are you experiencing God in your life?"

Aaron hopes to work for several years as a Clinical Officer, save money, then return to get his Bachelor's degree in Clinical Medicine and take a 6-month program in Medical Education, so he can be a fully-qualified teacher of other Clinical Officers. He previously wanted to become a surgeon, but along the way he discovered he loved to teach others.

James hopes to return to medical school to become a Medical Officer (doctor), or at least go for advanced training in Clinical Medicine in Reproductive Health. They are finding their way.

As of early 2022, they both returned to staff *His House of Hope* as outpatient services were reopened. We pray that God continues to keep them close to Himself as they seek how to best use their training, and if to get more education, to take care of their people and teach others to do the same.

Charles

When we returned in 2017 to work with some of the one million South Sudanese refugees in Moyo, northern Uganda, we found that Charles, the spokesman during the strike at *His House of Hope* who asked for forgiveness, lived a half-mile from us! While back in Yei, he told us he was married. In truth, he wasn't married, but had said that so the young women wouldn't harass him and try to draw him into a relationship. This was how he had dealt with the cultural and sexual pressures from his own people.

After leaving South Sudan, he became engaged, but the marriage never happened. Her father gave her to someone else. So, Charles married another of our former staff members, Rosalind.

"The other one didn't work out, so I got this one," he explained to me matter-of-factly, speaking of his new bride, just out of earshot (maybe). We observed during our time that marriage is a very different animal in East Africa; romance is rarely seen. He was working hard to provide for his wife, saving money to purchase land and build a permanent home for them. He was usually away in Juba, working.

A few months later, they announced they were expecting a baby. I confirmed her dates on ultrasound, and a few months later, repeated the scan to check that everything was developing well. They were expecting a baby boy. It was an encouraging experience to be a part of two of our former staffs having a child, in exile.

Charles was home over Christmas and New Year's, and joined me in going to the camps. I had told him that Yakani, another former staff member, was working at the health center to which we would go that day. When we arrived, they saw each other, hugged, and almost wept.

"It's really you!" Charles exclaimed to Yakani.

"I told him you were here, but apparently he didn't believe me!" I noted to both of them. I think he didn't dare hope to actually see another he had known from Yei.

We worked together that day, one on either side of me, each of them able to speak in four of the languages needed in that setting (Madi, Kuku, Arabic, and English). It was a good day. Along with my daughter Lillian, who had also worked in both places, it was a reunion of sorts for Bet Eman.

Charles was then a tutor (instructor) at the national midwifery school in Juba, South Sudan, teaching younger health professionals some of what he had learned at Bet Eman. He sent me copies of the curriculum and slide presentations he used in his lessons. It was encouraging to see one of those we had trained now training many others.

Each time he returned to work at the school, they traveled in convoy, along the same road between Juba and Nimule that Bond had traveled amidst so much carnage a few years earlier. It was not uncommon for one of the vehicles in the group to be shot at during the trip. He would text each time he departed and when he arrived, so we could be praying him along the way.

A week later, just after Charles had returned to Juba to restart the next session, he called early in the morning. Rosalind had had a gush of fluid. As they were both midwives, they understood what was amniotic fluid and how serious this problem was. She was only 25 weeks along. Back at Bet Eman, we had occasionally seen 29-week babies survive. In

(L to R) Yakani, Charles, Jeff, Lillian, Luru Health Center, Moyo Refugee Settlement, Uganda 2018

Moyo, I hadn't seen any less than 32 weeks do well—mainly because we didn't have staff like Charles.

A few hours later, I evaluated her at the hospital. She was undoubtedly ruptured. I wrote orders and admitted her to the hospital. The baby was still alive, and there were no signs of labor or infection. There was still a chance for life, if she remained uninfected and undelivered for many more weeks. We had to

leave town the next day. Charles remained in Juba, as it could be weeks before anything happened.

One week later, she delivered. Charles rushed back to Moyo, and called me while we were still in Kampala. Their baby boy was alive, and weighed about 2 pounds, larger than I expected. We discussed the treatment plan, and I sent him the protocols we used back at Bet Eman. With him caring for his son, perhaps there was a small chance for life.

Joshua, as they named him, lived about 24 hours. He tired out and stopped breathing. So many times, Charles had cared successfully for premature babies born to others. This, his first, would not be one of those who made it.

In the coming weeks, Charles stayed around Moyo, keeping busy with his building project. Near the end of his leave, they came over to our home. They shared the pictures of Joshua, we grieved together, and we looked to the future together; hopeful for what God would do, both in their family, and in his homeland. We prayed with them. There was much to lament; yet, there was still hope.

This was God's grace to us, that Charles and Rosalind lived half a mile from us in Moyo for that year and a half. He allowed us to do a little more life with our staff, to continue the healing from the way we finished our time in South Sudan.

Just before we left Moyo at the end of 2018, we went to his new home to say goodbye. He again shared his passion to work with premature babies. He expressed his sadness that *His House of*

Hope might never re-open. I felt the same, but looking at him, I remembered our "charge."

"When the Bishop told us to 'do something small, do it well, and let it be an example to South Sudan,'" I began, "perhaps it was meant to do nothing more than put a vision of what healthcare can be in South Sudan in the minds of a few such as you, Charles."
God gave us a glimpse of His mystery: Christ in our staff, the hope of glory.

Exit Strategy

Early in our time in East Africa, Logan and Olivia rode along with me from Nairobi to Kijabe Hospital, a well-developed mission hospital with over 60 years of history. As I sat with the medical director, he asked what scope of services and commitment to teaching we envisioned. He also asked what our exit timeline was.

"I would hope that in 10-15 years, we would transition out and hand off to South Sudanese professionals that know the Lord, to continue the work," I cast out before him.

He listened respectfully, then countered. "Think 30-40 years at least. It is a slow process, and South Sudan is just coming out of decades of war." I was floored. We certainly didn't see ourselves there for that length of time (I was 40 at the time).

As it turned out, we had just five years on the ground in South Sudan, a year of waiting, and another two in Uganda. Our plans are not His. But God is able, and perhaps He keeps us from achieving our "plans" to avoid thoughts that it ever depended on us. Buildings now sit empty, "underutilized" in our minds. We had plans, hopes, and dreams of further medical and spiritual work through *His House of Hope*. Yet, those in whom we invested do remain, and they have been changed through our time together, as have we. Hopefully, we have all been changed for the better—to know and follow the Lord more deeply.

All He truly called us to do was make disciples, even just two or three, in however many years He allowed us to remain. And He is Faithful.

What tangible "buildings" (tasks, projects, etc) are you holding onto in your life?

What relationships might God be asking you to focus on more than the tangible, outward structures in life?

Chapter 17

Kawaja Bye-Bye: Living as a Surrendered Stranger

For whoever wishes to save his life will lose it, but whoever loses his life for My sake, he is the one who will save it. –Jesus, in Luke 9:24

"Kawaja Bye-Bye!" they called out.

We heard the expression many times as we slowly made our way to and from town, mostly from the children that ran alongside our vehicle. They could almost keep pace with us, as we had to drive so slowly due to ruts and holes that would break most cars that didn't respect them. A few years later they installed road signs which warned of speed bumps along the road—which was humorous to us all, as the road was so rough that you could rarely get up enough speed to notice an intentional speed bump.

Why were they greeting us with "Bye-bye" when we had only just arrived? Did they want us to leave? We had only got there, and we had come to "help." And wasn't it rude to yell "foreigner" at someone?

The missionary life is full of paradoxes. This shouldn't surprise us, because so was Jesus' teachings. Surrender to have victory. Lose your life to save it. Missionaries are taught to live in these tensions, as they are undeniable and unavoidable in cross-cultural living. They are taught to embrace the paradox; or, "pair a ducks." Missionary kids are taught to reflect on the pair of ducks they all have: "yay ducks" (the good things that happen) and "yuck ducks" (those difficult, painful, messy things that happen). We hold on to both, not ignoring or throwing away the experiences. We lose the life we knew, saying "bye-bye" to things of this place (if called to do so), realizing we are strangers here.

And we trust that God's mystery will eventually shine through the messes we face.

Near the end of our time in East Africa, I was walking with our insightful, then sixteen-year-old daughter Eva through the busy market in Moyo, Uganda.

"I came when I was nine, but I still feel like I don't understand African culture. I think they look at the world in an entirely different way, and I won't ever understand them," she shared.

In that time period, she had also become unlike her peers in the United States. She and her seven siblings who grew up in East Africa were missionary kids (MKs), or now more broadly termed third culture kids (TCKs), a descriptor which also includes children of those stationed abroad in the military, international corporate jobs, or other foreign service. There are a surprising number of such "expatriates" living outside of their home culture. Our children would never fully be part of the "host" culture where we were serving, nor were they like kids their age in our "home" or "passport" country anymore. They may look like others in the US, but the breadth, depth, and difference of experience had fundamentally changed their worldviews.

When we visited Sudan in 2007, our children were the first "kawaja kids" most Sudanese had ever seen. We moved there in 2011 and the kids began making friends with the children at the orphanage. At first I thought they would have difficulty connecting, but within 6 months, they were finding ones they called friends. In retrospect, the children at Harvesters were TCKs like our kids. They were from various tribes in South Sudan, raised by a smattering of Kenyan, Ugandan, South Sudanese, American, and Malaysian staff and missionaries. They spoke a blend of English, Juba Arabic, Kakwa, and several other tribal languages. They had a unique way of looking at the world because those from multiple cultures taught them what was "normal". They struggled to fully fit in in other settings.

Early on, many missionaries want to be seen as one of the host culture, to be accepted, to bond, to belong. To some extent that does happen, especially if one stays for an extended time, makes effort to learn language and culture (which go together), and adopt some of the (acceptable) cultural behaviors and practices. We begin to blend a bit and our mutual understanding gets better. We learn to say things using the words they use, and we comprehend what others are saying with their expressions... well, some of the time.

"Can you please bring a trash can," I asked simply (or so I thought), as I once finished a C-section. Blank stares greeted me from our South Sudanese staff. "Sorry, a rubbish bin, please," I corrected myself. Eyebrows raised and looks of understanding washed over the staff's face, and the trash can was promptly produced. Sorry. Rubbish bin.

But as much as we learn and adapt, our worldview and values don't change substantially. We learned these as very young children, from our parents and those closest to us. Our worldview and values are the part of the iceberg below the surface, of which we aren't aware until some behavior (the part above the water) rubs us wrong. Depending on the ages at which our children came to Africa, though, some of their worldview and values were altered—making them unique and global in their outlook.

This is why re-entry to ones passport country is so difficult. Regardless of the age, it is a difficult process because one realizes anew that there is no place on this earth that is truly home.

"The only place I fit in is at the airport and with other TCKs," wrote a TCK friend to our daughter Lillie. I read that note and was impressed at his honesty and insight. I pondered his statement.

The next time we were waiting in the Nairobi airport for a flight back to Entebbe, Uganda, I looked around at our kids. We had all been traveling since the previous morning, having spent the entire night on the plane. Lillie was stretched out, asleep on the ledge next to the large glass windows overlooking the planes on the apron. The rest of them were slumped in uncomfortable seats, some listening to music with headphones, others reading books.

As I surveyed the scene, there were Africans, Asians, Brits, and Arabs engaged in similar activities. We had just transferred planes, once again going through the security drill. Four of our kids had carried a laptop computer, as we usually traveled with their schoolwork, and they dutifully took the laptop out, removed their shoes, put them all in plastic trays to be X-Rayed, and navigated the congested security checkpoint with several hundred other weary, smelly travelers from all parts of the world. And they just knew this was what you do when you travel.

When they called for our flight, I handed out the passports (which Elizabeth had labeled with their first names for quick distribution) and boarding passes. At the entrance to the jet way, the Kenya Airways attendant asked to see each child's visa, to be sure they could legally enter Uganda and wouldn't be turned away at immigration. Each child located his or her "Student Pass," which we had renewed just 3 weeks earlier at the Ministry of Internal Affairs in Kampala, and showed it to the lady.

Our children had such a strange skill set, unlike most kids their age. It was exhausting traveling and living this life, but it was the norm for them.

They came alive the most when they were able to connect with other TCKs. Whenever possible, we tried to allow for those times of connection. Other believers became our "family," just as Jesus pointed out to His disciples who had left their earthly families to follow Him.

One of the hardest questions for missionaries, especially TCKs, to answer is, "Where are you from?" Does the person want to know my passport country or my place of service? Which place of service? Where am I truly from? the TCK often wondered. I am a foreigner on this earth.

This awareness is healthy, in that the world is temporary. Our true home is a permanent one, a heavenly one, and one that is still not visible. Our true citizenship, where

TCK connections, Mombasa, Kenya 2018

we are from, is heaven. But it can be a lonely realization, and one that should compel us to draw closer to other followers of Jesus— especially our family. God calls families, and obedience is an act of faith that has an impact on the whole family. Abraham obeyed, bringing his wife and family with him. In it, all of them showed faith in the One who is Faithful. They were strangers on earth, but heirs of the God of heaven.

> *By faith Abraham, when he was called, obeyed by going out to a place which he was to receive for an **inheritance**; and he went out, not knowing where he was going. By faith he lived as an **alien** in the land of promise, as in a foreign land, dwelling in tents with Isaac and Jacob, fellow heirs of the same promise; for he was looking for the city which has foundations, whose architect and builder is God. By faith even Sarah herself received ability to conceive, even beyond the proper time of life since **she considered Him faithful** who had promised... All these died in faith, without receiving the promises, but having seen them and having welcomed them from a distance, and having confessed that they were **strangers and exiles on the earth.***

> *For those who say such things make it clear that they are seeking a **country of their own**. And indeed if they had been thinking of that country from which they went out, they would have had opportunity to return. But as it is, they desire a **better country**, that is, a heavenly one. Therefore God is not ashamed to be called their God; for **He has prepared a city for them**.* (Hebrews 11:8-16, NASB, emphasis mine)

We are all third culture kids, kawajas, strangers and exiles on the earth, but we are also children of God, looking forward in faith to our true home country.

Always a Kawaja

In the early days of the missionary life, we often desire to "fit in" with the culture—to not be the kawaja forever. In the "honeymoon phase," we mostly see the good and overlook the bad (and much of the in-between). As we adjust to our host culture, we start to see the difficult realities with which we don't identify. We can't ignore them forever. It becomes difficult to not be critical as we see the specific, ugly ways that they, like our passport culture, are not fully redeemed. When we get to the point of seeing many of the faults of the host culture, such as their intense jealousy of each other, we face the choice to love them as God does, even knowing their faults. The transition is helped when we are aware of our own cultural faults, such as materialism and proud individualism, just to name a few. This transition often happens after a year or more of living in that setting. For this reason, many agencies recommend that missionaries remain for at least two years in their first term.

Elizabeth and I would go walk or run the roads around our compound in Yei. It was good exercise, a protected time to talk things out, and excellent stress release. Except that every 50 meters someone yelled "Kawaja!"

"When will they stop yelling 'Kawaja!'?" we asked each other in a moment of frustration. This was after we had lived in South Sudan for five years.

Never, we realized. We will always be kawajas, in both our host culture and back in our passport culture. But this pointed us to the fact that our citizenship is in heaven. We belong to God, He belongs to us, and believers belong to one another. This last part is especially difficult to live out, because we are all broken. We wait and look to Jesus who has the power to make us glorious like Him.

*For our **citizenship** is in heaven, from which also we eagerly wait for a Savior, the Lord Jesus Christ, who will transform the body of our humble state into conformity with the body of His glory, by the exertion of the power that He has even to subject all things to Himself. (Philippians 3:20-21, emphasis mine)*

Why the Bye-Bye?

How do we live as kawajas in this world? There are aspects of life in either our home / passport culture, host culture, and our very inner being that we will never be able to fully embrace once we step cross-culturally. Part of our earthly life is "lost."

To what did we say bye-bye? What were we called to surrender?

Bye-Bye to Comfort. I love my office (wherever we may be living), with a big desk, where I can read, study, pray, and drink coffee, preferably at "o'dark thirty" in the morning before any of the kids are awake. Even before we were married, Elizabeth noticed that I preferred the huge desk in my small apartment above the church in New Orleans. She dubbed it my "command center." Wherever we moved, she made sure I had such a space to recharge and spend time with the Lord. The office in our big house on the hill even had a gas fireplace! It was super cozy. On a cold winter morning (the temperatures could reach -20 degrees Fahrenheit / -30 degrees Celsius), I would don a sweater and simply switch on the fireplace. Two weeks after moving into this wonderful home, we received the call about starting a hospital in Sudan. I knew I wouldn't have this particular comfy command center for too long.

The summers in southeastern Colorado were hot. For several weeks each July and August, the temperatures reached above 110 degrees Fahrenheit (43 degrees Celsius). Thankfully, it was a dry heat, though that is hot regardless of the humidity! We went from air-conditioned house to air-conditioned car to air-conditioned church or hospital or clinic. We in the West have gone to great lengths to make sure that our environment is roughly the same temperature the whole year round. Comfort is an unspoken value to us.

I feared practicing medicine in South Sudan because of the heat. I didn't like the feeling of being overly hot or constantly sweaty. I had the belief that I couldn't relax if I was uncomfortable. After about six weeks of living in South Sudan, we physically started to tolerate the heat a little better, but psychologically we still struggled.

After roughly six months, we psychologically began to surrender to the ups and downs (mostly ups) of the heat. We became very good at sweating. It was particularly noticeable during afternoon antenatal clinics during dry season. I would review patients while the midwife, several midwifery students, and eight very pregnant South Sudanese women (who had walked several miles in the blazing sun to get there) were crammed into the 10 x 20 foot room without much airflow. At times even the African staff and patients would complain as they fanned themselves with whatever piece of paper they could find, saying *"Sukun kalis!"* (much heat!). I would suddenly realize that droplets of sweat were pouring down my back and face, even as I simply sat still doing my work.

The operating theatre was hot on a whole other level. It was mostly airtight to prevent as many flies, dust, and germs from entering. The operating lights were an old, monstrous set donated from a generous hospital in Australia. They acted as a radiant warmer as well as a light source. We stepped into the room and donned cap, facemask, knee-high rubber boots, a thick cotton gown, and two pairs of latex gloves. We then stepped under the radiant warmer—I mean, the operating lights—and began the surgery. The operation sometimes required extreme physical exertion to stretch the tissue while the assistant pushed from above. By the end of it all, it was difficult to tell what was sweat, amniotic fluid, or blood.

Comfortable it was not. Most operating rooms in the West are super air-conditioned so the surgeon is comfortable. In truth, however, studies have shown that it is better for the patient if the room is above 80 degrees F. Our theatre was definitely better for the patient than the staff! Our African staff and visiting missionaries often complained of the heat, and occasionally passed out (which usually turned out to mean that they had contracted malaria). We learned to embrace the heat rather than mentally kick against it. This helped tremendously.

Our house reached 93 degrees F by midday and remained so until the next morning. The tin roof, thin plywood ceiling, and no insulation were a bad combination. During our second term, someone suggested a thin reflective insulation above our ceiling boards. We procured three large rolls in the US and hauled them back on the plane after medical leave. This thankfully kept much of the heat from entering and lowered the temperature by 5-10 degrees inside. Soon after, we did the same for the ceilings above the operating theatres. But no worries, it was still plenty hot for the patients' well-being!

Elizabeth worked hard to make our house a home where the kids could learn, grown, and feel secure. One area of the house had a twelve-foot table and shelves divided into cubicles for homeschooling. We had simple tables and desks made by local carpenters using the local lumber… mahogany and teak. The cost was minimal, though to purchase such furniture in the US would have cost tens of thousands of dollars! Elizabeth established my command center (an elevated desk with bookshelves) and hers (a sewing desk). They weren't fancy, but they were a place to step away, focus, and rejuvenate.

We had to say bye-bye to comfort, because of His call on our lives. We were comforted by the Lord, not by Him making our surroundings completely comfortable, but by a deep sense of being where He wanted us. We weren't happy to be there, but had a feeling of purpose and pleasure in Him—what I would call joy.

Bye-Bye to Family. Saying goodbye to family was very difficult. My family wasn't so hard to leave. My parents had divorced many years before, my dad passed away in 2003, and we lived 1,500 miles from my mom and stepdad in the US. We ended up seeing them as much while on the mission field as we did prior, and they were very supportive of this call on our lives.

Elizabeth's family was much closer—emotionally and geographically. Culturally, family is most important to them. Elizabeth's father was the only one in his family who emigrated from Cuba, when he was 25 years old, and he still carried the pain of being away from his family of origin. The family of Elizabeth's mom lived far away and had little to do with them, so Elizabeth and her brother Chris were all they had. Our decision to follow Jesus to South Sudan was perceived as a death in the family.

For the years leading up to our departure, it was the elephant in the room about which we never talked. Just prior to departure, often the night before our return or at the airport, the emotions came out and it was painful and awkward. Once back in South Sudan, we tried to keep in regular communication by Skype, email, and phone.

Still, we were absent for major life events. Just 4 months after moving to South Sudan, Elizabeth's sister-in-law, "Aunt Bev" to our children, died of metastatic colon cancer. We couldn't be there for the funeral, though Elizabeth "attended" by Skype, while lying on the bathroom floor, being sick with typhoid herself. A year later, Chris remarried, and we missed that too. There were birthdays and anniversaries. Her parents sold and moved out of the mountain home they had built by hand 30 years before. Comments were often made about our absence from these family milestones, which inadvertently felt like guilt daggers into Elizabeth's heart.

I wish I could say it got better, but it didn't. After we had made the decision to step off the mission field, her father had a "mini-stroke," from which he recovered well. He was diagnosed with diabetes. We were thankful to know that we could be near them again soon. Shortly after this, her parents were to celebrate their 50th wedding anniversary. Thanks to our friends Shelvis and Nancy who volunteered to stay with our children, we were able to make the trip from Uganda to Colorado to surprise them. We were grateful to be present at this important family event. God also coordinated it such that we arrived just hours before her dad's follow-up appointment for his mini-stroke and diabetes diagnosis.

We said bye-bye to family, and while we returned to them, a decade of absence surely took its toll on Elizabeth, her family of origin, our children, and me. Yet, we do trust the Lord is and will continue to work through our obedience to Him. He is making all of us, the missionaries and our extended families, more like Himself. As we and they allow Him to shape us.

Bye-Bye to pleasing others. Bringing eight children to the "most unstable political state" in the world was not a popular decision with most people. South Sudan topped Somalia and Afghanistan for this title during our last few years on the field. Few people were supportive; many quietly disagreed; some vocally disapproved. We were thankful for the few that encouraged us, like our Regional Leader with Pioneers, "Uncle Chris." He is a wise Ghanaian man who never demonstrated an attitude of power or pride about his position in the organization. Rather, he continually sought what was best for us, with primary concern for the safety and well-being of the children. We were grateful for the few like him who supported us as we followed Jesus as a family.

Leading a multicultural team in a new work generated many opportunities for others to not be pleased with us. As we read books on leadership, we realized that to lead is to say goodbye to pleasing all people and being friends with those we led. Someone would always be unhappy with our leadership. One had to be sure to be called to lead, and then seek to please God, not people.

Being medical director of a rapidly growing mission hospital also created staff members who weren't pleased with me. It was a difficult realization when those we came to serve expressed their dissatisfaction with us. At the same time, these interactions exposed my pride and desire to please others. Was I truly following Jesus in humility, able to learn from those I was leading? Or was I looking to the accolades of others for my validation?

It was an uncomfortable reality to face these truths about myself. I wish I could say that I have completely said "bye-bye" to these struggles, but I haven't. Day by day, the Holy Spirit continues to remind me to do my work as one who aims to please God, not others. When I walk in this truth, I am free. Free to lead and love others better.

Bye-Bye to self-dependence. Growing up as a competitive long-distance runner including the steeplechase event, I had a deep-seated sense of pride in my ability to keep on going whatever the barrier or obstacle presented. This was only fortified by the Biblical values of endurance, suffering, and not giving up. Elizabeth was equally as tenacious, and if told something couldn't be done, she assuredly took it on and completed the task.

However, we met our match physically and emotionally in South Sudan, as I have described in the preceding chapters. It was truly hard on the flesh, but as it forced us to say goodbye to dependence on our own abilities, it was good for our spirits. The illnesses, insecurity, immense medical needs, the laws we didn't understand, and the spiritual forces at work led us to see we could not depend on ourselves, but only God, who raises the dead. He is powerful, and He has given us the Holy Spirit as the true strength we need. He enabled our missionary team to do more than we were able to do in our own strength and skills.

It is His power, and simply our obedience, that enables us to walk in the way He has called us.

Kawaja Bye-Bye. Foreigner, say goodbye to the safe life, the sense of home that you once knew. We said goodbye to our life in the US, then had to say goodbye to the life God had granted us in South Sudan. After ten years of planning, preparing, and establishing *His House of Hope,* our family had to say farewell to the people, place and work in Yei. Then He called us to work for two years with the South Sudanese refugees and host culture, the Madi, in Moyo, Uganda. And then we had to say goodbye to those as well.

We are now forever changed. We had to say goodbye to the illusion that anywhere here is our home. We are foreigners and strangers on this earth. We are kawajas. Yet even as we trust Him, we see Him provide unexpected gifts that sustain us along the way. He gives us all of what we need, and some of what we want.

We live as surrendered strangers as we look to our true heavenly home and His mystery—Christ in us, the hope of glory.

What is "home" to you?

Have you said "bye-bye" to major things in your life?

Do you feel at home on earth, or like a surrendered stranger?

Chapter 18:
Moving Forward in the Mess and the Mystery

We live in the mess, but how do we move forward in it? We must embrace the mess, realizing that it may be the very means God intends to use, in us and in those not yet part of the kingdom of God.

Cling & Consider. *"Let us hold fast the confession of our hope without wavering, for He who promised is faithful"* (Heb 10:23). We cling to hope, not out of our grit but because of His greatness. Amidst the mess, we are tempted to despair rather than hope. We are told to *"consider Jesus...so you will not grow weary and lose heart (literally, 'faint in your soul'—which is the feeling of fear)"* (Heb 12:3). We need to cling to His truth and consider Jesus—daily.

We cling to Him by spending focused daily time with God, being saturated with His Word, and listening and thanking Him in prayer for myself and others. At a Pioneers leadership conference, a distinguished African speaker brought the message for the main plenary session. I looked forward to some deep truths, some spiritual nugget, some missional method to explode the work we were doing. His main point? **Have a daily quiet time with the Lord.** I was stunned again by the simplicity of this recurring truth, which I had been hearing since my early days of discipleship in college. We must minister out of a place of first being filled by Him.

I have found that I need to regularly read longer passages of Scripture so it continues to guide my thinking throughout the day. The world tries to drown out the truth He gives me in His Word.

Likewise, if my behavior begins to wander from His ways, I have to check how tightly I am clinging to His truth. Am I conducting myself in a worthy manner amidst the mess (Phil 1:27-28)? *"Only conduct yourselves in a manner worthy of the gospel of Christ... in no way alarmed by opponents..."*. My walk matters.

Love. We are known as followers of Jesus by how we love one another (John 13:35). How we manage the mess, cling to Him, consider Jesus, and love others has a big impact on our effectiveness in sharing the gospel.

In The Pineapple Story, a missionary in Dutch New Guinea (now Papua Indonesia) plants a pineapple field but repeatedly has the fruit stolen by locals.[1] He increasingly gets angry with them.

Finally, he surrenders the pineapple field to God. They keep on stealing the fruit, but the missionary, known to the locals as "Too-wan," doesn't become angry anymore.

Then one day they came to me and said, "Too-Wan, you have become a Christian, haven't you?" I was ready to react and say, "Look here, I have been a Christian for twenty years." But instead I said, "Why do you say that?" They said, "Because you don't get angry anymore when we steal your pineapples." This was a real revelation. Now I was living what I had been preaching to them. I had been telling them to love one another and be kind to one another, yet I had always been standing up for my rights, and they knew it.[2]

Later, the missionary struggled with his time being used up doing menial repair jobs for the locals.

I wasn't getting as much Bible translation done, but more and more people were being won to Christ. They kept saying, "Too-Wan has become a Christian. He tells us to love one another, and now he is starting to love us."[3]

The work that is being done by God in the life of the missionary is often the most effective witness for the gospel.

Seven years after we moved to East Africa, we met up again with Gloria, the nurse with whom we'd struggled in our first few months on the field. She had gone to another town in South Sudan and started her own ministry. Later, she fled South Sudan and ended up in the same town, same church in Uganda, as us! We were a bit wary, but Elizabeth engaged in conversation with her, and met with her several times.

One day after church, she approached us. "I want to ask your forgiveness for the way I acted seven years ago at Harvesters," she simply asked. It was a restorative moment for all of us. Perhaps the Lord had brought us back to this town in northern Uganda simply to allow the healing of our relationship. The unity of His followers is of great importance to Jesus. We see this in His final prayers for the disciples—for their unity (John 17).

There are two things that have been seen to impact Muslims deeply: Christians loving one another, and dreams.[4] We need to be doing ministry as a team, where we are put in the crucible of loving one another in difficult circumstances and dealing with issues of pride. Only then do those who are separated from Christ have a chance to see Christians love one another.

It may seem strange, but sometimes the best evangelism we can do is to love other Christian missionaries. People who are not a part of the family of God are waiting to see how His children treat one another, before deciding to follow Jesus. They need to know what kind of community they will be joining and depending upon if they make the choice to follow Jesus. For if they follow Him, they will be called to sacrifice their community, their identity, and often their very lives, for the sake of Christ.

We also need to pray for God to reveal Himself more and more through dreams. Followers of Mohammed know about Jesus, but need to be convinced that following Jesus, not Islamic law (sharia— "the way to water"), is the way to the water of eternal life.

Develop a Theology of Groaning and of Grace. It is normal to groan a bit as we struggle and suffer in the messiness of this world. *"...We groan inwardly as we wait eagerly for our adoption as sons..."* (Rom 8:23). We should expect, embrace, and engage with the mess, while pressing into the great mystery of God's grace to us. Deeper discipleship in the Church and missions requires us to understand where God is amidst our groaning, and to see His grace to us. We must develop what Ajith Fernando calls our "theology of groaning and grace" so we are not caught unawares when difficulty comes.[5] And the greatest difficulties are often with other believers.

As we groan in our relationships with one another, we must guard against bitterness. We must communicate often, forgive frequently, and not forget the grace and glory God has shown to us. "See to it that no one comes short of the grace of God; that no root of bitterness springing up causes trouble, and by it many be defiled" (Heb 12:15). Satan's scheme is to divide us through unforgiveness (2 Cor 2:10-11), and Jesus' prayer is for us, the Church, to be one because of the glory He has given us.

> Jesus, speaking to the Father, says, "The **glory** which You have given Me I have given to them, that they may be **one**, just as We are one; I in them and You in Me, that they may be **perfected in unity**, so that the world may know that You sent Me, and loved them, even as You have loved Me" (John 17:22-23, emphasis mine).

Don't ditch the Mystery of the Church. Jesus has given us Himself and His glory so that we, the Church, will be one, for the purpose of showing the world that God sent Jesus (John 17:23). The local and global Church is God's mysterious vehicle for communicating His truth to the world. The Church is a complex, messy organism. A Body. It is often easier to work only with a smaller mission agency and not bother with the Church, either in one's home country or on the mission field.

But beware. God established His Church, uses it to accomplish His work on the Earth, and will continue to do so after the missionary has gone. Circumventing His plans and methods is never a good idea. Just ask the ethnocentric prophet, Jonah.

Maintain the Presence and the Proclamation

One of the greatest keys to holding on to the mystery of what God is doing amidst the mess, is to maintain the presence (being Christ's presence to others) and the proclamation (speaking clearly about Christ when the time is right). How does one do this? Only with the power and presence of the Holy Spirit. I will suggest a few practical ways this may happen in our daily, messy lives.

Be still before God. When everything seems to be falling apart, as it often does on the mission field, God's direction to us is to "*cease striving and know that I am God*" (Ps 46:10, NASB). Other translations render this as "be still" or "relax" or "let go." To many of us overachievers in missions and ministry, the idea of responding to difficulty first by "ceasing" and then "knowing" seems impotent. How can stopping my efforts and simply "knowing" that God is God, help anything? Of course I know that He is God! Or do I really? Do I think and act like I know He is God, or do I think and act like maybe He is God, but He sure must need my help right now?

In the next breath, after God tells us to know that He is God, He doubly states "*I will be exalted among the nations, I will be exalted among the earth*" (Ps 46:10b, NASB). We often quote "be still and know that I am God" as an antidote to needless worrying. In context, it is a verse for the missionary in a mess. God is communicating that in the midst of natural disasters and wars that only He can cause to cease (Ps 46:9), we are to stop our efforts, know Him fully, and He will exalt Himself through our surrender to Him. Do we spend enough time still before Him? God had to remove the vision in my right eye at the height of my busyness, at the peak of my "useful service" in order to make me still before Him.

Martha was a busy ministry worker, yet Jesus chided her for being overly worried about "much service." Mary, on the other hand, sat and listened to His teaching. She had chosen the "one thing that was needed" (Luke 10:38-42). We must be careful not to end our missionary careers having done "much service" but having failed in the one needed activity—being still before God. If we are not immersed in His presence, how can we be His presence amongst those who need Him? Martha believed that Jesus was the Christ, but there is no record of others following her to the feet of Jesus, as there is with Mary. "*Therefore many of the Jews who came to Mary and saw what He had done, believed in Him*" (John 11:45; see also 11:20-45).

At age 92, Billy Graham was interviewed. The reporter asked him if he would have done anything differently in life and ministry.

"I would study more, pray more, travel less, take less speaking engagements. I took too many of them, in too many places around the world. If I had to do over again, I would spend more time in meditation and prayer and just telling the Lord how much I love Him and adore Him, and I'm looking forward to the time we're going to spend together for eternity," Reverend Graham responded.[6]

Previously, I would not have thought of "being still" as a mission strategy. Yet, I am beginning to see the evidence for it—in my life, the lives of others, and in God's Word. It is part—well, the lion's share, perhaps— of the ministry of presence. The more we are in God's presence, the more we embody His presence to others.

Love others through speaking, serving, & suffering. "The first thing I noticed when I met Mama Elizabeth was that she was learning our language. I said to myself, 'they must really love us!'" said Pastor Jimmy during a farewell fellowship with our local church in northern Uganda. He relayed how he had hated a certain tribe when he was young and living in another part of Uganda (before he knew Jesus). He displayed this hate with a complete resistance to learning their language—to the point of fighting with them if they didn't speak English to him and his friends. It wasn't until he became a follower of Jesus that Pastor Jimmy began to love, and learn the language of, the other tribe.

Learning to communicate in the tongue of the people is the first and most basic step to loving them. It is not a means to an end, in order to translate Scripture, or communicate important information. This may happen, and may be a great benefit of knowing their language. Rather, it is about valuing and loving the people enough to talk like a baby in their language, despite being over 40 years old and having several advanced degrees. To sound foolish in order to know and love them better.

As we enter peoples' lives and embed ourselves in their communities, we learn how to love them. We learn who they are. Through language we also learn their ways, their culture. We begin to see their different behaviors, beliefs, and values. We grow in our understanding of their need for the truth and grace of the gospel. And we can begin to serve them, hopefully in ways that empower them to also serve others.

Yet, it is often only as we suffer alongside them that we engage with those in the host culture. Many missionaries tell stories of being accepted by a people group only after going through a difficult situation, and remaining with the people. Through our efforts to love others, and willingness to suffer with them, we embody Christ's presence to those that don't know Him. We make Jesus visible to the world as we suffer, because as we suffer, we have Christ in us, the hope of glory. This is the "filling up what is lacking in Christ's afflictions" (Col 1:24) that Paul writes about.

Living with our eight children in South Sudan and northern Uganda involved loving the people as a family. It also involved suffering with the locals as a family. Just as their children got sick, so did ours. A local doctor visited our home in South Sudan and was shocked to see that our children actually lived in South Sudan with us! The lab tech from the hospital drew our children's blood countless times (his name brought a sense of fear, when we suggested they needed a test for malaria).

Our family's mission statement was to love the people of South Sudan as a family, and the investment of Elizabeth in the lives of our children was immeasurable. They were her disciples, as she taught them to love others by learning language, serving others, and making sense of the suffering in that place. Her work in this was key to the ministry of presence that Jesus was doing in and through us.

Teach others. Along the way, we must also proclaim the presence and truth of our God. People do a variety of good and bad activities in life. Other people usually ignore them, sometimes notice, and rarely bother to consider why they do those things. We can do good for others, and they will simply say, "Hmmm… that was a nice thing to do," and carry on with their lives. At a point when the Holy Spirit directs us, we must explain the why of our actions and point them to the Truth.

His power, our obedience. Our job is to obey. At certain moments, God may choose to proclaim His power through or around us, to lead others to know Him also. He seems to do this more often in cultures that have a fear / power worldview, that don't doubt the spiritual realm, but are interested in which god or spirit has the most power.

This is seen more often in tribal, animistic people groups. Miracles still happen, where they are needed, through those surrendered to Him and ready to obey.

Conclusion: *Seeing the Mystery through the Mess*

Expect. We didn't expect mission work to be so messy. We thought it would be difficult, but had no idea how deeply we would be affected by following Jesus amidst a different culture. We didn't anticipate the recurrent illnesses, loss of sight in one eye, weight of disapproval from family, depth of cross-cultural misunderstanding with staffs, strikes, accidents, hostility, riots from those we were serving, burden of administrative duties, endless human resource tasks, and conflict within our multicultural missionary team. It was far messier than we ever dreamed, and in ways we couldn't have imagined. *"Beloved, do not be surprised at the fiery ordeal (the mess) among you, which comes upon you for your testing, as though some strange thing were happening to you"* (1 Pet 4:12). In the end, we are thankful for the unexpected experiences through which the Lord walked with us.

Embrace. One should expect such mess, and embrace it. The temptation is to give up and never see the mystery that God is working through it. Rather than saying, "Lord, why?! This is not what we expected!" we want to move to the attitude of "What for, Lord?! How do You want to use this?" *"But to the degree that you share the sufferings of Christ* **(the mess)**, *keep on rejoicing, so that also at the revelation of His glory* **(the mystery)** *you may rejoice with exultation"* (1 Pet 4:13). We stopped praying for "smooth" travels, and instead prayed for peace regardless of the challenges we faced, wisdom to deal with them, and that God would be glorified in whatever happened. The crucible of travel in the developed and developing world often produced growth in us and opportunities to share the hope of Christ.

Engage. We also must engage with the mess. We are in the world and we operate within its systems, so we must engage with the details of the mess. When our employees went on strike, the indigenous church leaders came alongside us, and together we engaged with the staffs and local authorities. We listened to their grievances and learned the details of the Labour Law of South Sudan (which we didn't know existed at first!). It was messy and painful, but we had to engage with the details.

"The devil is in the details," the saying goes. This statement is true in several ways: the challenge is engaging with the details, and very likely, there is a spiritual attack happening via these messy details.

This sometimes included the painful reality that some people were a danger and should be avoided. As a result of the employee strike at our hospital, there were certain staff members whom we had to release and forbid from entering the hospital compound, because they had physically threatened other staff and missionaries. They were wanted by National Security for problems they had caused at *His House of Hope* and elsewhere.

The mess of the strike sifted our staff members, and from it emerged several to avoid, many who were simply following the group, and a few that sought to do right for the patients and in the eyes of God. And it sifted us too. The challenge to us as overseers of a mission hospital was to be "wise as serpents" (expect the mess) but remain "innocent as doves" (doing the right thing as we engaged in the mess, though we were tempted to react with anger, bitterness, and other shortcuts of the flesh). "*Make sure that none of you suffers as a murderer, or thief, or evildoer, or 'one who oversees others' affairs;' but if anyone suffers as a Christian, he is not to be ashamed, but is to glorify God in this name*" (1 Pet 4:15-16, NASB 'literal translation'). While messy and obnoxious at times, we see how the Lord was refining and disciplining us through the difficult details, because He loves us.

Paul engaged with the mess yet didn't lose sight of the mystery, the hope of glory because Christ was in him. He likewise recognized that certain people were a danger to be avoided. Near the end of his life, he writes to his mentee, Timothy, about the mess and the mystery he was facing in mission work.

The details of the mess are "sandwiched" between his certainty of the mystery:

"I have fought the good fight, I have finished the course, I have kept the faith; in the future there is laid up for me the crown of righteousness, which the Lord, the righteous Judge, will award to me on that day; and not only to me, but also to all who have loved His appearing" (2 Tim 4:7-8). Paul engaged in the fight, because it was necessary, but he never lost sight of the mystery of glory with which the Lord would reward him. He knew he was on the right side of the fight amidst the mess, and that when the Judge appears, he and the Church will love the fact that He has finally come to set things right.

Paul engaged in the messy details, naming specific people for Timothy to avoid or embrace. *"Make every effort to come to me soon; for Demas, having loved this present world, has deserted me and gone to Thessalonica; Crescens has gone to Galatia, Titus to Dalmatia. Only Luke is with me. Pick up Mark and bring him with you, for he is useful to me for service…Alexander the coppersmith did me much harm; the Lord will repay him according to his deeds. Be on guard against him yourself, for he vigorously opposed our teaching"* (2 Tim 4:9-15). This is likely the Mark that deserted Paul on his first missionary journey (Acts 13:13), and was the source of Paul and Barnabas parting ways on his second mission (Acts 15:38-39). At the end of his life, Paul appears to have reconciled with John Mark. **The last earthly prayer of Jesus was for the unity of believers, and this example reminds us that there is always hope for restored relationships, even amidst brokenness.**

Paul concludes with another affirmation of the mystery. *"The Lord will rescue me from every evil deed, and will bring me safely to His heavenly kingdom; to Him be the glory forever and ever. Amen"* (2 Tim 4:18). God will rescue us, but not necessarily from our physical plights. Paul recognized that His guarantee was to bring us to our true home, with Jesus in His heavenly kingdom. **Being surrendered strangers on this earth, our hope lies in Him keeping us until we reach home.**

Paul could see the mystery of glory, the completed quilt, amidst the scraps of broken people, seemingly fit only for the rubbish heap. Elizabeth embraced the mess of fabric pieces on the floor, knowing they could produce a beautiful quilt, just as God transforms the messiness of His followers to display His glory.

The message for the missionary, through the missionary, and to the global Church is one:

"For our momentary, light affliction (the mess) is producing for us an eternal weight of glory (the mystery) far beyond all comparison, while we look not at the things that are seen (the mess), but at the things not seen (the mystery); for the things seen (the messes) are temporal, but the things not seen (the mystery) are eternal" (2 Cor 4:17-18).

We are the Church, and we embody the hope of Christ to the world. We live in the mess and yet are called to share the mystery. The mystery is essentially about belonging. Belonging to Him, Him belonging to us, and us belonging to one another because we are His followers. This is discipleship, that we invite others to follow Jesus by our lives and our words. Managing the mysteries of God, doing mission work, is often messy, painful, confusing, and without measurable outcomes, but we cling to hope and continue on because we are His and He who called us is faithful.

How have you seen messiness as you follow Jesus?

How well do you **engage** in messy details? Do you fear and avoid conflict?

How are you holding up under the mess of the world? Are you weary?

In what ways could you grow as a "manager of the mysteries of God?"

In what areas of your life do you need to 'cease striving'? How do you plan to do this?

Epilogue:
The Mess and the Mystery of Returning "Home"

We arrived back in Colorado the first few days of January 2019. We left lush vegetation and hot, crowded streets in Moyo, Uganda, to find our little town in rural America to be cold (physically and metaphorically), seemingly lifeless and deserted. Few people roamed the streets, but rather remained locked in their houses to stay warm and look at screens. During our absence from US culture, smartphones became a must-have, multiple classes of diabetic medications were invented, our town of 4,000 people gained four legal marijuana dispensaries, and being one particular gender became optional. However, the first question as I performed an ultrasound was still "boy or girl?"; new fetal DNA testing made it possible to know the sex of a baby at 10 weeks of gestation; and ironically, gender reveal parties became a fad. Parents even became angry if I couldn't tell them the fetal sex in time for the gathering, as out-of-town guests had already purchased plane tickets.

Our US home of nine years had been rented out to three sets of renters during our eight years away, the last one using our 120-year-old Victorian as a kennel for pit bulls – without our knowledge or permission. Many of the floors and doors were ruined. We spent the first three weeks completely sanding and repainting the house. Fortunately, our kids were old enough— and eager—to do much of the work!

More important than the house, relationships were changed.

"Africa messed you up," said one friend to a daughter of ours. (Begging the question, what had American culture done to *her* in the intervening eight years to say such a thing?)

"Stay away from the Perrys," said a youth in our home church of twenty years, to a boy who was new to the church. "They're nothing but trouble." This message was relayed to one of our daughters, after the young man had worked with her for a few weeks. He rather enjoyed her, and added his own thoughts, "I don't see what he was talking about. You're not so bad."

Around this time, our house was egged, someone threw a rock and shattered our front door glass, and the back of Elizabeth's car was smashed.

Kids have less filters. They either speak their thoughts openly, or parrot what their parents say in the privacy of their home, but would never say to our faces.

Relationships were few and far between. People didn't know what to do with us. Their lives had moved on, without us as a regular presence. Previously we were missionaries, out *there*, garnering interesting stories but not a part of their daily lives. Now we are *returned* missionaries, no longer *out there*, but part of their present existence again. Few are able or interested in listening. Life is busy, and most have no "hook" on which to hang our experiences in their own lives. They can't relate to us, and feel they have nothing to offer. So, they distance themselves.

One of our daughters was thankful to have a close friend, whom I will call Rae. Rae's family was very helpful to us over the years, storing our belongings in their barn for several years. Rae and our daughter were inseparable. They were almost always together either at our house or theirs. She started to feel like part of the family, often remaining for dinner. I participated in a men's Bible study with her father, and we joked that we were co-parenting.

During their many hours together, our daughter noticed some "spells" coming over Rae, during which she stared into space and could not be roused. She had several of these episodes sitting at our kitchen counter, witnessed by our family. Once, our daughter didn't hear from Rae for four days, and when she finally responded, it turned out that Rae had had another episode, fallen, hit head her head on the bathroom sink, and lost consciousness. When she came to, the police and EMT's were trying to wake her. Having grown up hearing medical stories, our daughter rightly concluded she was having seizures ("absence seizures"). They were becoming more frequent, so she expressed her concern to Rae.

Rae talked with her parents, and later responded. "The choices about my health are *not* for you to decide," she stated emphatically.

Thereafter, Rae was abruptly withdrawn from relationship with our daughter. They were no longer allowed to spend time together. I called her father and asked if we had done something to offend them, and he replied, "No, she just needs to rest and focus on her diet to get better." After over a year of near daily interaction, nine months of no contact ensued. During that time, Elizabeth and I dropped by their house unexpectedly, to attempt to have a conversation, but were turned away by Rae herself, who said her parents weren't home (though we could see her mom in the window).

The day after Thanksgiving, we received a chilling phone call from an acquaintance. Rae was found dead that morning, apparently having suffered a grand mal seizure during her sleep. Our daughter was devastated. Not only was her friend gone from this world, but any hope of reconciling in this lifetime had passed as well.

Our daughter courageously went to the funeral, though not invited nor welcomed, and stood in the back with another friend. It was a *long* year of grieving, not only her death but the death of the hope of restoration of friendship. She engaged in counseling with a local church. A dear family friend came alongside her, even taking her to the gravesite and remaining there while she processed unresolved feelings.

Amidst this time of loss, when asked, someone in the community was brave enough to share what Rae's family was saying about her death. The story was that *we* had given Rae "marijuana candy"— made by our children at home— and this led to her seizures and eventual death. This, despite the fact that our son had worked harvesting hemp (marijuana with lower concentrations of THC) for several days with Rae's dad at her dad's request. Our son ultimately quit after three days because he couldn't stand to be around the odiferous plant. Our family despises the legalization of marijuana, seeing the increase in addiction to other substances, crime, and emergency room utilization since Colorado led the rest of the nation in declaring it "just fine."

Sadly, most in our small community who knew both our families, remained silent. We heard this family was asked to leave their church, and we still occasionally see them around. But the confusing, unresolved events and relationship lingers, and we can't begin to understand what is going on for them in their loss and grief.

Over a decade before, when in the throes of culture shock and adjustment in South Sudan, a more experienced missionary warned us. "It's harder coming back," she stated. *Surely not harder than this?!* we countered silently, not daring to believe she was right. But she was. And now we see for ourselves. **It is a lonely, misunderstood road.**

The radical changes in society infiltrated our own ranks. One of our young adult daughters told us she believed she was transgender, and began transitioning to be a man by taking testosterone injections. The rest of the family wrestles with what it means to love her, yet remain faithful and true to our God and His Word. And we continue to wrestle with that, even to the time of this writing.

A year after our return, the worldwide COVID-19 epidemic hit. In the initial stages of lockdown, with its shortages of basic supplies, fear, and cessation of normal activity, it felt strangely familiar to much of our time overseas. Our return was downright *messy*.

We could choose to *obsess* over the mess of return, or instead *see* the mystery of Christ and His Body, continuing to work. The Lord continues to bring key, supportive individuals into our lives to encourage us as we try to adjust.

Our former pastor, Glenn (the one from Chapter One) and our former lawyer (now a judge) join with me weekly to run, talk, and pray. Both of them visited us in South Sudan back in 2012, so they have some appreciation of where and what we lived. We wrestle through our own personal sin patterns and the challenges in our churches, homes, and community. Elizabeth does the same with the judge's wife, walking and talking things out early each Wednesday morning.

Pastor John and Ruth Ann led a small church in our area, and they were a soft spot for us in our return. They insisted on us joining them for an occasional weekend at their mountain home, which they had acquired years before. He was one of the few individuals that asked with interest what we and our children had experienced in East Africa. *And they listened well.*

They handed us a key to their home, and refused to accept it back. Less than two years after our return, he succumbed to COVID-19, leaving his wife a widow in her early fifties. At his funeral, Elizabeth leaned over and said to me, "the man leading worship at the piano is going to be Ruth Ann's next husband." I raised my eyebrows, surprised, but remembering her prediction of the armed robbery back in South Sudan, I didn't contradict. Sure enough, just over a year later, we were attending their wedding!

Steve was a family friend, and he grafted into our families' relationship wonderfully. Steve and Ruth Ann likewise insist their home in the mountains is our home. They too listened and were a soft spot for us. On a recent visit, we led worship together at the small church near their home—the *mystery of belonging* accentuated by corporate worship.

The Allen family is also a consistent encouragement to our family. Not only did their church help us re-acquire a family vehicle upon our return, but they *heard* us. When the accusations about our family were flying about the valley (regarding Rae), Millie spoke healing words to Elizabeth. "You *know* that's not true. Satan is the father of lies."

Then there's the handful of supporters who refuse to stop supporting us financially, since we remain as *Pioneers* Associates, and our account is still active. They believe God still has plans for us in global missions, and want us to have funds to go. In fact, we started planning a trip to Papua New Guinea during the pandemic, to encourage and provide some extra medical manpower to a mission hospital. As of this writing, one of our daughters is serving at that location as a teacher's assistant, and we hope to join her for a month of her time there.

God is faithful.

Our mission agency, *Pioneers*, prompted us to attend a week-long debrief within two months of our return. This was key in preparation for the mess we face in re-entry. Later, we participated in a group study over two months, processing through the book "Returning Well." These punctuated spaces of common experience help us feel like we are not going crazy. We are not alone in our struggles.

Less than a year after our return, the Lord connected us with our "back-alley neighbors" who were finally ready to sell their family home next door to us. We recognized its good bones, and the proximity to us made it ideal to create a space of respite for missionary families. After six months of renovating the property as a family, Elizabeth opened "501 Blue," a missionary guest house which she operates, utilizing her gifts of hospitality. When not needed for missionaries, it is listed on Air BnB, and these profits cover costs, allowing us to offer it free of charge to those in missions and ministry. In the years it has been open, we have hosted missionaries that serve in Russia, Ukraine, Bangladesh, Malaysia, Mexico, Guatemala, China and pastors serving throughout the US.

After many years of living far from our parents, God unexpectedly allowed first Elizabeth's parents, and then my mom to relocate to our neighborhood. It is a precious gift to live together in the community with them.

I returned to the same job as I left ten years earlier. It felt like what I mentioned in the introduction, when the disciples went fishing after Jesus was crucified and resurrected—strange and anticlimactic. It was difficult coming from the raw, deep medical needs of a refugee camp to a climate-controlled clinic with a new electronic health records system to learn. But God is faithful, and He continues to give me favor in the medical community in which I "grew up" as a doctor. Some patients that I cared for over my first decade in Colorado returned to me as their doctor. I was happy to just be a "worker bee" again, and not the medical director. This didn't last long. Less than a year and a half into our return, overnight, the doctor who led our group developed an infection in his spine (vertebral osteomyelitis) and nearly died. I was called on a Sunday evening to assume leadership the following morning. For the next five months, I was the interim medical director, but I readily handed the reins back to him upon his return to health.

One year later, he stepped down, and I immediately told the Lord I was not accepting the role. Over the next week, however, He gently impressed upon me to take the job for the third time (I had served in this capacity prior to leaving for South Sudan also), and truly stop complaining about what I was being asked to do. He continues to show me how I need to grow as a leader, and challenges me to walk the hard yards of learning leadership even more.

Elizabeth and I have found that our return is not what we wanted or expected. We are daily challenged to grow in submission to the Lord. We say "I want to do Your will, Lord," but when He shows us what is to be done, we often reply, "but not THAT, Lord!" As we experience slander, unresolved relationships, and have the experience of *living misunderstood*, we more deeply understand that our citizenship is not where our passport says it is.

We continue at our home church. The Lord has not released us, and we continue to grow in relationships with this local Body of Christ. We try to put our "heads down and bums up" as we seek to teach and share God's word. Five years later, some relationships are still unresolved, which grieves us.

Several of our children are pursuing long-term cross-cultural mission work. One is a pilot, one is in nursing school, and another is volunteering as a teacher's assistant overseas and plans to return to pursue a teaching degree. Others are seeking the Lord's direction for *their* paths. Some are not actively walking with the Lord, though they know *of* Him. These are their stories to tell, and are still being written.

Return is *messy*. *Not* easy. But God is good and faithful, and we delight in the *mystery* that we can know Him.

August 2023
Colorado, USA

Endnotes

Chapter 2: A New Playing Field
1. *Day of Devastation, Day of Contentment: The History of the Sudanese Church across 2000 years*; Werner, Anderson, Wheeler, 2010: Paulines Publications Africa, Nairobi.

Chapter 4: Kasulu: Discipleship is Messy
1. Walt Viera, Family Life Ministries, personal communication, 2014.
2. *Living in the Grey*, author not noted.
3. John H., personal communication, August 2018.
4. *The White Nile*, Alan Moorhead, 1960: Harper & Bros, New York.

Chapter 9: The Neglected Middle
1. *Spirit of the Rainforest*, Mark A. Ritchie, 2000: Island Lake Press.
2. *Free from Deception*, James Wio, 2010: Sudan Literacy Center.
3. Columbia International University class notes, Prof. Philip Steyne.
4. "The Flaw of the Excluded Middle," Paul Hiebert, Missiology: An International Review, Vol X, No 1, Jan 1982.
5. Wikipedia—"Bacchus," accessed April 2018.
6. "Ephesians," Dr. Stuart Briscoe, conference in Greece, March 2018
7. Orestes G. Pino, personal communication, 2017.
8. *Victory over the Darkness*, Neil T. Anderson, 2013: Regal Books.

Chapter 12: A *COG* in the Wheel: Belonging
1. *Encountering Theology of Mission*, Ott, Ch 11.
2. *Africa Bible Commentary: a one-volume commentary*, Tokunboh Adeyemo, general editor, 2010: Zondervan, Grand Rapids, MI.
3. http://edition.cnn.com/video/#/video/

bestoftv/2013/02/02/nr-brooke-baby.cnn?iref=allsearch

Chapter 13: Abscess of the Soul: *Pride, Power, and Control*
      1.   *The Rest of God*, Mark Buchanan, 2006: Thomas Nelson, Nashville, TN, 72.
      2.   Ibid, 72.

Chapter 15: Mechanical Messes & Mystery Managers
      1.   *Jesus Through Middle Eastern Eyes*, Kenneth Bailey, 2008: InterVarsity Press, Downers Grove, IL, 203-04
2.   https://mymodernmet.com/kintsugi-kintsukuroi/

Chapter 18: Moving Forward in the Mess and the Mystery
      1.   *The Pineapple Story: How to Conquer Anger* (Oak Brook, IL: Institute in Basic Life Principles).
      2.   Ibid.
      3.   Ibid.
      4.   https://www.rzim.org/watch/ravi-zacharias-at-the-mormon-tabernacle
      5.   *Jesus Driven Ministry*, Ajith Fernando, 2002: Crossway, 140-43.
      6.   https://youtu.be/1dsi7hHfXKY (Billy Graham Interview)

Made in the USA
Las Vegas, NV
31 October 2023

80047660R00177